TO SAM.

All the Best.

From.
    All att the. Jordon. School.
        2013/14.

GUNDOGS

Their Past, Their Performance and Their Prospects

A GROUP OF SHOOTING DOGS.

POINTER, SETTER, SPRINGER & COCKER.

GUNDOGS

Their Past, Their Performance and Their Prospects

❧ DAVID HANCOCK ❧

THE CROWOOD PRESS

Previous Books by the Author

Dogs As Companions – 1981
Old Working Dogs – 1984 (reprinted 1998 and 2011)
The Heritage of the Dog – 1990
The Bullmastiff – A Breeder's Guide Vol 1 – 1996
The Bullmastiff – A Breeder's Guide Vol 2 – 1997
Old Farm Dogs – 1999
The Mastiffs – The Big Game Hunters – 2000–06 (six editions)
The Bullmastiff – A Breeder's Guide – 2006 (one volume hardback edition)
The World of the Lurcher – 2010
Sporting Terriers – Their Form, Their Function and their Future – 2011
Sighthounds – Their Form, Their Function & Their Future – 2012

First published in 2013 by The Crowood Press Ltd,
Ramsbury, Marlborough, Wiltshire, SN8 2HR

www.crowood.com

British Library Cataloguing-in-Publication Data
A catalogue record for this book is available from the British Library.

ISBN 978 1 84797 492 1

Page 1: Studies of Three Spaniels by Edwin W. Cooper.
Page 2: A group of shooting dogs, 1864.
Page 3: Setters were called spaniels; Cocking spaniels were not a separate breed.
Page 5: The Springer: a 19th century engraving/aquatint.

Typeset and designed by D & N Publishing, Baydon, Wiltshire

Printed and bound in India by Replika Press Pvt Ltd

CONTENTS

THE SPRINGER.

DEDICATION

This book is dedicated to the skilful pioneer gundog breeders who developed these remarkably gifted dogs for our appreciative use. They made function the main criterion in their breeding plans yet bequeathed to us handsome animals admired and favoured far beyond the shooting field. It is now for us to honour their memory, and respect the sporting dog heritage that they established, by breeding dogs they themselves would have coveted. Breeding functional dogs, gundogs especially, is a moral duty as well as a means to an end; we really must, in times when appearance is all, strive to protect the distinguished breeds of gundog from valueless exaggeration and unsound anatomies, in the misguided pursuit of purely show ring success. The casual seeking of 'breed points' ahead of stable temperament and a physique not suited to the gundog function is a betrayal of all that the pioneer breeders strove for in their honourable quest for an outstanding field dog. A sound gundog is a healthier gundog and that goal is the only true basis for the ethical breeding of subject creatures, especially those whose whole purpose is to serve us. Let us make the twenty-first century the one in which the very best interests of these quite admirable dogs were given the highest priority. They truly deserve it.

Laverack's Monument at Whitchurch, Shropshire – the plaque.

Mrs A. Butter with early Labrador, Dungavel Jet, 1911.

Shooting Party by John Beer, 1889.

The Gamekeeper by John Emms, 1843–1912.

PREFACE

Most men who shoot appreciate the services of a good gundog, both as a quester and 'flusher' and as a retriever of dead and wounded game, particularly that which may fall in places not easily accessible to the gun himself. Many men find that working a gundog gives them as much, if not more pleasure than the actual shooting and, apart from increasing the bag, a well-trained dog enhances a day afield whether you are shooting alone or in company.

P.R.A. Moxon, writing in *The Farmer's Book of Field Sports* edited by Colin Willock (1961)

Gundogs, developed and bred for their biddability, their strong desire to serve, their reliable temperaments and robust physiques, make ideal companion dogs – because of those very qualities. But unless gundog owners respect their dogs' instincts, their innate desire to *work*, to be active, to be employed and then provide an outlet for such valuable instincts, they will end up with unfulfilled frustrated pets. It's a real responsibility owning a dog from one of the gundog breeds. Of course it is vital to feed them, care for their physical needs and safeguard their health. But

there is a distinct requirement to consider too their spiritual needs, their inherited instincts, their deeply-implanted desire to 'use their noses'. Give them sensory stimulation! Give them spiritual release! Let them be *gundogs*!

Much is made quite rightly of conserving precious old buildings; far less is made of the similar need to conserve our living heritage. The sporting dog is part of Britain's living heritage; in the next decade we could not only lose some of our hounds of the pack, but betray our sporting forefathers by breeding gormless gundogs, timid terriers and supine sighthounds. The threats are manifold: animal welfare activists, financial pressures, demands on land and – perhaps often understated – the ignorance of a mainly urban dwelling population of the spiritual needs of sporting breeds. These dogs were not fashioned as companion dogs, however good they may be in that role. They had a *use*.

As our various breeds of dog were developing, function fashioned form. Breed type often reflected local preferences or breeders' whims, but the phenotype of each breed was decided by function, not by preference or whim. Terrain or country usually

Grant's 1840 painting 'Shooting at Ranton' on display at Shugborough Hall in Staffordshire.

decided, in pack hounds, the size of the hound, just as the grouse moor shaped the setter breeds. Colour and coat texture apart, most terrier breeds used as earth-dogs resemble each other. The need for retrievers in the shooting field gave us our highly popular retriever breeds, which were proficient enough to find wide-ranging employment away from the sporting world. A change in the needs of shooting men brought a whole range of hunt-point-retrieve all-rounder breeds to us, as versatility triumphed over specialization. But whatever their place of origin, every gundog breed developed from a *function*, not cosmetic appeal.

In these pages I have striven to depict gundogs from past times through the medium of sporting art. I am very much aware that dog writers of the past, Victorian ones especially, copied from each other and did little research outside Britain. It pays breed historians, rather than carelessly parroting previous writers, to look, for example, at the Golden Retriever superbly captured by Grant in his *Shooting at Ranton* of 1840 – long before stories of Russian imports and circus dogs were circulated. It's important that breed historians are aware of the paintings in the Bowes Museum in County Durham of the Bowes family, with a fine yellow Labrador depicted as long ago as 1848. Charles Towne's 1818 painting *Pointers in a Stable* and Sir William Beechey's portrait of *Richard Thompson and Pointer* at the end of the 18th century depict a

ABOVE RIGHT: Portrait of Josephine Bowes by Antoin Dury, 1850.

RIGHT: Pointers in a stable by Charles Towne, 1818.

Pointer very much like the French breed of pointing dog, the Braque Français. In 1713 Desportes produced his depiction of the *Earl of Burlington's Pointers*, with one of them having a distinct continental pointer look to it. James Barenger, too, in his *Awaiting the Flush* of 1811, depicts in the left-hand dog the French Braque influence on our Pointer stock. The casual acceptance that our Pointer originated in Spain rather than France is challengeable. This I discuss in the coverage of the gundog breeds that follows.

Whilst researching this book I have become increasingly aware of the sporting motives, breeding philosophy and, often, noble aspirations of the pioneers in each gundog breed. I believe that unless you are aware of their intentions and the thinking behind them you cannot fully appreciate the dogs of today. I have therefore made full use of quotes and illustrations from those early times, in each gundog breed, to provide the reader with such essential fundamental background. I have striven to give the dedicated talented breeders, who gave us these superb breeds, a voice. I have also given space to the expert show ring judges whose after-show critiques provide so much of value to the future breeding plans of pedigree gundog breeders. These are very rarely mentioned in books on dogs.

The general public may not work their gundog pets, but all gundogs require activity and stimulation; they need exercise as well as human company. These breeds were selectively bred, not as hearthrugs but as

ABOVE LEFT: *Portrait of Richard Thompson by Sir William Beechey, 1753–1839.*

LEFT: *Awaiting the Flush by James Barenger, 1811.*

shooting field assistants, and developed over centuries for *function*. A fat Labrador tells you more about its owner than any words of excuse from that owner. An excessively coated Cocker Spaniel, with overlong judges-wig's ears, illustrates human indulgence beyond any canine need. We betray the pioneer breeders of these magnificent breeds when we elect to ignore their proven criteria and follow our less well-informed whims. These breeds need responsible ownership, they deserve conscientious patronage, they have earned our best endeavours on their behalf. This book is not a multi-breed book containing advice on rearing, training, breeding, care and maintenance and exhibiting; it's a celebration of the gundog function, the contributing breeds, their form, their function and worries about their future. Sportsmen owe a massive debt of gratitude to these remarkable dogs, for, without, their enthusiastic service, the sport of shooting would become just a firing range exercise. May gundogs be treasured for centuries to come; they richly deserve our very best custodianship.

Earl of Burlington's Pointers by Desportes, 1713.

If we take the large classes of English Setters that a Kennel Club or Birmingham Show brings together, and compare them with the Field Spaniels of to-day, we see at once a very marked distinction – differences so wide that, unless we reflect on the influences that have been at work in producing both, we cannot realise that they are from the same stock. But ever since dog shows began Setters have been undergoing alteration in form, and the long, low, workmanlike Setter of a quarter of a century ago has been changed to a lighter, more leggy, and – and, in appearance at least – less enduring animal; whereas the Field Spaniel has been bred lower on the leg, and with longer body – so that the divergence is now greater than ever it was in the history of the group.
British Dogs by Hugh Dalziel (Upcott Gill, 1888)

An old friend of mine insisted that a thoughtful Providence had sent the gundogs of this world to be of use to man. I preferred to look at it in another way, suggesting that man had been endowed with an intelligence that enabled him to mould animals to his advantage.

British Dogs by A. Croxton Smith (1945)

ACKNOWLEDGEMENTS

The author is grateful to the staff at Sotheby's Picture Library, Christie's Images Ltd, Bonhams, Arthur Ackermann Ltd, David Messum Galleries, Richard Green & Co., The Bridgeman Art Library, The Bowes Museum, Rountree Fine Art Ltd, The Nature Picture Library, The National Art Library, The Wallace Collection, R Cox & Co., Lane Fine Art, The Kennel Club, The American Kennel Club, The National Trust, The Royal Collection – Photographic Services and private collectors (especially the late Mevr A.H. (Ploon) de Raad of Zijderveld, Holland, who gave free use of her extensive photographic archive of sporting paintings), for their gracious and generous permissions to reproduce some of the illustrations used in this book.

AUTHOR'S NOTE

A number of the illustrations in this book lack pictorial quality but are included because uniquely they either contribute historically to or best exemplify the meaning of the text. Old depictions do not always lend themselves to reproduction in today's higher-quality print and publishing format. Those that are included have significance beyond their graphic limitations and I ask for the reader's understanding over this.

Where quotes are used, they are used verbatim, despite any vagaries in spelling, irregular use of capital letters or departures from contemporary grammar. For me, it is important that their exact form, as presented by the author originally, is displayed, as this can help to capture the mood of those times.

Spaniel and game, engraving of 1854.

THE CHANGING FORTUNES OF GUNDOGS

The main body of this family is composed of Spaniels proper, the Setters and Retrievers, while pointing dogs and diminutive allies are the miscellaneous members of the group. Head characteristics are rather broad skulls which are convex or 'domed' across the top, well-defined stop, fairly thick, long and pendant ears, loose lips, and rather full round eyes. Body formation is generally lithe and muscular, with the back slightly sloping to the set-on, legs of substantial but not coarse bone, and feet fairly large with toes that are capable of spreading out on soft earth. Tails are naturally long (except in some foreign Pointers which are purposely docked, and most British Spaniels), tapering and flagged with long fine hair on the underside. Coats are always soft, usually medium in length and well feathered. Employment is usually in flushing, setting, pointing and retrieving game.

Dogs in Britain by Clifford L.B. Hubbard (1948)

Native Breeds Admired

Britain has every reason to be proud of her contribution to the breeds of gundog in the world. Our sportsmen, supported by the landed families, developed the renowned breeds that are still active in the field today – pointers, setters and spaniels – although some of these breeds sadly are little used in the shooting field. If you want sheer style on the grouse moor, a dog that excels at flushing, starting or springing game, or a specialist retriever for picking up, our sporting breeds are still supreme. But if you want a dog that is capable of hunting game, pointing out where it is and then retrieving it to hand when it is shot, then you must choose a breed from overseas. In a later chapter I suggest that this should be rectified – that we in Britain should develop our own 'hunt-point-retrieve' breed. It is strange that British gundog breeders, revered the world over,

Partridge Shooting; an engraving by C. Catton after George Morland, 1763–1804.

Partridge Shooting by James Barenger, 1804.

The Artist with Two Pointers by Ben Marshall, 1767–1835.

have not responded to the contemporary demand for all-round skills in a gundog. As the paintings of George Morland, James Barenger and Ben Marshall illustrate, our Pointers once used to retrieve, as did some setters, as the Paul Jones painting of 1859 shows. Dog breeders are not usually so slow to respond to the marketplace, as our exports of gundogs in past centuries demonstrate.

Retrieving Setter by Paul Jones, 1859.

Popularity has its Price

This book is a tribute to the gundog, whether a bird-dog, a water-dog, a decoy-dog, a flushing dog, a retrieving dog or a versatile all-rounder. Modern living presents many problems to sporting dogs, ranging from contemporary lifestyles that do not suit such active creatures to unwise unskilled breeding, often in the unashamed pursuit of money. But for some breeds, especially some gundog breeds, there is a special danger from their being appreciated, wanted, coveted and therefore over-bred – their sheer popularity. The sport of shooting is thriving; it is vital that the hard-working dogs providing irreplaceable support in the field to this sport are well-served, not just by trainers and shots once mature, but by their breeders, breed clubs and parent bodies. It would be good to see an energetic organisation like the British Association for Shooting and Conservation (BASC) extending their remit still further in the promotion of healthier, better-bred and sounder gundogs, as well as the conservation of our native minor gundog breeds.

Challenge to British Breeds

If you look at the annual registrations of gundog breeds with the Kennel Club (KC), you can quickly see the fairly recent popularity nowadays of the hunt-point-retrieve (HPR) breeds from the continent. In the first decade of the twenty-first century, twice as many German Short-haired Pointers (GSPs) were registered here as our own native breed of Pointer; 1,000 more Hungarian Vizslas were registered than the combined totals of our Clumber, Field, Sussex and Irish Water Spaniels; more Weimaraners were registered than all our native setter breeds put together. More Italian Spinoni were registered than the combined totals of our Curly-coated Retrievers, Irish Red and White Setters and two of the minor spaniel breeds. Less than fifty years ago, only around 540 GSPs, 330 Weimaraners and under 100 Hungarian Vizslas were registered each year and no Spinoni. But nearly four times fewer Irish Setters were registered in 2000 as in 1975. Is this entirely down to sheer merit in the newly popular foreign breeds or an indication of our fondness for the exotic, the casual pursuit of novelty or copycat fashion-following?

Even fifty years ago, the shooting men went for British gundogs; not any more. The preference for hunt-point-retrieve breeds has largely caused this, but our national fascination with all things foreign plays a part too. The sustained popularity of the Labrador and Golden Retrievers and the English Springer and Cocker Spaniels must not be allowed to mask the worryingly small numbers of far too many of our native gundog breeds. In succeeding chapters I discuss this alarming decline in numbers in far too many of our long-established British breeds.

There is also a regrettable fickleness in the fancying of gundog breeds. Take the Gordon Setter as an example: in 1908, 27 were registered; in 1927, 74; in 1950, 100; in 1975, 255; in 1985, 586; in 2001, 288; in 2009, 192 and then 306 a year later. Such

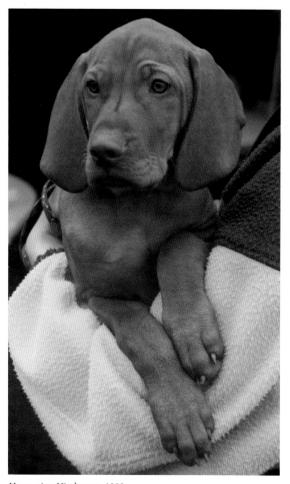

Hungarian Vizsla pup, 1998.

Three Springer Spaniels by Reuben Ward Binks, 1944.

The Many Colours of the Cocker Spaniel (courtesy of Dogs In Canada *magazine).*

comparatively wide fluctuations in a small breeding population calls for extraordinary shrewdness from breeders if top-quality dogs are to be bred and a virile gene pool maintained. Another of our native gundog breeds, the English Setter, is declining alarmingly, with 240 being registered each year either side of the First World War, as many as 1,700 in 1980, a drop down to 768 in 2000, then further drops in 2009 (295) and 2011 (234). To lose 1,500 registrations in 30 years is a dramatic loss of patronage and of enormous concern to breed enthusiasts. This cannot be put down purely to changes in shooting habits.

Fashioning Fame

If you look at the list of the twenty most popular breeds of dog, as registered with the Kennel Club in 2011, you see a wide range of types. There are terrier and spaniel breeds, gundogs and herding dogs, foreign breeds and British ones, toy dogs and working breeds. The Labrador Retriever easily heads the list, with nearly 40,000 registered, as in the previous four years. The Golden Retriever and the Cocker and English Springer Spaniels feature high in the popularity stakes, with all three breeds proving popular overseas too. The fashion-following of the dog-owning public can be seen in the changing fortunes of two British breeds: the Cocker Spaniel and the Fox Terrier. In 1910, over 600 Cockers and 1,500 wire-haired Fox Terriers were registered. The wire-haired Fox Terrier was top dog from 1920 to 1925 and again from 1928 to 1935. It was still the third most popular breed half a century ago. Eighty years ago it was the third most popular breed in the US too. Now fewer than 700 are registered here annually, only one third of the numbers registered in 1956.

The Cocker Spaniel was top dog here from 1936 to 1953, with over 7,000 registered each year in the 1950s. In the US in 1977, as many as 53,000 were registered, the breed having been top there even thirty years before. The registrations here of Cockers went up by 1,600 between 1989 and 1998, with the breed moving into third place here in 2000, with 13,000 registrations. Unlike the Fox Terrier, this is a story of sustained popularity. There seems no discernible reason for such varying fortunes. The Fox Terrier has lost its working role but perhaps the rise of the Jack Russell has contributed to its fall. The Cocker Spaniel is not worked as much as it once was, but the steady rise of another small spaniel breed – the Cavalier King Charles Spaniel – has not affected its numbers. It is now more popular than the English Springer Spaniel.

Labradors: FT Ch Peter of Whitmore and Ch Type of Whitmore by Maud Earl, 1914.

Golden Retriever Vesta of Woolley by Reuben Ward Binks, 1928.

Success Stories

The gundog breed success story of the twentieth century here was undoubtedly that of the Labrador Retriever, with the Golden Retriever, the Cocker Spaniel and the English Springer not far behind. In his *Dogs since 1900* (1950), Arthur Croxton Smith wrote:

> The year 1903 was memorable in the history of Labradors, which had hitherto been little known except among a few select sporting families… I must admit that before 1903 I had never seen one… Then in that year a class was provided for them at the Kennel Club show at the Crystal Palace.

In 1908, 123 were registered, in 1912, 281, in 1922, 916, by the 1950s 4,000 were being registered each year, in the 1980s 15,000 a year, rising to nearly 36,000 in 1998 and over 45,000 a year after that. No other breed in the history of purebred dogs can match that rise in popularity. This degree of popularity calls for visionary breeding control, both a voluntary one at breeder level and firm leadership at the top, both at breed club and KC level. Sadly, this has not been entirely successful and far too many unsound unhealthy dogs have been born – and bred from – to respond to public demand. The breed, and indeed the public, deserve better and I argue for that in succeeding pages.

Threat from Abroad

Is there a need to restrict the often whimsical way in which fresh foreign breeds are imported into this country? Coming along behind the German Short- and Wire-haired Pointers are the Stichelhaars and the Langhaars; behind the Large Munsterlander is the small variety and then there are the French braques and epagneuls, as well as the Dutch dogs: the Stabyhoun (Frisian Pointing Dog) and the Drentse Patrijshond, with the Italian Spinone and Bracco, the Portuguese Pointer and the Slovakian Rough-haired Pointer already imported. I am full of admiration for these breeds and have seen many of them at work in their native countries. I would like to see talented, well-bred specimens from those breeds gracing our shooting fields but I would not want them to gain ground here at the expense of our own breeds. As I argue in Chapter 3, we are more than capable of creating our own hunt-point-retrieve breed from native working stock.

Stabyhoun or Frisian Pointing Dog (courtesy of Dutch Kennel Club).

RIGHT: *Drentse Partridge Dog (courtesy of Dutch Kennel Club).*

BELOW: *English Pointer, depicted by F. Deiker in 1880, happily retrieving feathered game, whilst distracted by fur.*

Portuguese Partridge Dog (courtesy of Portuguese Kennel Club).

Threats from Within

One of the less satisfactory aspects of the purebred dog industry in breeds that still work is the tiny contribution to the gene pool from the top working dogs. In the retriever world, the early dogs nearly always had field trial champions in their five-generation pedigree. Nowadays, with over 50,000 retrievers being newly registered with the Kennel Club each year, only a very small percentage have that input. Gundog experts who take the view that if the top working dogs are good then there is little wrong with the breed are not living in the real world. It is illuminating, too, to note that the only group of sporting dogs still earning their keep in the field and whose breeders still register their stock with the KC is the gundog group. Racing Greyhounds, hounds of the pack and working terriers do not feature in KC lists. Working sheepdogs never have. This is discussed in the concluson.

Changing Fortunes

Generally speaking, in the world of dogs, kennel clubs keep the breeds going and sportsmen keep the functions alive. Our Kennel Club does stage field trials, working tests, agility and obedience events but it is sportsmen who *use* hounds, gundogs and terriers as sporting assistants. The KC oversees the world of the pedigree gundog; in every decade, in the world of the show gundog, the faddists are at work, sadly in far too many breeds. Sporting dogs, like the setters, were once famed for their lung-power; now they are mostly slab-sided in the chest, despite the evidence that such a structure enhances the likelihood of bloat. A Cocker Spaniel can, it appears win Best in Show at Crufts with ears that defy the breed standard. 'Oh, doesn't he know,' I can hear the gundog gurus proclaim, 'that there is a division now between working and show gundogs?' My response is two-fold: firstly, nearly all the gundogs taking part in the working tests I have judged were show-bred; secondly I am prepared to bet that many readers of sporting magazines buy their gundog from a show breeder. In later pages, I make regular reference to the views of show-ring judges; this is usually overlooked in books on dogs but here provides extremely valuable insight into the state of each gundog breed and is *of value to the future breeding of each breed.* I have also made full use of registration figures to illustrate the changing fortunes of each breed; popularity does not bring security to a breed, but a lack of it can spell disaster for limited gene pools.

Fads may be passing indulgences for fanciers but they so often do lasting harm to breeds. If they did harm to the breeders who inflict them, rather than to the wretched dogs that suffer them, fads would be more tolerable and certainly more short-lived. What are the comments of veterinary surgeons treating the ill-effects of misguided fads? In his informative book *The Dog: Structure and Movement*, published in 1970, R.H. Smythe, himself a vet, wrote:

> Many of the people who keep, breed and exhibit dogs, have little knowledge of their basic anatomy or of the structural features underlying the physical formation insisted upon in the standards laid down for any particular breed. Nor do many of them – and

Curly-coated Retriever and Pointer by John Emms, 1895.

this includes some of the accepted judges – know, when they handle a dog in or outside the show ring, the nature of the structures which give rise to the varying contours of the body, or why certain types of conformation are desirable and others harmful.

Every gundog owner needs to know what his dog is *for*! This is covered in later chapters.

Celebratory Survey

I have striven in this book to promote the best long-term interests of gundogs; it is a book intended to be a celebratory survey of the gundog breeds, covering their origin, evolution, employment, essential form and their future. It is not a manual covering animal husbandry, training and breeding. It aims at the production of better gundogs in the years to come, with a renewed respect for their needs and best interests. Gundogs represent a very special collection of breeds both native and imported; they were developed by skilled breeders for a precise *sporting* function. It is our duty to continue the inspired work of those pioneers in each breed who bequeathed these precious breeds into our care. These words are intended to encourage just that.

The discovery of the gun superseding the use of the falcon, the powers of the Dog were directed to the new acquisition; but his fleetness, wildness and courage, in quest of game, rendering him difficult to manage, a more useful kind was established, with shorter limbs and less speed…

Cynographica Britannica by Sydenham Edwards
(1800)

There was great competition amongst English sportsmen at the beginning of the nineteenth century to secure the ideal gundog. There were plenty of breeds to choose from because gundogs had appeared long before the gun in England. Springers had flushed game for the falconer. 'Crouchers' had driven partridges or quails into a net and setters had been developed for the same purpose.

The British Dog by Carson I.A. Ritchie (1981)

Black Retriever with Duck by Reuben Ward Binks.

CHAPTER 1

ORIGINS AND ANCESTRY
GUNDOGS – BEFORE THERE WERE GUNS

The cross-bow, the arbalast and the stone-bow (both variants on the cross-bow) were becoming increasingly used in sport. With blunt bolts or stones for killing birds they were an effective weapon. Other methods of securing birds and small game, such as decoying, netting, trapping and liming were becoming increasingly common as the Middle Ages drew to their close and the protection of the 'fowls of warren' became correspondingly ineffective. Yet still the immense wild bird population showed little signs of suffering from these persecutions.

Hunting and Shooting by Michael Brander (1971)

Pre-Firearm Hunting

Strictly speaking, once you have named a distinct group of dogs as 'gundogs', their history begins with the invention of firearms. But hunters were 'armed' long before the introduction of firearms, with the spear, the bow and arrow, the boar-lance and the bolt-firing weapons to the fore. The net could also be described as a weapon, being used to capture rabbits or envelop game birds indicated by setting dogs. Before the invention of firearms, hunters were reliant on dogs that could indicate unseen game and not run in, as well as those that could retrieve valuable bolts, especially from water, when used on wildfowl.

In the late middle ages, the netting of birds was not a simple matter; dogs had to be trained to find the quarry and 'hold' them whilst crouching expectantly but with immense patience. To further deter the birds from taking off, a kite-hawk, a device resembling a bird of prey, would be flown over them. Alternatively, a falcon could be positioned above them, either flown free or at the top of a long pole, within sight of the birds. Each stratagem ensured the birds clung to the ground, so enabling the hunter to proceed. Once the targeted, transfixed birds were grounded by this system, the netsmen could advance with their net and trail it over the prone dog and cast it over the stupefied birds. Gamekeepers would often spread obstacles in open fields to prevent game being poached in this manner.

Pot Filling

Shooting birds with a gun was initially regarded as pot-filling rather than sport. The sporting way was locating them with 'setting dogs' which then lay

Spaniels taught to crouch from Blome's Gentleman's Recreation, 1686.

low to allow the hunters' net to be drawn both over them and the crouching dogs, or *chiens couchant*. There are many setters to this day that instinctively crouch low rather than stand and point in the classic pose. In continental Europe a draw-net or tirasse was employed; this involved the dogs crawling slowly towards the stationary birds, gradually driving the alarmed but not flight-prone birds towards the approaching netsmen. In such a way, the dogs 'worked' the birds into the net, rather as a well-trained collie urges sheep to move but not run. The value to the hunter, both here and on the continent, of a dog which instinctively found game on the ground, indicated its find, then almost hypnotised it into staying on the ground until a net descended on it, must have been priceless.

The rapport between sportsman and setting dog was captured in *The Sportsman's Cabinet* of 1803, with these words:

The Setting Dogg & Partridges from Blome's Gentleman's Recreation, 1686.

That the setting dog has more continual and intimate relations with man, than almost any other of the species; he hunts within his view, and almost under his hand; his master affords him pleasure, for the pleasure is mutual when the game is in the net; which being shown to the dog, he is caressed if he has done right, corrected if he has done wrong; his joy in the first instance, or his remorse in the latter, are equally apparent, and in this mutual gratification is formed the very basis of reciprocal affection.

We may well have lost that particular intimacy with our gundogs as operating distances increased with developing shooting methods.

Dogs of the Net

I am inclined to believe that the earliest sporting

Hawking from a drawing by Francis Barlow, 1626–1704.

16th Century Hawking Dog.

dogs, other than hounds of the chase, were the dogs *'da rete'* (of the net) and the water dogs that would retrieve bolts, arrows and wildfowl which had fallen into water. The 'oysel' or bird dogs of the sixteenth century were much more setter-like than anything else. I take the view that the expression *chiens d'arret*, or stop-dogs, is more likely a corruption of *chiens de rets*, the French word *'rets'* meaning a net or a snare. Terms like *chien couchant, chien d'oysel* and *chiens de rets* were used for dogs working to the net before the distinct breeds for this task evolved. In his *The Master of Game* of 1410, Edward, Duke of York, called all bird dogs spaniels but pointed out that some could be trained for the net, referring to them as 'couchers'.

In his ground-breaking book *Of English Dogs* of 1576, the Cambridge scholar Dr Caius was recording:

When he hath found the bird, he keepeth sure and fast silence, he stayeth his steps and will proceed no further; and with a close, covert and watching eye, layeth his belly to the ground, and so creepeth forward like a worm…whereby it is supposed that this kind of dog is called *Index,* 'Setter', being indeed a name most consonant and agreeable to his quality.

Half a century later, Gervase Markham was writing: 'It is meete that first before I wade further into this discourse, I shew you, what a Setting dogge is: you shall then understand that a Setting Dogge is a certaine lusty land spaniel, taught by nature to hunt the partridges, before, and more than any other chase.' He also referred to the taking of pheasants by bird-liming bushes, supported by spaniels.

Heron-hawking Party by Henry Alken Snr, 1821 (note larger 'setting spaniel').

Spaniels, too, were used with the net and the hawk. The use of names for types and uses of dogs was more than loose in past times. The Irish called the setter the English Spaniel for quite some time, while the poet John Gay referred to the setter as 'the creeping spaniel'. All longer- or rougher-haired sporting dogs, not used as hounds, were once clubbed together as spaniels. The cocking spaniel was also called the gun spaniel. In his *Rural Sports* of 1870, Delabere Blaine disputes a Captain Brown's statement that, 'The true English-bred spaniel differs but little in figure from the setter, except in size', writing that, 'It is evident Captain Brown here thought only of the large sporting spaniel. Both springers and cockers are used in greyhound coursing, and the excellent scenting qualities of each usually enables them to find every hare in their beat.'

Nicholas Cox, in 1677, was stressing the value of the spaniel in hawking, writing: 'How necessary a thing it [the spaniel] is to falconry I think nobody need question, as well as to spring and retrieve a fowl being flown to the mark, and also in divers and other ways to help and assist falcons and goshawks.' But was he writing of spaniels or setters or even, before the days of purebreeding, of a blend of the two? The veracity of sources matters too; Dr Caius was a scholar not a sportsman and undoubtedly had his leg pulled by the latter; Cox was a shameless plagiarist who used material on French dogs as though it came from England; Markham was a clever and prolific journalist who often wrote beyond his knowledge.

Netting the Quarry
When real sportsmen write you soon get a marvellous impression of the essence of the sport itself. In an article headed *The Setter and Grouse*, 'Nimrod' in a sporting magazine of 1837, described the practice of an old-fashioned squire in Flintshire, Peter Davies of Broughton Hall:

The old gentleman took the field in good style, being accompanied by a servant to hold his horse when he

Medieval Hawking with Hounds (in Germany) from an 1860 drawing.

dismounted, and two mounted keepers in their green plush jackets and gold-laced hats. A leash of highly-bred red and white setters were let loose at a time, and beautifully did they range the fields, quartering the ground in obedience to the voice or whistle. On the game being found, every dog was down, with his belly close on the ground; and the net being unfurled, the keepers advanced on a gentle trot, at a certain distance from each other, and drew it over them and the covey at the same time. Choice was then made of the finest birds, which were carried home alive, and kept in a room till wanted, and occasionally all would be let fly again, on ascertaining their fitness for the spit. Modern sportsmen may consider this tame sport, and so in fact it is, compared with the excitement attending the gun; but still it has its advantages. It was the means of preserving game on an estate, by equalising the number of cock and hen birds – at least to an extent – and killing the old ones; no birds were destroyed but what were fit for eating; and such as were destroyed, were put to death at once, without the

chance of lingering from the effects of a wound, which is a circumstance inseparable from shooting.

Sounds like ethically acceptable sport to me, awaiting a comeback.

The Fowler's Dog

A number of old books on sporting dogs describe the setter as the fowler's dog and link the pointer breeds only with the introduction of firearms. In the seventeenth century on the continent and in the early eighteenth century in England, the braques and pointing griffons were developed, probably benefiting from the blood of the hounds, like the bracke and the scenthound griffons (or Gayffons as Markham misnamed them in 1630) in central Europe. In England, the setter breeds and the Pointer developed separate loyal bands of devotees, with the Rev Simons writing in 1776:

The setter cannot be *degraded* into a pointer; but the pointer may be elevated to a setter, though but a

A Spaniel (a setter then described as a spaniel).

second class. The setter is only of service where there is room to run a net, so must be hunted accordingly. Whole coveys are the just attention of the setter...The pointer as has been the setter, is broke from chasing we well suppose, to which the sight of the game had hitherto been the stimulus. *Now,* although he will hear the whirl and departure of the birds it is more than probable the report of the gun will agitate him into the forgetfulness of duty and the urge to pursue.

The gundog had arrived.

One may be sure that the soldier, or more often the sailor, returned from adventures overseas, having seen the deadly effects of a 'handgonne' on the enemy, was not slow to try it on the rafts of wildfowl in the marshes, or even on the king's deer in the forests, although a slow match and a stand was necessary. Such a man who had possibly travelled half way round the known world was not likely to submit tamely to having his liberty curbed on his return home.

Michael Brander, *Hunting and Shooting* (1971)

RIGHT: *Prototypal English Setters, from 18th century tableaux, English School.*

BELOW LEFT: *The Itinerant Poulterer by J-C Bonnefond 1818, depicting a French Epagneul.*

BELOW RIGHT: *Shooting on the Wing, etched by S Gribelin for Blome in 1686.*

Pheasant Retrieving by James Ward, 1812.

The Sportsman by George Maile, 1824.

Shooters outside a Cottage by Seffrien (John) Alken, c.1825.

The Water Dogs

THE ROUGH WATER DOG. This is a most intelligent and valuable animal. It is robustly made, and covered throughout with deep curly hair. It exceeds the water spaniel in size and strength. It is much used as a retriever by shooters of water-fowl. No dog is more easily taught to fetch and carry than this; and its memory is surprising. This variety is the Barbet, of the French, and is often called the German or French Poodle. Some are of a snowy white, others black, and others black and white.

Those few words, in *Cassell's Popular Natural History*, published towards the end of the nineteenth century, will have little meaning for today's sportsmen. They know a great deal about the gundog breeds of today but not a great deal about the ones that went before. Yet without the water dogs, we would not have the retrieving breeds of today. Stubbs once portrayed '*A Rough Dog*' and it is forever described by art historians inaccurately; it is a fine depiction of a rough water dog. This type of dog gave service to man the hunter long before the invention of firearms; here was the foundation stock. Their value has been overlooked in the passing of time; in *The Sportsman's Cabinet* of 1803, there are nine pages devoted to them, but few books on sporting dogs today even mention them.

Stubb's A Rough Dog, depicting a Large Water Dog of that time, c.1790.

European Variants

In the ancient world anyone found guilty of killing a water dog was subject to a most severe penalty. The first written account of a Portuguese Water Dog is a monk's description in 1297 of a dying sailor being brought out of the sea by a dog with a black coat of rough long hair, cut to the first rib and with a tuft on the tip of the tail, the classic water-dog clip. Water dogs came in two types of coat: long and harsh-haired or short and curly-haired. The French Barbet displays the former, the Wetterhoun of Holland and our Curly the latter; the Portuguese Cao de Agua or Water Dog features both.

In Dr Caius' *Of English Dogs* of 1576, he described the Aquaticus, a dog for the duck, but blurs the water dog with the spaniel. He does, however, in 1569 provide his naturalist friend Gesner with an illustration of a Scottish Water Dog, retriever-like but with pendant ears. Writing in 1621, Gervase Markham recorded: 'First, for the colour of the Water Dogge, all be it some which are curious in all things will ascribe more excellency to one colour than to another as the blacks to be the best and the hardier; the lyver hues swiftest in swimming ... and his hairs in generall would be long and curled...' In 1591, Erasmus of Valvasone wrote a poem on hunting, which will appeal to Lagotto fanciers, referring to 'a rough and curly-haired breed that does not fear sun, ice, water ... its head and hair resemble that of the ram, and it brings the bird back to the hunter merrily.'

Function Decided Type

Gundog breeds today are rightly revered and their sporting prowess as well as their breed type, which originated in function, perpetually prized. Sportsmen in early medieval times, however, knew the value of setting dogs and water dogs, the original retrievers, more than any of their successors. The invention of firearms did away with the need to recover arrows or bolts, as well as increasing the range at which game could be engaged. The setting dogs adapted from the net to the gun and survived, but the water dogs of Europe lost their value and many became ornamental dogs, like the Poodle.

Some water dogs survive as breeds, with the Irish Water 'Spaniel' still causing discussion over whether it is a spaniel or a retriever. This type of dog, quite often black, liver or parti-coloured, had one

Sir John Maxwell of Pollock, a mezzotint by Charles Turner after James Howe, depicting a hawking party with small spaniels, a pointer and a water dog.

physical feature which set it apart from most others – the texture of its coat. It is so easy when looking at a Standard Poodle in show clip to overlook their distinguished and ancient sporting history. And how many breeds recognized as gundogs can match their disease-free genotype? Anyone looking for a water retriever with instinctive skills, inherited prowess, a truly waterproof coat and freedom from faulty genes should look at the Standard Poodle, but stand by for ignorant comments from one-generation sportsmen, unaware of its heritage.

The Standard Poodle is a living example of the ancient waterdog whose blood is behind so many contemporary breeds: the Curly-coated Retriever, Wetterhoun of Holland, Portuguese and Spanish Water Dogs, Lagotto Romagnolo, Pudelpointer, Barbet, Irish and American Water Spaniels and the Boykin Spaniel. I suspect that the Hungarian breeds, the Puli and the Pumi, used as pastoral dogs, may, judging by their coat texture, have water dog ancestry, as may the French breed, the Epagneul de Pont-Audemer. The Tweed Water Spaniel was behind our hugely popular Golden Retriever. The old English Water Spaniel's coat sometimes emerges in purebred English Springers.

Although our breeds of retriever were not developed until comparatively recently, the use of dogs as retrievers by sportsmen is over a thousand years old.

Traine him to fetch whatsoever you shall throw from you...anything whatsoever that is portable; then you shall use him to fetch round cogell stones, and flints, which are troublesome in a Dogges mouth, and lastly Iron, Steele, Money, and all kindes of metall, which being colde in his teeth, slippery and ill to take up, a Dogge will be loth to fetch, but you must not desist or let him taste food till he will as familiarly bring and carry them as anything else whatsoever.

So advised Gervase Markham early in the seventeenth century on the subject of training a 'Water Dogge' to retrieve.

Half a century earlier, the much quoted Dr Caius identified the curly-coated Water Dogge as 'bringing our Boultes and Arrowes out of the Water, which otherwise we could hardly recover, and often they restore to us our Shaftes which we thought never to see, touch or handle again.' Such water dogs were utilized on the continent too; in *The Sketch Book of Jean de Tournes*, published in France in 1556, we

ABOVE: *Portuguese Water Dog of 1908.*   BELOW: *Barbet of 1904.*

see illustrated 'The Great Water Dogge', a big, black, shaggy-headed dog swimming out to retrieve a duck from a lake. This sketch could so easily have been of the contemporary Barbet, still available in France (and now here), acknowledged as an ancient type, and used to infuse many sporting breeds with desirable water-dog characteristics. The dog depicted could also represent the modern Cao de Agua, the Portuguese Water Dog. These European water dogs are the root stock of so many modern breeds.

Ships' Dogs

Not surprisingly such dogs were favoured by the sea-going fraternity – fishermen, sailors and traders. The dogs were trained to retrieve lines lost overboard and used as couriers between ships, in the Spanish Armada for example. In time, such dogs featured in the settlements established along the eastern seaboard of the New World by British, Portuguese, Dutch and French traders. Water dogs exist today in those countries: the Barbet in France, the Wetterhoun in Holland, the Curly-coated Retriever and the Irish Water 'Spaniel' here and the Portuguese Water Dog there. The latter, still favoured by fishermen in the Algarve, has either a long, harsh, oily coat or a tighter curly coat. The Barbet has the long woolly coat, the Wetterhoun the curly coat.

Of these three, the most distinctive is the Cao de Agua, now gaining strength in this country. An ancient Portuguese breed that can be traced back to very remote times, it has great similarity with the Spanish Water Dog, now being restored to that country's list of native breeds, and the Italian Water Dog, the Lagotto Romagnolo, also being resurrected. Overseas kennel clubs do, unlike ours, try to conserve their national canine heritage. There is evidence that such breeds were regarded as sacred in pre-Christian times, any person killing a water dog being subject to severe penalty.

The highly individual water-dog clip led to the Romans referring to such dogs as 'lion dogs'. This clip, with the bare midriff and hindquarters but featuring a plumed tail, does give a leonine appearance. The modern toy breed, the Lowchen (meaning little lion dog) displays this clip and is a member of the small Barbet or Barbichon (nowadays shortened to Bichon) group of dogs, embracing the Bolognese, the Havanese, the Maltese, the Bichon a poil frise and the Coton du Tulear.

Fishing Dogs

Important historical information on ships' dogs used as fishing dogs in the south of England can be found in the words of the 6th Earl of Malmesbury, contributing to the Labrador Retriever Club's booklet *A Celebration of 75 Years*, published by the club in 1991. He wrote:

My great-great-grandfather needed a good retrieving water dog, and a companion in the home. He found both qualities in the little Newfoundlander (later to be renamed the Labrador, which was a less cumbersome name). How did these dogs develop their retrieving instinct? It was customary for the fishing boats in Newfoundland to carry dogs. These dogs developed their retrieving instinct in two distinct ways. Fish

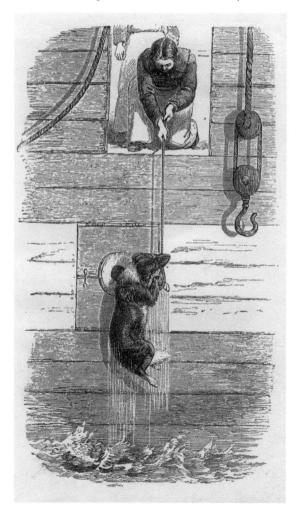

Fishing Dog from Hutchinson's Dog Breaking of 1909.

hooks were not as well made as they are today. A large fish, when brought to the surface, might free itself from the hook. A dog with a special harness would be lowered from the deck – grab the fish – and be hauled back on board with, hopefully, the fish still in its mouth… I know from my own experience that many of these dogs have still inherited this retrieving of fish.

Preserved in the Natural History Museum outpost at Tring is a 'Trawler Spaniel', a parti-coloured dog, just under a foot high, resembling the small sporting spaniels found here and on the Continent, often included by artists in family portraits.

The Earl went on to point out that when his ancestor was importing dogs from the Newfoundland Fishing Fleet unloading in Poole Harbour, the fishing industry in Christchurch and Bournemouth harbours was intensive and the need for dogs extensive. Further north, the great retriever authority, Stanley O'Neill, recorded that his father was Superintendent of Grimsby Fish Docks, and he went with him to visit every port where fish was landed in England and Scotland, writing:

I saw hundreds of water dogs around Grimsby and Yarmouth which were ships dogs, and it was well

Trawler Spaniel, preserved at the Natural History Museum, Tring.

known that a cross with them to improve retrieving from water had been the origin of the curly-coats. In 1903, at Alnmouth, he saw men netting for salmon with a dog with a wavy or curly coat and of a tawny colour.

When he asked about the dog he was told it was a Tweed Water Spaniel. Such a dog was behind many of our emerging land retrievers, with what became the Golden Retriever gaining from this type and coat colour. In his *The Complete Farrier* of 1815, Richard Lawrence wrote: 'Along the rocky shores and dreadful declivities beyond the junction of the Tweed and the sea of Berwick, Water dogs have received an addition of strength from the experimental introductions of a cross with the Newfoundland dog… the liver-coloured is the most rapid of swimmers and the most eager in pursuit.' The genotype of the purebred Newfoundland includes two different factors for the brown coat. Landseer Newfoundlands can be piebald red or bronze; the American vet Leon Whitney has reported both blues and reds, and Clarence Little, the American coat-colour inheritance expert, has recorded the tan point pattern in pedigree Newfoundlands.

The Water 'Spaniels'

The dark liver is the classic water dog colour, as the American and Irish Water Spaniels, the Wetterhoun and the Lagotto display today. The Wetterhoun, once famed as an otter-hunter, and the Lagotto, still famous as a truffle-finder, also feature liver and white, as our own now extinct water spaniel did. It is of interest that the Newfoundland, once described as the Great Retriever, was depicted by Ben Marshall in his well-known painting of 1811 as being black and white and covered in small tight curls. Our ancestors bred dogs with waterproof coats to support them in their ship and shoreline tasks. As the show ring now fashions so much in the pedigree dog world, it is important that judges of water dog/spaniel breeds insist on the coat texture of the entry before them is traditional and does not become the subject of exaggeration. These dogs had to have a waterproof coat to survive and we should honour that heritage. Later on, in this book, I argue for the restoration of the English Water Spaniel to our list of gundog breeds.

Unfounded Grouping

The kennel clubs of the world have become seriously confused by the water-dog breeds, regarding them as having different origins and functions, and therefore meriting different groupings. In Britain, our KC originally allocated the Spanish Water Dog and the Lagotto Romagnolo to the new sub-group of Utility Gundog – with the Kooikerhondje within the Gundog group, where they joined the Irish and American Water Spaniels. It places the Poodle in the Utility group and the Portuguese Water Dog in the Working group, with the Barbet, now becoming established here, awaiting allocation. From 2014, however, the Spanish Water Dog and the the Lagotto Romagnolo will be reallocated to the Working Group and the Kooikerhondje to the Utility Group. (What kind of functional test could be designed for them there?) The FCI places the water dogs in their own sub-group, section 3 of Group 8, which embraces the retrievers and spaniels and includes the Barbet, possibly the most ancient water dog. They place the Irish and American Water Spaniels in this sub-group too. (The Poodle is grouped with the Toy breeds.) I agree with such an arrangement. It can, however, affect specialist knowledge amongst judges at shows held here and those on the continent of Europe.

The Poodle

The Poodle of today came directly from the curly-coated variety of water dog, as indeed, less directly, did our Curly-coated Retriever, the Wetterhoun of Holland and the surviving water spaniels. Seen nowadays as a non-sporting dog, the Poodle has

ABOVE RIGHT: *Small Water Spaniel and Water Dog of Italy by A. Innocente, c.1770.*

RIGHT: *Standard Poodle in working clip.*

a creditable sporting pedigree – the Rev. Harold Browne's retrieving Poodles being much admired at the start of the twentieth century. The Germans referred to such a dog as a Pudel; the French spoke of a Canne Chien or duck dog, which became in time Caniche, the modern French name for a poodle, whilst the Russians wrote of a Podlaika, *laika* meaning a bark-pointer, like the Finnish Spitz.

I have yet to meet a French sportsman who is proud of the Poodle, but I admire them. They are clever dogs and the standard variety is underused as a gundog. Clipped to resemble a Curly-coated Retriever, they look workmanlike and utilitarian, rather than exhibition items. A French shooting man, so anxious to distance his country from the Poodle, assured me that they were Russian in origin and German in development. He cited the Pudelpointer and the Schafpudel as German variations on the type. The word Pudel is German and the French do call the breed the Caniche, derived from Chien Canard (Canne Chien) or duck dog. My French colleague insisted that the French water dog was the Barbet and the German the Pudelhund. The corded Poodle, or Schnur Pudel, has been dubbed the Russian Poodle. The nineteenth-century German cynologist Dr Fitzinger listed six different varieties of the breed, but maintained that the standard version originated in northwest Africa.

The standard Poodle in a solid black coat, in a working trim, can be confused with a Barbet and even the smaller Portuguese Water Dog, just as the American and Irish Water Spaniels can appear one breed to the general public. We expect the standard Poodle to be at least 15in high and have a harsh textured coat, in any solid colour. The FCI expects the standard Poodle to be 17½–23½in and have a woolly coat.

The Barbet

The advent of firearms led to many changes in the use of dogs in the hunting of feathered game. No longer were the dogs just required to bring back the valuable arrows or bolts but they were expected to retrieve shot game on land as well as from water. The finding of shot game on land, especially as the range of munitions increased, demanded top quality scenting powers, the persistence of a hound and the biddable qualities of a sheepdog. In due course, the breeds of land spaniel developed alongside the water spaniels, which usually had a high proportion of water-dog blood, as their coat texture revealed.

The Barbet in France was one of the prototypal water dogs and after nearly becoming extinct in the nineteenth century, yet probably predating the Poodle, was once clever enough and versatile enough

Ben Marshall's portrayal of the Newfoundland, 1810.

to be favoured by French poachers and continental travelling families. They were used by French fishing communities and may have contributed blood to the Newfoundland on the Northeastern American seaboard. Certainly, some of the early Newfoundlands had a distinct Barbet look to them. They are strapping dogs, powerful swimmers and clever dogs with great energy. It would be good to see them being used by wildfowlers, as they are well equipped to be really good water retrievers.

The Irish Dog

The Irish Water Spaniel, affectionately known as the whiptail, is a rich dark liver-coloured gundog, with a coat of crisp tight ringlets, free of any woolliness, but containing the natural oiliness of the water dog group of dogs. Just under 2ft high, strongly made but compactly built, the breed is shown here as a spaniel but enters field trials as a retriever, yet another sign of the KC's misunderstanding of water dogs. In his *The Dogs of the British Islands* of 1878, 'Stonehenge' gave the view that this was the by far the most useful dog for wildfowl shooting then in existence and quotes a breeder called Lindoe as stating 'Notwithstanding their natural impetuosity of disposition, these spaniels, if properly trained, are the most tractable and obedient of all dogs, and possess in a marked degree the invaluable qualities of never giving up or giving in.' That sums up the character and potential of the 'wild Irishman', with highly experienced sportsman James Wentworth Day, in his *The Dog in Sport* of 1938, describing him as 'one of the finest

William Poyntz of Midgham by Gainsborough, c.1750, depicting a sportsman and his waterdog.

Irish Water 'Spaniel' retrieving in Holland, 1986.

water-dogs in the world… the best dog out of Ireland for the all-round shooting man.'

Their blood is valued by wildfowlers too. In *The Countryman's Weekly* of 21 March 2012, Derek Robinson described how his Labrador cross Whiptail performed in the field: 'The hunting ability and nose is far better than any Lab while his coat is dense and coarse, drying so much quicker than a spaniel's. It is wildfowling that he's been trained for…' Never over-popular, their annual registrations with our KC averaging just over 100 a year, it would be good to see their grouping as a gundog breed rethought and their recognition as a rather special breed assured.

The American Dog

The American dog has a distinct look of the Irish dog about it but unlike the other types of water dog is scarcely known here. Only 15–18in high, solid liver, brown or dark chocolate, their coats can range from the close curl of the water dogs to the marcelled coats of the water spaniels. Long used as a wildfowlers' dog, American sportsman and writer Freeman Lloyd, in his *All Spaniels* of 1930, stated that:

> There was a fine old breed or strain of liver-colored water spaniels of the flat or wavy-coated variety which was much in use in several parts of the United States and Canada. There were others with curly coats and often long tails, more or less related to the water spaniels of Ireland. Here was a spaniel strong enough for anything…

As with the Cocker Spaniel and the Staffordshire Bull Terrier, the Americans have stabilized their own type and established new breeds of dog, if mainly in the show world. The American Water Spaniel has recently been imported here but it will need immense efforts to get it established.

The Portuguese Dog

This ancient Portuguese breed, recognized by our KC not as a gundog, but as a 'Working Dog' in the group for such dogs, can be black, white, shades of brown or parti-coloured, with two distinct types of coat: long and loosely waved or short, dense, fairly harsh and curly; it is around 20in high, weighing around 45lb. These dogs are usually given the classic water dog clip from the last rib. Now well known here, with around 100 registered a year, it would be good to see the curly-coated variety used by wildfowlers and their latent sporting instincts encouraged.

The Spanish Dog

This water dog breed *is* recognized by our KC as a gundog and was first seen in Britain in the 1970s. When I was based in Gibraltar half a century ago and visited Spanish ports at the southern end of that country, you could find dogs of this type as all-purpose dogs there and even as herding dogs further inland. Around 18in high, in the same coat colours as the Portuguese dog, they can be naturally bob-tailed, have a woolly curled coat, even corded, but are not given the classic water dog clip. They are justifiably

American Water Spaniel – Ch Clair's Corkey of 1905.

becoming quite popular here as a companion dog, with nearly 200 registered with the KC in 2011, but I have not heard of their employment as a gundog in Britain, despite their correct grouping.

The Italian Dog

This breed, known as the Lagotto Romagnolo, and used there as a duck retriever and as a truffle hound, is the same size as the Spanish dog but comes in a wider range of colours. Originally a water retriever from the lowlands of Comacchio and the swamps of Ravenna, this breed moved on to become a valuable truffle locating dog in the plains and hills of Romagna, being recognized as a breed internationally in 1995. Its coat can range in colour from solid white to parti-coloured white and brown or orange or roan. Its texture is curly, dense, woolly and in ringlet form. Recognized here as a gundog breed, thirty-five were registered in 2011 and I can see this attractive breed steadily increasing its popularity.

The Dutch Dog

The Frisian Water Dog is of a type found all over Europe in past times, including Britain. Our English Water Spaniel, once listed by the Kennel Club, now lost to us but easily restored if ever we regain our national pride, was in this mould. The Portuguese, the Spanish, the Italians, the French and the Americans have retained and treasured their water dogs; we have, in our reckless pursuit of all things foreign, forsaken ours. The Dutch too have conserved their ancient breed. The Frisian Water Dog, or Wetterhoun, is a curly-coated, solid black or brown or part-coloured 2ft-high dog, rather like a smaller Curly-coated Retriever. As their name suggests, they excel in water and are robust working dogs rather than ornamental pets. As a breed they are not recognized in Britain but exhibited at European and world dog shows.

ABOVE RIGHT: Spanish Water Dog.

RIGHT: Lagotto Romagnolo.

Wetterhoun from Holland.

The Water Dog Legacy
Distinctive Coats
I have seen purebred Labradors with tightly curled coats and we have all seen English Springer Spaniels with very curly coats. I suspect the linty coat of the distinctive Bedlington Terrier owes its origin to water-dog blood, perhaps that of the Tweed Water Spaniel, once known in the area where the Bedlington was developed. The early Airedale Terriers, bred originally as waterside terriers in the Aire valley, had noticeably curly coats; this is now frowned on, the word crinkle-coated being preferred. The now extinct Llanidloes Setter also sported this tight, densely curled, waterproof coat. The Tweed Water Spaniel blood in the Golden Retriever is, however, not only acknowledged but prized. Our ancestors knew the value of water-dog blood.

It may not suit the misplaced pride of the shooting man of today to acknowledge the blood of poodle-like dogs in his working gundogs or associate such dogs with his sporting image. I see it as a matter of gratitude more than anything else. It may be difficult to accept a shared origin between a strapping Curly and a toy Poodle, a sturdy Wetterhoun and a diminutive bichon, or a lion-clipped tiny Lowchen and a whiptail. But, as the Chihuahua and the Great Dane dramatically illustrate, different purpose has led to different development; ornamental dogs are expected to be small, retrievers have to have substance and stamina.

The liver and the black coat colours of the ancient water dogs and their unique curly texture have survived and surfaced in many of today's breeds, whether sporting or non-sporting in use. Their fondness for and durability in water lives on too, whether the breed is linked to Ireland or Holland, Italy or Spain, France or Portugal, America or Britain. Water dogs are the rootstock of many of our sporting breeds, whether they have lost or retained the typical coat texture and colours of their distant ancestors. The water dogs of Europe have contributed a great deal to our sporting heritage and more should be made of the debt we owe them, in breed histories for example. May those of Italy and Spain, now saved from extinction, go from strength to strength. And how about recreating our Tweed Water Spaniel?

Portuguese Water Dog – curly-coated variety.

'Curly-coated Labrador' from purebred parents.

This very description of water-dog differs materially in size, as well as in the length and rigid elasticity of the coat, from the smaller and more delicate, as well as more domesticated breed under the denomination of the water-spaniel, it becomes only necessary to recite such distinguishing traits of his utility as are but little known to that part of the sporting world who are situate in the centrical and inland parts of the kingdom. Upon the sea-coast, the breed is principally propagated, where they are mostly brought into use, and held in the highest proportional estimation; but along the rocky shores, and dreadful declivities, beyond the junction of the Tweed with the sea at Berwick, the breed has derived an addition of strength from the experimental introduction of a cross with the Newfoundland dog, which has rendered them only adequate to the arduous difficulties and diurnal perils in which they are systematically engaged.

The Sportsman's Cabinet (1803)

The Decoy Dog

It is forgivable in these days of high-quality, increasingly accurate, much longer-ranged sporting firearms to overlook the fact that a century and a half ago shooting was, literally, very much more a hit-and-miss affair. Gundogs, especially those supporting wildfowlers, had to be rather special dogs, versatile and skilful, as well as extraordinarily robust. Our trusty retrievers still serve us well in this respect but the widespread use of decoy dogs, to bring the wildfowl either within range of the guns, or to entice them along ever-narrowing netted channels, is unappreciated. Much of the construction of duck-decoys here was inspired by the Dutch. They have conserved their decoy dog, the Kooikerhondje; we have lost ours – perhaps to Canada!

Colonists' Needs

How valuable must have been the dogs that accompanied settlers to 'new' countries in past centuries. Hounds, gundogs and herding dogs must have been a godsend to those carving out a new life in primitive conditions. The dogs the settlers brought with them would not have conformed to any contemporary standard, but earned their keep and were valued for what they could do, not what they looked like. Bob-tailed, shorter-haired collies may now be called Australian Shepherds and been developed as a breed in North America. But the breed type has long been known in Britain and is still favoured in the Black Mountains on the English-Welsh border. The

Wild Fowling on the Norfolk Coast in 1830, with red decoy dog in forefront.

Throwback to collie-like red decoy dog.

Chesapeake Bay Retriever may well be the sandy-brown rust-coloured Norfolk Retriever transported and the Nova Scotia Duck Tolling Retriever the Red Decoy Dog of the Fens resettled in a new location.

The dog used as a decoy in duck hunting often worked in partnership with tame ducks to entice their wild relatives along ever-narrowing netted or caged channels until they were made captive. George Jesse, in his exhaustive *Researches into the History of the British Dog* of 1866, described how, in the Fens of Essex, dogs resembling the 'colly' were used with tame ducks to entice wildfowl into tunnel-nets. Throwbacks to this collie-like, red-coated, lavishly tailed, clever, agile dog still occur in country areas; their luxuriantly furnished tails are flourished exorbitantly when alert to feathered game. There were once as many as 188 duck-decoys located in England, mainly in the easternmost counties.

Coat Colour Significance

In Ralph Payne-Gallwey's book on duck decoys of 1886 there is a good depiction of a red decoy dog working with a black water dog; it displays the appealing red-gold coat once common in Golden Retrievers before it was diluted in a closed gene pool. I see this colour in working Cockers but, not being favoured by show fanciers, it is not bred for, despite its distinctive hue. This coat colour is remarkably difficult

A Lincolnshire Duck Decoy, late 18th century.

to pick up when working gundogs or patrolling with guard dogs at night. Coat colour matters more in working conditions than many show breeders realize. A heavily feathered tail also has its uses, not just as a rudder in water or in providing balance on tight turns.

The skill of the decoy dog lies in giving the inquisitive ducks only fleeting and tantalizing glimpses of its progress, usually its tail's progress, through the reeds and undergrowth, taking great care never to frighten them or even give them cause for suspicion. Before the use of firearms and indeed in the days when their range was very limited, these dogs must have been enormously valuable to duck-hunters. For the humbler hunters they represented the difference between eating or starving. In the nineteenth century, just ten decoys around Wainfleet in Lincolnshire produced 31,200 head in one season, mostly for the London markets.

Universal Features

The distinctive feature of dogs used in this way was the well-flagged tail. Their colour was usually fox-red, leading to some being referred to as fox-dogs, partly also because foxes will entice game by playful antics in a very similar vein. Clever little fox-like dogs have been used in many different countries in any number of ways in the pursuit of game: in Finland, the red-

Sportsman with red decoy dog/retriever and Pointer by E.P. Shuckard, 1872.

Sportsmen with red decoy dog and water dog, early 18th century.

coated bark-pointer Spitz breed transfixes feathered game by its mesmeric barking whilst awaiting the arrival of the hunters; in Japan, the russet-coated Shiba Inu was once used to flush birds for the falcon and the Tahl-tan Indians in British Columbia hunted bear, lynx and porcupine with their little black bear-dogs, which were often mistaken for foxes.

The Use of the Piper

In his *Duck Decoys* of 2001, Andrew Heaton writes on decoy dogs:

> A dog trained and used in working a decoy in this manner needs to be extremely obedient, able to respond to silent commands and carry out its duties without taking notice of the encroaching wildfowl. The dogs were traditionally given the name of Piper. Such dogs tended to be fox-like in form, small with a bushy tail and a reddish coloration.

Ferrets, cats, tame foxes and even a rabbit have been tried in this role but proved untrainable. The KC's standard for the breed of Nova Scotia Duck Tolling

Retriever stipulates that the breed should be easy to train, with a constantly moving heavily feathered tail, and playful. I do hope the breed retains the red-gold coat and does not become off-white like the Golden Retriever. Small red-coated retrievers were once very common in Britain and depicted by such artists as Ferneley, Van Dyck and Shuckard.

At the end of the nineteenth century 'ginger coy dogs' were frequently to be seen alongside the lurchers in gypsy camps, especially in East Anglia. James Wentworth Day, the celebrated country sports writer, refers to them in his *The Dog in Sport* of 1938, linking them with the 'Fen Tigers', the rough countrymen who cut sedge and dug peat from the Fens and were skilled wildfowlers. In his mammoth *Dogs – The Ultimate Dictionary of over 1,000 Dog Breeds* of 2001, Desmond Morris describes the Red Decoy Dog as a small rufous dog employed to lure wildfowl into nets and suggests that their behaviour in doing so was modelled on comparable behaviour in foxes. Because no pedigree breed in this mould has been handed down to us, very little reference is made nowadays to these gifted and at one time invaluable dogs, rather as the ancient water dogs are rarely acknowledged in the histories of our gundog breeds. Both decoy dogs and water dogs were usually handled by the humbler hunters like farm labourers and gypsies and so very little has been written about them.

Dutch Expertise

In Europe it seems that the Dutch in particular had perfected the art of duck decoying, with the word itself coming from their word *endekoy*, a duck cage. The first duck-decoy in Britain was built by a Dutchman, Hydrach Hilens, just over 300 years ago in St James's Park for Charles II. Such a decoy usually consists of a small shallow pond secluded by trees with a number of 'pipes' leading off it, each about 200ft long. These pipes or caged tunnels are 20ft wide and 13ft high at their entrance but narrow right down to the decoyman's net.

Along the curve of the pipe the decoyman (or *kooiker* in Holland) is concealed behind reed-screens. One of the few remaining in Britain is a joint venture between the National Trust and the Berkshire, Buckinghamshire and Oxfordshire Naturalists' Trust at Boarstall. This decoy is marked on the 1697 map of the Manor of Boarstall in the Buckinghamshire

County Record Office. Tame 'call ducks' are no longer used here but Daniel White, who worked this decoy for over sixty years, used six large Rouen call ducks. The yearly average of duck taken here at the end of the nineteenth century was 800. I believe there are only four *kooikers* still operating in Holland but they have retained their specialist breed of decoy dog, the Kooikerhondje, a small red and white spaniel-like dog; one of these is now working at the Boarstall decoy. A Nova Scotia Duck Tolling Retriever is working at the decoy on the Berkeley Estate in Gloucestershire. England has lost its native red-coated decoy dog, which surely could still have been useful if only to those wishing to ring, photograph, paint or just study wild duck.

Both the Nova Scotia Duck Tolling Retriever from Canada and the Kooikerhondje from Holland are now established here. They make attractive companion dogs, with happy natures and a handsome appearance. The Canadian dog is around a foot and a half high, and comes in all shades of red or orange, with lighter markings under the tail and white markings on the chest, toes and tip of tail. The Dutch

Nova Scotia Duck Tolling Retriever.

dog is a little smaller, mainly white with orange-red patches breaking up the coat.

Kooikerhondje – Dutch decoy dog.

LEFT: English Duck Decoy Scene of 1897, with our red decoy dog.

BELOW: English Decoy dog at work in 1897.

Duck Luring

Some wildfowlers, hunting the open shoreline, have used decoy dogs to lure ducks within shooting range by throwing sticks for the dog to retrieve and arousing the natural curiosity of the birds. The skill of the hunter lies in throwing the stick for the dog the right distance at the right moment so that the ducks are not frightened away by the menace of an advancing dog, but made curious by the enticing waving of its bushy tail. The dog makes a normal retrieve of the stick but does so in a playful manner with plenty of tail-wagging. This decoy dog does not entice the birds by deliberately frolicking about, as foxes have been seen to, but is used essentially as a retriever of sticks. This playful retrieve does, however, lure the duck within range of the hunter's gun. This is actually more work than play; before the use of firearms with appreciable range, such dogs would have more than earned their keep.

The Nova Scotia Duck Tolling Retriever is widely favoured in Scandinavia, where working tests are held for them. A tolling working test is a hunting trial using canvas dummies in lieu of cold game, embracing tolling and retrieving, aiming to rehearse and instil basic retriever skills. Tollers are expected to feature the true retriever double coat, the outer for waterproofing, the inner for insulation. The toller has been described as a hunter's dog, rather than a trainer's dog. They can often follow their instinct rather than their handler's wishes! They can vary in size and weight of bone, as well as degrees of obstinacy, but their handy size, handsome appearance and soft natures have won them many loyal fanciers.

I see many resemblances to the Golden Retriever in the Canadian decoy dog both in its sunny nature and its perpetually waving tail. A Golden was quite recently used as a decoy dog in East Anglia, charming many visitors. We may not, in these sophisticated times, need all of the wide-ranging skills of our dogs, but they need to have them exercised and we should respect their innate desire to be active, their instinctive interest in hunting and their inherent talent for serving mankind.

Completion of a successful Dutch Decoy.

A 'kooiker' at work with his dog in Holland.

Wildfowler Challenge

The Welsh have their springer spaniel and the French their Brittany, both featuring that attractive rich red with white coat, although the French dogs are more often red-roan. To see a sporting dog in this rich red hue, working in the sunshine, active and enthusiastic, is for me one of the most satisfying sights on any shoot. Their coats seem to glow with health and vigour. It is often a colour favoured by wildfowlers and may be more than a preference in colour; so many breeds with waterproof coats have a reddish look to them. The old Norfolk Retriever was said to have had a reddish coat, as did the Tweed or Ladykirk Spaniel, the Norfolk or Shropshire Spaniel and the English Water Spaniel. They live on in our surviving gundog breeds perhaps but we have lost part of our sporting dog inheritance. One day a keen wildfowler might take on the worthy task of re-creating them; that would be an appreciable contribution to our fast-disappearing canine sporting heritage.

> There is another dog, called, Down East, the Tolling Dog, which hails from Newfoundland... Suppose you had a dog that bred true to type, was an unexcelled cold-water retriever and would 'toll' ducks for you... This dog is trained to perform antics in the sedge; now in sight, now down in the grass, appearing and disappearing, until the curious ducks begin to swim in, little by little, to satisfy themselves what it is all about. They seem to have no fear of the toller which is a rather small dog, and soon are in range, when the gunners up and at 'em, whereupon the toller swims out, retrieves the slain, and again begins his antics... Such is the toller, seemingly a breed produced by crossing the English retriever on the well-known Labrador... Mr HAP Smith of Nova Scotia is at present the principal breeder of these dogs.
>
> Warren H. Miller, (former Editor of *Field and Stream*), *The American Hunting Dog, Modern Strains of Bird Dogs and Hounds, and their Field Training* (1919)

Victorian Gundogs

> I consider dog shows necessary for the maintenance of the high standard of the various breeds, but they are often abused by exhibitors for pecuniary benefit and self-advertisement, rather than for the benefit of the dogs. There are too many dog shows. Fewer, with better prize-money, would, I am sure, do more for the advancement of the different breeds, besides making the winners of more value. The only way to prevent fraud is to insist on all dogs being registered.
>
> *The Twentieth Century Dog (Sporting)* by Herbert Crompron (1904)

It was in 1865 that the first field trial of pointers and setters was held at Southill, on the property of the late Mr. W.H. Whitbread, who was the proprietor of one of the largest estates in the county of Bedford. This was about the time when, owing to the improved system

Victorian Field Trial, Bala, North Wales, by George Earl (active 1856–83).

of agriculture and the tillage of the land, pointers and setters were beginning to lose their vocation. Still, there are many who look back to the period when, with stubbles – reaped with a sickle – half way up to the knees, they had shot over a brace of pointers and setters and enjoyed it infinitely more than the battues which are now the fashion of the day.

Fred Gresham, writing in *Dog Breaking* by 'Wildfowler' (1915)

Input of Nobility

Queen Victoria's long reign witnessed huge changes to Britain, and the world and the world of dogs was no exception, undergoing changes with far-reaching implications. Britain had a wide reputation as a breeder of livestock; the existence of the Empire ensured that British sporting styles and social trends soon spread all over the globe. When, in the days before quarantine, British landed gentry went on sporting tours, their dogs went with them. When British livestock was exported, the herding dogs went too. When the British emigrated or went to work for extended periods in places like India, their dogs went with them. In the second half of the nineteenth century British dogs, sporting dogs especially, became known and highly rated in most parts of the world. In her *The Hungarian Vizsla* (1985), Gay Gottlieb relates how, in 1880, Zoltan Hamvay imported the English Setter and Julius Barczy de Barczihaza brought in the Irish Setter and both were bred to the native dog, the Vizsla. It was the fashion in Hungary for the aristocracy to bring in English

gamekeepers, who understandably brought their retrievers with them and in due course the best were bred to the local bird dogs.

In Victorian times, the nobility and landed gentry had a huge influence on dogs, sporting breeds especially. There were 200 packs of Foxhounds, with the Duke of Beaufort and Lords Donerail, Portsmouth, Coventry and Bentinck taking a keen interest. The Dukes of Gordon and of Richmond kept Deerhounds, as did Lords Seaforth, Tankerville and Bentinck. Lord Bagot showed Bloodhounds and Lord Wolverton ran a pack of them in Dorset, later sold to Lord Carrington in Buckinghamshire. The Marquess of Anglesey kept Harriers and Sir John Heathcote-Amory favoured Staghounds. Lord Lurgan's coursing Greyhound Master McGrath won three Waterloo Cups out of four. The Duke of Atholl maintained a pack of Otterhounds. In Borzois, the Duchess of Manchester owned a huge specimen bred by Prince William of Prussia. Noble families made a significant contribution to the gundog breeds: Lord Tweedmouth in Golden Retrievers, the Earl of Malmesbury and Lord Knutsford in Labradors, Viscount Melville in Curly-coats, the Earls of Sefton, Lichfield and Derby in Pointers, the Duke of Gordon in his type of setters, the Earl of Tankerville and Lord Waterpark in English Setters, and the Duke of Newcastle, Lords Middleton and Spencer in Clumbers. This is an impressive list, and a very noticeable difference between the patronage of breeds of dog in Victorian times and now is the almost negligible involvement of the nobility nowadays.

Gamekeepers at Maer Hall, Staffordshire, 1890.

Once, their interest guaranteed support for many breeds, a higher profile for the Kennel Club and the promotion of dogs for their sake rather than the bank balance. However, I believe it is fair to state that the major contribution to the development of breeds as such came from lower down the Victorian social scale, from the more plebeian fanciers, as well as the dedication of the squires and yeomen breeders. In gundogs, for example, the likes of Llewellin and Laverack achieved longer-lasting impact, whilst in the Foxhound world the legendary 'Ikey' Bell restored soundness at a time when so many Masters of Foxhounds had lost their way – the strange seeking of 'great bone' handicapping hounds when hunting.

LEFT: *Athole Estate Keepers, Scotland, late 19th century.*

BELOW LEFT: *Ernest Smith, Gamekeeper, Oakedge, Staffordshire, c.1900, with his retrievers.*

BELOW RIGHT: *Victorian Gentleman with his black retriever (courtesy Bucks County Museum).*

The Squire's Friends by Frank Paton, 1892.

On Point by Maud Earl, conveying the sheer intensity of the Pointer's stance.

The wider spread of wealth and more time for leisure had an impact on the dog scene; dog shows became fashionable, field trials were introduced and both hunting and shooting became 'must-do' events in the countryside. Shows and trials brought a need for registration so that a dog's identity could be verified. As the range and frequency of shot increased so the needs of sportsmen in their supporting dogs changed too. In the hunting field the better breeding of hounds received much more attention. Companion dogs too were influenced by greater foreign travel and the subsequent introduction here of exotic breeds from distant places. At the same time came more focus on animal welfare, the moral repugnance towards some barbaric so-called 'sports', greater concern over the plight of street dogs, draught dogs especially, and a move towards more enlightened training and less 'breaking' of dogs.

Stern Judgements

Some of the Victorian judges were very forthright in their views on the show dogs appearing in front of them. In *The Kennel Gazette* of July 1888, at the Kennel Club Show the English Setter judge, W. Sargeantson, wrote: 'I hope I may never again have to judge such poverty-stricken classes.' The Irish Setter judge, C.C. Ellis, wrote: 'With the exception of a few the Irish Setters were bad...' The Pointer judge, W. Sheild, commented: 'I only have to say that pointer breeders should pay more attention to breeding dogs with typical heads and hazel eyes; there were pointers in the show carrying heads of the shape of the bull terriers' and with eyes like cat's eyes.' The Spaniels judge, J.S. Cowell, noted in the black Field Spaniel entry: 'The Bitches were a very poor lot.' In the same publication in July 1889, the retriever judge at the Olympia show, the great Pointer man William Arkwright wrote:

It is quite extraordinary to me how judges can award prizes to so-called retrievers, which are manifestly unfit for their work from the badness of legs and feet and clumsiness of shape, because they have the fleece of an Astrakhan sheep on their backs; one can understand reporters being so deluded, but surely judges should not forget that the retriever is intended for sporting purposes and not to decorate a furrier's shop. That many of them do so err is painfully evident on reading over the list of prizes won by some of these monstrosities of the show bench.

Such overt, unrestrained criticism can do good, but you would never see it in *The Kennel Gazette* of today, despite the campaign for a gundog entry that is 'fit for function'. Total honesty in the Victorian show ring judges shaped the breeds we have before us today.

Higher Profile

Royal patronage and the obsessive interest of the nobility in field sports gave some types of dog a higher profile, but the desire to produce dogs that closely resembled their parents and bred true to type, a fall-out of the show ring, led to the production of purebreeds. Of course, before that, breed type had been established in many cases with Greyhounds, Harriers, Beagles, Pointers and Deerhounds usually looking like their ancestors. But from now on closed gene pools were to be respected and purity of breeding revered. For the first time in dogdom, it was not just a case of breeding good dog to good dog – both parents had to be registered and out-crossing was frowned upon. This ethos has persisted more in the gundog world than, say, the terrier world or the hunting field.

English Setters searching for air–scent by P.E. Stretton, 1884–1919.

The Shooting Party by J.F. Herring Jnr (1815–1875). Note the moderate feathering on the setter in the foreground.

A Day's Grouse Shooting in Aberdeenshire 1889 by C. Suhrlandt (German) with two Gordon Setters (centre stage) and three brace of English Setters in the cart.

This pursuit of breed purity has had a marked effect on the well-being of the dog. Breeding from a closed gene pool is fine when things are going well but disastrous when inbred faults and genetic flaws are encountered. The Victorian era may have given us the breeds but it has also given us the problems arising from inbreeding, conducted for a century in some cases. Our lives have been enriched by the breeds of dog handed down to us by our Victorian ancestors; now we must use scientific advances and increased veterinary knowledge to capitalize on and not be penalized by the admirable pioneering work done by the Victorians. This is the great challenge for sportsmen who prize their breeds in the new century. The old century, the twentieth, saw huge changes in shooting habits and marked differences in gundog breeds and this is covered in the next section.

> If any argument was required to prove the immense value of high breeding and pedigrees, the condition of foreign countries might be cited in regard to sporting dogs as to what it was twenty years ago and what it is now. Formerly, foreigners were entirely dependent on dog dealers for all kinds of pointers and setters, and they were only too fortunate if they got any value at all for the money they expended. Good field performers might occasionally be found … but in proof that the importations from England were mostly moderate was the abuse bestowed upon the English dog traders by Frenchmen generally… I never saw a good dog that was bred in France from such dogs… Such dogs have no pedigrees, as dealers' dogs never have … many of the

puppies resembling droppers more than anything else.
> 'Leatherhead' writing in *The Kennel Gazette*,
> October 1884

In referring to foreign gundogs it must at the outset be understood – as it is generally acknowledged by the sportsman of other lands than our own – that the British breeds used in the process of fowling are far superior to their foreign relatives… It is only fair to our fellow sportsmen on the Continent, however, to remember that our Setters, our Pointers, our Spaniels and Retrievers, have all been derived from strains imported into these islands from abroad.
The New Book of the Dog by Robert Leighton (1912)

Twentieth-Century Gundogs

With the almost total suspension of breeding activities during the 1st World War period (1914–1919) breeders had a very uphill task to re-establish the breed, but they are deserving of the highest praise and admiration for their efforts, as with the very scant material to hand, in the course of a very few years the Cocker was flourishing more than ever and had gained its present popularity by peaceful methods, by steady progress, and did not burst on the world with a flourish of trumpets, but step by step consolidating its position steadily as it went along.
The Cocker Spaniel by H.S. Lloyd (1924)

The effect of the War is easily seen in the registration figures. In 1942 and 1943 there were only two dogs registered, and the whole decade did not average 10 per annum. Challenge certificates were suspended with dog shows in mid 1939 and the last field trial was held in 1938. It was 1948 before the Field Spaniel Society was able to meet again and we owe much to those who gathered then and by careful breeding from the few dogs left, raised registrations as high as 45 in 1950.

The Complete Book of Gundogs in Britain by Roger Hall Jones (1974)

If in the last fifty or sixty years hunting conditions have changed so also have shooting conditions altered. Before the advent of the reaping machine and latterly the binder and reaper, a Pointer or Setter was almost a *sine qua non* to the man who loved his gun. Now, alas, how different! Except in a few cases, and those mostly over the Border, there is practically no use for those fascinating dogs, for of all Gundogs, there are none, perhaps, that appeal more to the lover of all that is best in a day's shooting.

The Early Life and Training of a Gundog by Lt-Col G.H. Badcock (1931)

All the gundogs have ample opportunities of showing their worth at field trials, many of which are held in the course of a season. The first of its kind took place at Southill in Bedfordshire in 1865, and the numbers gradually increased, but the greatest expansion took place after the Great War. The general effect has been to raise the working level of these dogs, to produce a degree of efficiency that was probably unknown to our great grandfathers, although dogs meant so much to them in their sports.

British Dogs by Arthur Croxton Smith (1945)

ABOVE LEFT: *A prize-winning Cocker Spaniel of the mid-20th century.*

LEFT: *Hunting Party on a Moor by G.D. Armour (1864–1949).*

Edwardian gundog training session.

1930s gundog group photographed by Constance Adams.

Effects of Wars

In the first half of the twentieth century sporting dogs were under threat, gundogs especially. Two World Wars saw many a famous kennel disappear and a subsequent rise in gundogs becoming purely pets had a lasting effect. Either side of 1900 it was not unknown for a keen wealthy sportsman to own several hundred gundogs, as William Humphrey exemplified with his kennel of over a thousand gundogs. The demands of two World Wars saw an end to such extravagance. The extraordinary popularity of the gundog breeds in the first fifty years of the last century was led by the unprecedented rise of the Labrador Retriever. The half-century ended with the introduction of the HPR

breeds and their adoption by increasing numbers of sportsmen in the UK.

If you look at the Kennel Club registrations in the period 1900–50, you can soon identify the mixed fortunes of the gundog breeds. The two wars made their mark; looking at gundog figures in 1914 and then again in 1919 shows the effect: English Setters 127 in 1914, 64 in 1919, Gordon Setters from 18 down to 2, Irish Setters 149 to 65, Pointers 146 to 28, Retrievers, Curly-coated 53 to 8, Flat-coated 370 to 97, Goldens 58 to 28, Labradors 363 to 131; Spaniels, Clumber 92 to 25, Cocker 501 to 344, Field 119 to 24, Irish Water 30 to 11, English Springer from 53 a surprising rise to 71, Welsh Springer 23 to just 2 and

Prize Golden Cocker Spaniels of 1922.

Sussex a small increase from 3 to 7. These are tiny numbers on which to rebuild a breed.

In 1927, over 1,300 Irish Setters, over 1,400 Labradors, nearly 4,500 Cockers and over 1,300 English Springers made their debut; the age of the pet gundog had arrived. The show ring too made its mark. Gundogs could triumph because of their looks rather than their performance. Dual-purpose dogs were still comparatively common and show ring judges nearly always had knowledge of gundogs at work in the field. Away from the shooting field, however, the needless undesirable indulgences crept in: over-furnished legs and tails, upright shoulders, especially in Pointers, and added weight in Clumbers. The latter were nevertheless still tighter-eyed than they are today and far less cloddy. King George V, in the 1920s, shot over the lighter type but exhibited the heavier dog.

Structure and Regulation

The field trial movement expanded significantly in the first part of the twentieth century. In 1901, meetings were few; by 1913 they had increased to twenty-seven and by 1938, as many as eighty were held. The early years of the twentieth century saw too more structure and regulation in the gundog world. In 1907 the Kennel Club instituted field trials for retrievers, after earlier attempts had led to The Retriever Society being founded in 1900. About this time, dogs from the same litter could be registered as a Lab if smooth-coated and a Flat-coat if wavy-coated. So, in 1916, crossbred retrievers were allowed to be registered; ninety-three were registered as such in 1923. There was a place also for 'gamefinders', allowing dogs of any ancestry but with some retriever blood to be registered. The English Springer Spaniel was recognized as a breed

Judging at the Golden Retriever Show near Pangbourne in June 1937.

RIGHT: Three high-quality 'Noranby' Golden Retrievers owned by Mrs W.M. Charlesworth, 1930s.

BELOW MIDDLE: Three generations of 'Banchory' champions (grandsire left and sire right).

BOTTOM: Top Labrador 'Peter of Faskally' at the Trials, 1911.

in 1902; breed clubs began to appear, with the Curly club starting in 1933 and the Goldies club forming in 1912. The year 1904 was an important one for Labradors, when Holland-Hibbert's Munden Single received a Certificate of Merit, on the first appearance of Labs at a field trial.

One regrettable feature in spaniels was the 'bassetization' of Field Spaniels, which produced low-slung specimens with long backs and shortened legs and was only rectified when the Field Spaniel Society set to work. Until the formation of the Irish Water Spaniel Association in 1926, little had been seen of these dogs in public and it was the policy of the newly formed body to organize field trials to test their breed. The British Gordon Setter Club came into being at the end of the 1920s, which did much to revive interest in the breed.

Although Irish Setters have long enjoyed a reputation as working dogs, they had not been run much at English field trials until Mrs F. Nagle founded a kennel of them at Sulhamstead, near Reading. In 1929 and 1935 her Sulhamstead Brantome d'Or won the KC Derby for Pointer and Setter puppies, with her Carrie d'Or coming fourth in 1932 and Bluff d'Or third in 1933. The breed's registrations went from 308 in 1921 to 1,359 in 1927, such was the interest in the pet/show world.

It was, paradoxically, the field trial world which kept the English Setter going. From 1911 until 1925, Captain Gilbert Blaine used his English Setters to work with trained falcons near Caithness. He needed to have fast, wide rangers that had really good 'long' noses and never made false points. In both 1913 and 1922, Capt Blaine killed over 200 brace of grouse with his peregrines.

Later on, Lorna, Countess Howe, added English Setters and Pointers to her strong kennel of gundogs.

LEFT: *English Springer Spaniel FT Champion 'Banchory Bright', 1927.*

BELOW: *Champion English Setter 'Mallwyd Sirdar' of 1906.*

It was largely through her influence that Labradors have enjoyed more fame as dual-purpose dogs than any other gundogs. The Labrador Retriever Club was founded in 1916, with her as its secretary; she did her own breaking and was the first of her gender to judge a KC trial. Registrations of this breed went from 140 in 1910 to 1,410 in 1927 and have never looked back. The English Springer, too, triumphed, going from 70 in 1910 to over 1,320 in 1927. In 1950, over 4,000 Labradors and over 2,000 English Springers were registered. In 1999, over 33,000 Labradors and over 12,000 Springers were registered with the KC. These two gundog breeds have truly been *the* sporting breeds of the last century.

Continental Influences

But the post-Second World War sportsman had a new shooting style to pursue and a different type of gundog to support it. Army officers stationed in Germany saw the all-rounders, the HPR breeds, and liked what they saw. With little or no experience of these multi-purpose gundogs, these expatriate sportsmen, using mainly German short-haired pointers, became very impressed by their capabilities and realized the potential of a pointer-retriever. This breed was similarly imported into America after the Great War and so became established there so much earlier. For us, it was just another example of our bringing talented sporting dogs across the channel, a timeless exercise. This time however, unlike previous centuries, their blood would be kept distinct and not used to strengthen the performance of native stock. In the gundog world, this, together with the gundog breeds entering the pet market in unprecedented numbers, was a significant legacy of the first fifty years of the twentieth century. The Second World War devastated many breeds but also led the gundog registers opening up to new breeds from the Continent.

With the HPRs from Germany leading the way from the 1950s, (in 1953, thirty-four Weimaraners were registered with the KC; by 1983, a total of 7,088 had been registered) the all-round gundogs from other mainland European countries soon followed. The second half of the twentieth century saw these talented dogs establish themselves here, whilst three of our native breeds, the Labrador Retriever, the Cocker and the English Springer Spaniel went from

strength to strength. This may have been to the detriment of less-favoured native gundog breeds, like the Field, Sussex and Clumber Spaniels, the Curly-coated Retriever and the Pointer. By the end of the nineteenth century, we had lost our native water spaniel, failed to preserve the distinctive milk-white Llanidloes Setter and overlooked the Irish Red and White Setter as a distinct breed. At the end of the twentieth century, there were worrying signs that we might be losing the less fancied spaniel breeds from our breed lists and shooting fields.

The Field Spaniel rallied from only two registrations in 1960 to thirty in 1970, seventy-eight in 1980 and 121 in 1990. The Sussex Spaniel recovered from only thirteen registrations in 1960 to achieve 127 in 1990. The Irish Water Spaniel too steadily gained ground, with just over thirty in 1960 and 1970 to 144 in 1990. Meanwhile Cocker Spaniel registrations doubled in the thirty years between 1960 and 1990, those of the Labrador quadrupled and the English Springer's increased tenfold. But in those thirty years the Weimaraner figures went from seventy to over 1,800, and over 100 Brittanys, GWHPs, Vizslas, Large Munsterlanders and Italian Spinoni joined the lists. I get the impression that proportionately more HPRs are worked than our native gundog breeds. I do hope one of our unsung, unspoiled, quite admirable gundog breeds, the Curly-coated Retriever, is not allowed to disappear, as its registrations are worryingly low. Do we really need a further 45,000 Labradors each year?

Foreign Arrivals – Domestic Neglect

A hundred years ago, British shooting men would have scoffed at the idea of a German pointer eclipsing our Pointer within the coming century, but it has happened. Styles of shooting have changed and gundogs are now owned by a wide range of people; they were once the preferred breeds of country dwellers and landowners, but not any more. The key question is not about preferences or popularity, but whether these attractive talented dogs are being bred wisely. All these gifted gundog breeds were developed by knowledgeable, dedicated, often inspired breeders. Sometimes misguided cliques have half-ruined a breed, as the once-bassetized Field Spaniel and the heavyweight Clumber Spaniels exemplify. Happily the Field is now soundly bred and the Working Clumber fraternity have done a great

LEFT: FT Chs Scotney Phillip and Yvette, Pointers owned by Lord Rank.

BELOW LEFT: German Short-haired Pointer.

Over-furnished setters, Cockers with over-long ears, Clumbers with red-raw eye-rims, Labradors with Rottie heads, Golden Retrievers featuring a white coat, English Springers resembling liver and white Cockers more than their own breed (mainly in working stock, admittedly), a lack of substance in Pointers and most regrettably the disturbing presence of upright shoulders and a lack of drive from the hindquarters – these are all betrayals of the gundog heritage passed down to us. The braver (or better-informed) judges pick up such points and record them in their post-show reports; but who is listening? Temperament, too, is rarely bred for as a desired feature, being usually an expectation rather than a top priority despite most pups going to pet homes. Will the twenty-first century witness the loss, too, of working instincts, neglected in the second half of the twentieth century, in our gundogs?

Changing Tastes

It is interesting to compare the KC registrations of gundog breeds at the beginning of the twentieth century and the end. In 1908, fifteen breeds were recognized, as well as 'interbred' and 'crossbred' retrievers; in 1999, thirty-three breeds were recognized, eleven of them HPR breeds. Only purebred gundogs featured. Of the fifteen gundog breeds listed by the KC in 1908, their fortunes were markedly different by the end of the century;

job with their breed. But unwise exaggerations and worrying aberrations do still crop up across a wide range of anatomical features. We need to continue the best achievements of the twentieth century whilst correcting any excesses.

by breeds, with the 1908 figures first and the 1999 ones next, the list shows: English Setters 240 against 627, Gordon Setters 27 against 317, Irish Setters 189 against 1,391, Pointers 152 against 824 , Curly-coated Retrievers 163 against 90, Flat-coated Retrievers 474 against 1,315, Golden Retrievers 0 against 12,730, Labradors 123 against 33,398, Clumber Spaniels 182 against 105, Cockers 535 against 13,445, Field Spaniels 286 against 75, Whiptails 38 against 72, English Springers 46 against 12,409, Welsh Springers 38 against 522, and Sussex Spaniels 19 in 1908 and 89 in 1999. The days of the companion gundog had very much arrived. Shooting needs had changed and certainly the ratio of gundogs worked to gundogs not worked by their owners had changed forever. The owners of companion dogs have no incentive to test their dogs' instinctive skill; show fanciers do not win rosettes for their dogs' scenting, marking or retrieving talents. This affects the anatomy desired in their dogs.

Damning Critiques

It is dispiriting to read extremely worrying comments on gundogs, in the ring at championship shows, by approved judges, on dogs clearly entered by their proud owners as potential winners. Most of these seriously flawed dogs are bred from; it is a chilling thought.

I have in mind comments like the following from gundog judges in 2006, on entries based on twentieth-century stock. Golden Retrievers: 'many exhibits were unbalanced, too straight in shoulder and long in body'; 'many lacked substance and strength in quarters', and, 'I was disappointed in the dogs' heads, some far too big and heavy'. Gordon Setters: 'Some exhibits who looked very good stacked, let themselves down on movement and quite a few lacked muscling'. GWHP: 'Movement leaves a lot to be desired'. Weimaraner: 'I am saddened to say that I was bitterly disappointed by the limited number of exhibits that carried the true qualities in type, construction and soundness that makes up this beautiful aristocratic breed'. Welsh Springers: 'too many dogs were lacking the correct extension and return of the foreleg underneath the body when viewed on side movement'. Some of these flaws went uncorrected in the late twentieth century and these are not minor matters.

Pointers from Germany now outnumber our own.

And it gets worse! Take Labradors, a very uncomplicated breed. Critiques in 2006 include these comments: 'front movement remains a cause for considerable concern', 'what is happening to our wonderful Labrador head?', 'we do need to give our serious attention to the front construction, particularly the numerous short and upright upper arm that the breed currently displays'. But a recently introduced gundog breed, the Italian Spinone, records comparable problems, with judges writing: 'construction is not so good, far too many dogs were steep in shoulder and short in upper arm', and, 'wealth of dogs very poor in front…with steep short upper arms'. Do contemporary gundog breeders appreciate the link between sound construction and correct movement? Is the legacy of the twentieth century in gundogs an unfortunate, however gradual, move away from the ability to function in the field towards a rosette-chasing desire to concentrate on cosmetic appeal in the show ring? That is an honest enquiry, not a stern accusation. In the conclusion, I make wide-ranging recommendations for an improved future for our gundog breeds.

National Responsibility

The immense rise in the popularity of pedigree dogs in the twentieth century, with 22,000 registered in 1921 and, by 1999, around 80,000 gundogs alone being registered each year, has not been all good news for the dogs themselves. As sporting dogs are increasingly denied an outlet by today's urban activists, all those who care about our superb gundog heritage need to be watchful. These superlative breeds came to us after the devotion and breeding skill of past enthusiasts. They bequeathed to us handsome dogs with immense field capability based on sound construction and an innate desire to work. We surely owe them and these fine breeds the same commitment. The twentieth century allowed us the choice of either capitalizing on the remarkable legacy of gundog men such as Laverack, Llewellin, Shirley, the Duke of Gordon, Arkwright, Farrow, McCarthy, Fuller and the Earl of Malmesbury or abandoning our renowned gundog breeds to the fashions of the times.

LEFT: Gundog Working Test 1990.

BELOW: The Welcome Newcomers:
LEFT: German Wire-haired Pointer depicted by Holzstich in 1897.
RIGHT: German Long-haired Pointer (Ansichtskarte, 1915).

It is always worth a study of the gundogs of a century ago to judge whether we have kept faith with those devotees who bequeathed us these superb dogs. The bitches produce the pups, we design the litter. In the next section, I take a look at today's litters and ask if we are perpetuating sound gundogs.

It is not necessary, in a work of this kind, to discuss the vexed question of the influence of canine exhibitions on the sporting dog. Much good has been done by these; but alas! also much evil. The sporting dog, however, has suffered less than most other breeds, and, on the whole, in the writer's opinion, distinct benefit has accrued, except in the case of the spaniel breed. This is due to the fact that dogs of other breeds have not been tampered with to the same extent as the spaniel has been by 'fanciers', whose handiwork is seen in the numerous grotesque creatures which appear on the bench, and, with considerable difficulty, are able to walk a few times round the judge's ring. With these, however, the gamekeeper has nothing to do. The breed is right enough, but by selection a non-sporting class has produced an animal unfitted for work owing to the exhibitors' want of knowledge and the apathy of other classes. One must remember, however, that those are selected specimens, and that it is possible to find animals of the same breed which are quite fit and able for field work.

The Keeper's Book by Sir Peter Jeffrey Mackie (1924)

In the modern world of driven shoots and breech-loading shotguns, pointers and setters are something of an anachronism: a living, and sometimes working, reminder of past times when shooting was a more leisurely and less commercial pursuit. Our native game birds, the grey partridge on agricultural land and the red grouse on the moor, were the main sporting quarries in those days and they were shot over pointing dogs. The time of the big battue, the reared pheasant and the commercial shoot were yet to come, though the dual pressures of technological innovation and Victorian fashion would eventually bring about a decline in popularity of the pointing breeds as working dogs.

Working Pointers and Setters by David Husdon (2004)

Today's Gundogs – Are They Sound?

We would therefore advise the discerning reader to attend these exhibitions – not to walk round when the dogs are benched, but to make a point of being present at the judging, to plant himself stolidly down opposite the ring, and to scrutinize carefully every animal in it…he will then appreciate what a heavy-loaded shoulder, slack loins, or bad feet mean in hard day's work. This is by no means learnt in a day, though some people have an instinctive eye for the points of an animal.

The Keeper's Book by Sir Peter Jeffrey Mackie (1924)

Show Stock Appraisal

If you are aware of how our gundog breeds evolved, prize our gundog breeds and have an interest in seeing them perpetuated in their classic mould, then, even if you don't show dogs, it pays to visit a conformation dog show for them from time to time. I would recommend an outdoor show; the dogs enjoy it more and the setting is far more appropriate. For as long as sixty years, I have been visiting the Bath Dog Show, now held in an attractive rural setting at Bannerdown, between Bath and the M4 motorway. I believe that this location, thanks to the vision of Labrador breeder Geoff Waring and his wife, is now owned by the Bath Canine Society. I first attended as a mid-teens kennel-boy to a Bath vet, who was

Brittanys wait their turn.

also the show vet, in the late 1940s. I have long been appreciative of the instruction I received on breed

points and the conformation of the dog whilst touring such a show with my employer vet and his fellow Bath vet, Manson Baird, the Deerhound breeder. The 2007 gundog entry at their old show would have disappointed them. (Since then, I have seen some of this entry's offspring – and *their* offspring.)

Sadly the foreign gundog breeds were more impressive than our native ones, although the Weimaraners ranged from oversized specimens to distinct weeds. The Brittanys I admired; the German pointers looked the fittest, especially the wire-hairs; the Spinoni lacked muscular development, which gives any sizeable dog very ugly movement. The Vizslas varied undesirably, some over-boned, some too fragile, with wide variations too in the movement, perhaps because many were stiff-hocked, some were loose in the shoulder and a few were lacking coordination on the move. This can come from a mismatch between the fore and hindquarters, with weakness at the back making the dog pull itself along. It should always be a joy to see a sporting breed moving, without effort, using that appealing slingy action, with real spring in the step, feet hardly leaving

ABOVE LEFT: *The Italian Spinone.*

LEFT: *The Wire-haired Hungarian Vizsla.*

the ground, shoulders moving freely and genuine power coming through from the rear. The absence of this in some of our native gundog breeds on display made dismal viewing.

I don't think I have ever seen so many poor setters in one place, Irish Setters especially. This is such a handsome breed, and when soundly constructed and in top condition, is a joy to observe. The distinctive coat saved some of them from being Salukis! But then some of the Pointers on display resembled dish-faced Greyhounds. The clear lack of muscular development made me wonder if these dogs ever got exercised. The slab-sidedness made me doubt that their breeders themselves had ever strode out across a moor and experienced the lung power needed for sustained field work. Today's Pointers are Whippets compared to their ancestors, which were much more hound-like and strongly made. An even more worrying feature in the Pointers and setter breeds was the presence of upright shoulders. What was truly depressing was

RIGHT: *Red Irish Setters at the Bath Dog Show 2009.*

BELOW: *Pointers in the Ring.*

to witness dogs being awarded cards with such a handicap. A front action like a carriage horse is not a pretty sight in bird-dog breeds once revered the world over for their stamina.

Encouraging Signs

The spaniels, however, cheered me up. There were some excellent Cockers, English Springers and a couple of high-class Welsh Springers. It was so good to see minor spaniel breeds, like the admirable Field, the bustling Sussex, the distinctive Irish Water and the handsome Clumber, although I will never get used to seeing a sporting spaniel at the weight of the show Clumber. The only gundog I saw struggling with the heat was a heavily skirted American Cocker Spaniel; I really would not wish to take one home after a long day in the mud! I wonder too about the wisdom of breeding a dog with such a deep and abrupt 'stop'; it has never been anything other than a man-imposed feature and I know of no vet who favours it. Does a gundog actually *need* such a feature? Is it a benefit or a disadvantage? If it is desirable, why does no other gundog breed gain from it?

The retrievers have long been my favourite gundogs. Their popularity is richly deserved, but has its downside. There are some top-class retriever breeders in Britain but the widespread appeal of Labs and Goldies has diluted the quality. A modest retriever breed like the Curly-coat and a workmanlike one like the Chessy always seem undervalued by the public. Such underrated breeds need our support and would benefit from greater field use. At this show there were some disappointing Flat-coats, a whole ring full of over-coated Goldens and several rings full

ABOVE LEFT: Pointer with Pups by S.L.D. Simonsen (Denmark, 1898) – stronger dogs altogether.

LEFT; The Cocker Spaniel Class.

of overweight Labs. Sportsmen may not be surprised by this but many country-dwelling gundog fanciers unacquainted with working stock buy their pet gundogs from kennels willing, it seems, to show off their flawed dogs to the world in this way; whatever happened to 'show condition', or, for that matter, owner pride?

Sustained Criticism

Thinking I might have been over-critical, a day or so after the show I went into my archives and consulted the critiques of the gundog judges at Crufts in recent years. The Kennel Club boasts that here you find the best of the very best; what did their appointed judges report? Here are some judgements: Crufts 2004, Weimaraners: 'so many of the dogs were in soft condition and lacked muscle tone…short steep upper arms were the norm'. Flat-coats: 'We still have too many upright shoulders, short straight steep upper arms… Mouths are another big problem…'. IWS: 'I found too many short necks, upright shoulders…' Sussex Spaniels: 'How do some exhibits get past judges?' American Cockers: 'I was dismayed to find so many poor fronts.'

ABOVE: *A rather sombre Sussex Spaniel.*

BELOW: *Heavyweight Clumber Spaniels.*

TOP: *Relaxed Field Spaniels.*

BOTTOM: *American Cocker Spaniel – heavily skirted.*

These are the dogs that would have been the parents of the exhibits I saw in 2007; their faults are being perpetuated. If Crufts is reckoned to be the place to find excellence, the judges seem to have difficulty in doing so. Crufts 2005, Flat-coats: 'bad mouths and poor construction were only too evident…'. Welsh Springers: 'Movement varied from being correct and positive to downright unsound. This is due almost entirely to bad construction. Short upper arms, no depth of chest…'. Crufts 2006, Clumbers: 'Truly I was disappointed by the number of unsound exhibits…'. Labrador dogs: 'I was appalled at what some people had qualified…'. In other words, there were dogs at Crufts without quality. After the 2007 show, judges in five gundog breeds reported poor movement. Many of these exhibits have been bred from and their faults passed on. Below I have spelt out some of these potentially pernicious flaws that are cropping up in succeeding litters.

Persistent Faults

It's worrying to read of certain faults persisting in some gundog breeds down the years. The great Flat-coat breeder, H. Reginald Cooke, was writing in *The Kennel Gazette* of December 1908: 'I think more attention should be given to neck and shoulders. Though much improvement has been made, one still sees too many dogs with short necks and straight shoulders.' A century later and the Crufts judge for the breed is concerned about the entry, stating that they 'need to have a good reach of neck sloping into well-placed shoulders', expressing considerable worry about the front movement in the younger classes. Show judges in this breed have reported several times in the past few years their concern over upright shoulders and short upper arms in the breed. The front assembly of a retriever is an essential element in its ability to retrieve sizeable game over a long period on a hot day in difficult country; it is not merely a show point for faddists.

Sporting dogs, gundogs especially, the Setter breeds and the Pointer in particular, were once famed for their lung power; now they are uniformly slab-sided in the chest, despite the evidence that such a structure enhances the likelihood of bloat. A Cocker Spaniel can, it appears win Best in Show at Crufts with ears that defy the breed standard. The gundog breeds carry surprisingly heavy items of shot game

in their mouths using their temporal muscles ahead of their masseter muscle. This results in a soft mouth. Marked cheek development is undesirable in any gundog breed if the soft-mouthed virtue is to be retained. But I see many Labradors with the head and cheek muscles of a Rottweiler. I doubt very much if such a Retriever also displays a soft mouth. I worry too about some gundog breeds beginning to feature too deep a stop; cleft palates and very deep stops all too often go together. Why seek a feature that can *harm* the dog?

Fit for Function?

The Crufts judge of Labrador bitches at the 2000 show concluded that: 'I had two overall concerns…excess weight and movement… Some promising bitches spoilt their chances by moving close behind or were pinning in front.' The KC claims that this show contains 'the best of the very best' in each breed exhibited. For Labradors at this premier show to be overweight and display faulty movement is alarming. At this same show, the judge of the Labrador dogs (males) observed: 'I had a few heads resembling Pyreneans [that is, Mountain Dogs] rather than Labradors, on the move there were feet coming towards me that were more like lily-pads and shoulders that made me despair. The latter point not being helped by excess weight…'. If these are the top dogs in this breed in the show world, what are the rest like?

Working Ability

It is depressing for any admirer of dogs that can work to read a prominent KC member declare a few years back that people don't want their terriers to go to ground, their Border Collies to herd sheep or their gundogs to retrieve game, they just want pets. What a betrayal of trust, an admission of defeat! A breed that is not physically able to carry out its original task has no right to bear the name of that breed. It is not a question of whether it has to but whether it is able to undertake its historic role – indeed, whether it is truly a member of that historic breed at all. Do we really want retrievers with no capability for retrieving?

Working Anatomy

In his timeless textbook on gundogs *The Early Life and Training of a Gundog* of 1931, the eminent trainer of that period, Lt-Col G.H. Badcock wrote:

Cocker Spaniel – with ears defying the Breed Standard.

No animal can move without propelling power, and that comes first from the loins, which should be broad and strong; secondly from the shape of the pelvis, which Nature in her wisdom has built in the galloping dog in the form of a crouch, and the more this is intensified the better the propelling power. The last bit of mechanism to fit in with propulsion is the hock, to me the most wonderful joint of all to dissect and examine. Very truly did old Jorrocks remark: 'No fut, no 'oss; no 'ock, no 'unter.'

Show ring judges today can become obsessed by the angle at the hock but not many test the strength of the exhibit's loin.

Crufts as a Livestock Show

Of course, there are some excellent gundogs at Crufts and there are excellent breeders of dual-purpose gundogs too. What we need to do is eject from the show ring – not even allow them to be exhibited – dogs with the kind of structural flaws highlighted by the top show ring judges themselves. It's not good enough for them just to go cardless; they should be thrown out of the ring before the judging even starts. A dog show is a livestock show or it is nothing. Dogs that qualify for Crufts with blatant faults represent a severe judgement on the show ring judges who provided them with qualification. In the wake of that admirable TV documentary *Pedigree Dogs Exposed* (2008), quite remarkable changes are being made in the show dog world. After the sad and predictable attempts to 'shoot the messenger' rather than heed the message, immediately after that hard-hitting programme, the Kennel Club has grasped the nettle over such serious matters as excessive exaggeration in many breeds and I give them credit for that. The Bateson Report on dog-breeding in the UK will in time benefit pedigree gundogs, whether worked or shown.

Commendably, the Kennel Club is at last striving to perpetuate a working anatomy on its entry; they ask for fitness for function, they ask for gundog judges to attend field trials. Over the last century the KC has not done all it could to perpetuate the working capabilities of the revered breeds of pedigree dog entrusted to its custodianship. Gundogs were developed over many centuries by dedicated master-breeders to perform to a high standard in the field; to

be worthy of the responsibility now entrusted to our generation, we simply have to perpetuate these breeds in their time-honoured mould. Many superb working dogs make excellent pets. All dogs kept as pets are spiritually happier if their instinctive behaviour is exercised.

Registry Control

The KC studbook should never merely be a register of births but a record of sound stock. How else can dog owners wishing to own purebred animals be given a service for their registration fee? A livestock studbook has to be much more than a breeding record; domestic animals are not free to choose their mates. We cannot elect to do that for them unless we act responsibly. Breeders of working gundogs are protected in many ways by the performance of their stock; their brand's reputation is their sales pitch. The general public seeking a gundog as a companion dog is at the mercy of breeders, breeders that really do need pressure to breed sound, typical, healthy dogs and that pressure can only come from the body registering the breeders' stock as healthy. A breed's popularity should instil greater quality control in breeders, not just the need to produce puppies.

Fickleness of Fashion

Today's favourite breed can so easily become tomorrow's victim breed. And gundogs are too precious for us to allow them to become such victims without a fight. Fashion is fickle and breeds can suffer cruelly from it. If you look at the advertisements in the sporting press for gundog pups from the highly popular breeds, most are from parents neither hip-scored nor eye-tested. If only the public would insist on health screening for their prospective purchases, it would put an important new dimension into breeding plans. I have seen puppies advertised at high fees without the high hip score of their dam or sire being stated during subsequent enquiries. Hip dysplasia is a complex disability but inheritance is a major factor. It is surely of paramount importance for working dogs of any breed to be clear of potentially crippling disabilities.

The Best of the Very Best

The KC's slogan for Crufts for many years has been to describe the entry as 'the best of the very best'.

Undoubtedly there are good dogs there; but what are the judges, alleged to be the best too, saying? Here are some judges' comments on the gundog entry of 2012: Flat-coated Retriever bitches: 'I am however concerned that some exhibits in the lower classes were very slight, lacking in bone, which is required to carry out a day in the field, also front movement was poor due to incorrect upper arm and lay of shoulder.' Irish Setters: 'I did find quite a lot of upright shoulders which we must all look out for.' English Setters: 'I do feel that some breeders are not paying enough attention to this [that is, correct anatomy for speed and endurance] and consequently we are seeing dogs which are weak in those aspects – some with a lack of angulation, some with elbows turning out and feet turning in, some with sickle hocks, etc, all of which contributes to a lack of forward reach and rear drive, thereby causing them to tire more quickly...more noticeable in the dogs.' Pointers: 'I think that front angulation is still a problem, we are seeing brisket well above the elbows, short necks, no extension in front on the move and we are seeing more over-angulation in the hindquarters.' Irish Red and White Setters: 'There were several exhibits with flat splayed feet and weak pasterns...'. At Crufts! Of course, the judges had great praise for most of the exhibits but gundogs that qualify for Crufts get bred from, and with these basic faults in evidence, that is of some concern.

It is lazy to argue that sportsmen know where to get a good gundog, so what is the problem? Our famous gundog breeds deserve the loyal support of knowledgeable dog men and should not be abandoned to show ring incompetents. Of course there are really good British gundog breeders, quite capable of producing outstanding dogs. But what about the mainstream system for perpetuating the gundog breeds, our native gundog breeds especially? I saw better Flat-coats in Finland a few years ago than those at the Bath show. Their breeding system and judging method is so superior to ours; it clearly produces better dogs. And so we muddle on, with the Kennel Club boasting about the sheer quality of the dogs on parade at Crufts, despite what their own judges are saying. Perhaps every gundog breed needs to mirror the work of the Working Clumber people – the satisfaction of seeing a working anatomy restored in so many breeds would surely delight the heart of any true gundog devotee. Show breeders are often accused of favouring flashiness ahead of soundness and if that is true, breed clubs and especially breed councils just *have to* redress this. It's vital for today's breeders to know how their breed was shaped, what decided its form. This I cover in the next chapter.

Whether retriever or pointer, we want a level mouth, neither undershot nor overshot – the former condition is almost never seen, but the so-called snipy muzzle is a common defect in our retrievers at the present time, and a bad one... The chief points, therefore, to be desired in a working dog are a good head and eye, light shoulders, strong loins, powerful thighs, and compact feet. Given these in our chosen puppy, and we start well with an animal better than our neighbour's, while we hope to make him above the average in other respects.

The Keeper's Book by Sir Peter Jeffrey Mackie (1924)

Irish Red and White Setters.

Working Clumber Spaniels.

CHAPTER 2

THE SPECIALISTS

The Bird Dogs

There is a remarkable self-denial in a setter or a pointer. The hound gives full play to his feelings; chases and babbles, and makes as much noise as he likes, provided only he is true to his game. The spaniel is under no restraint, except being kept within gunshot. The greyhound has it all his own way as soon as he is loosed. And the terrier watches at the rat's hole, because he cannot get into it. But the pointer, at the very moment when other dogs satisfy themselves, and rush upon their game, suddenly stops, and points, with almost breathless anxiety, to that which we might naturally suppose he would eagerly seize. He seems to feel, 'this is my master's and not mine; and here I am till he comes up, or the birds are off of themselves.'

Those words, from *Cassell's Popular Natural History* of over a century ago, sum up very neatly the unique hunting style of the bird dogs. Their innate skill lies not in the raw pursuit of their trade but in controlled delay, unlike every other canine characteristic in the sporting field.

The Pointer of England

Most organized game shooting in Britain in the twenty-first century involves engaging the birds from a set position, or battue, and awaiting driven birds. For some, and they often consider their choice to be that of the *real* sportsman, shooting over dogs that range ahead and then indicate hidden game is the way. As the great Pointer man William Arkwright wrote in his *The Pointer and his Predecessors* of 1906:

I do not expect to convert many unbelievers by this chapter on shooting over dogs, and I am not sure whether, in the present plethora of shooters, it would even be desirable to open the eyes of the multitude

to its attraction. I believe that fondness for this style of sport must be innate; for there is a mysterious attraction in the sport, though it does not appeal to every constitution and is hardly to be defined in working-day prose. Where the soil is congenial this grace pf perception bursts into flower sometimes early, sometimes late – now in the kennel-yard, now on the mountainside. When was it implanted? None can tell that; but once established in a man's heart it can nevermore be uprooted.

For those with this 'implant' there is no other way. To enjoy this method fully it's vital to understand the work of the dogs, and their origin.

Early References
In his book, Arkwright quotes from a most interesting letter from the US vice consul in Valencia in 1900:

In this part of Spain there are no pure-bred sporting native dogs of any kind. The famous breed that existed here for three centuries – the Gorgas…are now extinct or so crossed with inferior breeds as to be indistinguishable. They were very nearly pure white, and much lighter than the old cylindrical Navarrese dog. Tradition says they were of foreign origin, the first pair being presented by an Italian prince…

In England, Thomas Fairfax, in his *The Complete Sportsman* of 1689, wrote: 'When you have got your gun, a turn screw, worm and flints ready, call your pointers.' In John Gay's poem published in 1711 in his *Rural Sports,* he mentions Pointers and states an origin in Spain or Portugal, as was the common view at that time amongst writers. The Earl of Powys introduced a breed of rough-haired Pointer from Lorraine to his gundog kennel in Suffolk; the movement of pointing dogs amongst sportsmen to and fro across the channel was by no means rare.

Drury, in his *British Dogs* of 1903, notes that the first *record* of the Pointer in Great Britain is the Tillemans' painting of the Duke of Kingston with his kennel of Pointers in 1725. He commented that the latter were the 'same elegant Franco-Italian type as the pointing dogs painted by Oudry and Desportes at the end of the 17th century.' Richardson, writing in 1847, describes seeing Italian pointers in Scotland, only about a foot high, but remarkably staunch with superb noses. The French have long had two sizes in their national pointing breed, the smaller – the Braque Français de petite taille – being just over 18in at the withers. Our native Pointer is expected to be over 2ft high at the withers, with no smaller version.

'And as one talks of a greyhound of Britain, the boarhounds and bird-dogs come from Spain'. Those are the words of Gaston Phebus, the famous Comte de Foix who, at the end of the fourteenth century himself owned over 1,500 sporting dogs. A century and a half later, the great canine authority of his day, Conrad Heresbach, was writing: 'Spanish dogs, zealous for their masters and of commendable sagacity, are chiefly used for finding partridges and hares. In the quest of bigger game they are not so much approved of, for they for the most part range widely nor do they keep as near as genuine hunting dogs.' A fair conclusion from those words might be

that at the time both these authorities were writing the then powerful nation of Spain was producing the best bird dogs and dominating the European market for them. Their *origin* – like that of our Greyhound – may well be rooted elsewhere.

No Foreign Name

It was most unusual in Victorian books on dogs, gundogs especially, for any link to be made between our developing breeds of setter and pointer and those on mainland Europe. A concession was usually made over the origin of our Pointer, the most prolific authors without exception firmly linking this breed with Spain. My preferred dog historian, the underrated Scot James Watson, wrote in his masterly *The Dog Book* of 1906:

> When sportsmen got a gun so improved as to admit of shooting flying as a regular and not as occasional practice, which we consider was possible as early as 1680, they thereupon made us of this dog, that had the faculty of locating game and stood still in place of rushing on as the spaniel did to put up game... They gave to this dog a name which indicated what he did – point to where the game was. Had he come from abroad, is it not likely he would have come with his foreign name?

Tillemans's painting of the Duke of Kingston in Thoresby Park, 1725.

In his *Cynographia Britannica* of 1800, Sydenham Edwards tells us that 'The Spanish Pointer was introduced to this country by a Portugal Merchant, at a very modern period, and was first used by an old reduced Baron, of the name of Bichell, who lived in Norfolk, and could shoot flying...' The Portuguese Pointer is much more like ours than, say, the heavier Burgos Pointer from Spain.

It is worth studying the wealthy and well-informed William Arkwright's classic work *The Pointer and his Predecessors* on the question of the origin of our native Pointer. Despite the time and money he clearly spent searching not only Spanish but other continental archives too, he could produce no convincing evidence of a Spanish origin for the breed. But the historical evidence that can be produced demands the most careful scrutiny before definitive statements can be made. I do not believe that the Pointer of Britain originated in Spain or indeed that pointers as a functional type of dog sprang from there, as is usually claimed. It is important though to clarify the nomenclature being used. There are French, German, Italian, Danish, Portuguese, Spanish and English pointers, with several different breeds of pointer

RIGHT: An 18th century French Pointer.

BELOW: Spanish Pointer of 1801.

within some of those countries. A pointer is a type of short-haired (usually), hound-like bird dog, rather than one breed. It is misleading and inaccurate, and perhaps overly nationalistic, to dub the Pointer of England as *the* pointer, despite its deserved world-wide reputation.

European Dogs

The Edwardian writer, Rawdon Lee, in his *Modern Dogs – Sporting Division* of 1906, accepts that the French had their own pointers before the Spanish Pointer was introduced into Britain at the beginning of the eighteenth century, going on to state that in the latter part of this century, 'Pointers far removed from

the imported Spanish dog in appearance, were not at all uncommon in England and they could easily have been brought over from France.' In his *The Art of Shooting Flying* of 1767, Page remarks: 'Pointers. – As nothing has yet been published on these dogs…I am inclined to think that they were originally brought from other countries, though now very common in England.' I am inclined to think they were originally brought from other countries too – France, Italy and Spain, with distinctive types from each country of previous development. The modern English Pointer is much more like the French Braque St Germain than the old Navarro and Burgos Pointers from Spain and the modern Bracco Italiano and, in the Preface, I refer to paintings that illustrate a French influence.

Hound Influence

Arkwright's Pointers had considerable influence in the making of today's dog; his all-black Pointer came from the Greyhound cross and an increasing number of contemporary dogs, both in Europe and America, exhibit the tucked-up loin, the tighter lips and low-set tail from this Greyhound blood. The Pointer of Britain has the eye and the eyesight of a sighthound, certainly no trace of the sunken eye of the scenthound breeds. In temperament too, the Pointer has more in common with the cool, aloof, reserved, rather introverted Greyhound than the gregarious, much

ABOVE LEFT: Arkwright's Pointer Ch Seabreeze by Reuben Ward Binks, 1908.

LEFT: Arkwright's black Pointer Leader, born 1895.

more extrovert and certainly noisier Foxhound. (I am told there is an outstanding kennel of solid black Pointers in the Czech Republic. A decade or so ago, a breeder in Wales, Peter Woodford, produced an all-black litter, the first for nearly a century).

Arkwright himself wrote that 'the French were the chief admirers of the Italian braque… And after a time, though the heavier type of their own and the Navarrese braque still survived, it was quite eclipsed by the beautiful and racing-like Italian dogs with which Louis XIV and Louis XV filled their kennels.'

The ability of the domestic dog to indicate unseen game by standing in a frozen posture staring hard at it has been utilised since ancient times. The Greeks identified a breed of dog in Italy, called the Tuscan, perhaps the ancestor of the Spinone, which was covered with shaggy hair and would actually point to where the hare lay hidden. Wolves have been known to display the same capability, however, and many non-sporting breeds of dog have also demonstrated this instinctive trait.

This scenting skill, supported by the classic pointer stance, has been of great benefit in the shooting field, especially in the days when 'walked up' as opposed to driven game was the favoured style. In the quest for improved scenting powers, the outcross to the Foxhound was made and some experts, like William Humphrey, famed for his 'of Wind'em' Pointers, have claimed to be able to spot Pointers with Foxhound blood in them from their tendency to seek ground scent as opposed to air scent. This is the expected penalty from using tracking dog blood. In 2012, I heard glowing reports of Wilson Young's FT Ch Fearn Mate of Burncastle, a dog excelling on distant air scent as well as closer ground scent.

Family Base
Professor J.M. Beazley has traced the origin of our modern English Pointers back to seven discrete families and shown how these original family groups led to the emergence of two main lines of descendants from 1840 to 1980. This may indicate a small gene pool but that doesn't mean the sealing of type forever more. Genes act randomly and type has to be actively sought. For me, our contemporary Pointer is too lightly constructed, too Greyhound-like. The Pointers depicted in paintings from past centuries show dogs with far more substance. It was sad to read the

critique of the Pointer judge at Crufts in 2009, which stated, 'The movement on the majority of these dogs and bitches was quite unbelievable, from crossing in front, upright in pasterns, upright in shoulders and it became very soul-destroying watching so many bad unsound movers.' For such a magnificent English gundog breed at our premier dog show to exhibit such serious faults is truly distressing. Unsound movement is a heavy and needless handicap for a bird dog.

> I remember well that, as a boy, I used to go and shoot at a very good grouse moor called Strathavon, near Tomintoul, with Colonel Legendre Starkie, who had a great kennel of pointers and Gordon setters. I remember the particular style and excellence of a black and white pointer; he used to stand to birds with his stern straight up in the air. This was not quite right, but Colonel Starkie liked him especially from his striking likeness in appearance and ways to a foxhound. On this subject he writes to me: 'Shot, like many of my pointers, had three crosses of foxhound in him from three different kennels, Osbaldistone, Sir Harry Goodrich and Captain J White. All these men had a famous breed of pointers, and each one of them had used the foxhound cross. This gave to their progeny endurance, and good legs and feet and pace.'
> *The Queen's Hounds and Stag-hunting Recollections* by Lord Ribblesdale (1897)

The Setters

Favoured Colours
In the time of the Stuarts, the setting dog was used to hold game birds to ground, often with a hawk overhead to keep the birds from flying, while a net was carefully drawn over them. Then, with the introduction of firearms, and later 'shooting flying', setters were needed, along with pointers, to indicate and then put up feathered game. In pursuit of this function, the setting dog breeds developed both here and on the continent and were widely traded, with a high value on a trained and effective dog. Whilst our setter breeds were evolving here, so too were the epagneul breeds in mainland Europe. It is foolish for setter breed historians to claim a long and pure lineage for their favoured breed. Good setters were mated to other good setters irrespective of colour.

The Old English Setter of 1830.

The landed gentry went on their Grand Tours, sometimes taking their dogs with them through Europe and sometimes coming back with a dog that had impressed them. It was easier to bring foreign dogs into Britain in every previous century than the twentieth. In 1563, Lord Warwick wrote to his brother, the Earl of Leicester, from Le Havre: 'I thank you for sending me so fine a horse. In return, I send you the best Setter in France…'

In time certain coat colours were favoured by individual sportsmen both here and abroad. The epagneul breeds varied all over mainland Europe but all had that definite setter appearance: feathering on the tail and legs, a distinct occiput and enormous style when seeking game scent. In Holland the Drentse Patrijshond and Stabyhoun emerged, in France the Epagneul Français, in Germany the Munsterlander (and later the Langhaar and long-haired Weimaraner). In Britain, distinct strains were stabilized, often exemplified by their coat colour, with far greater variety than nowadays.

Setter colours ranged from the liver and whites of the Prouds at Featherstone Castle, keepers Laidlaw at Edmond Castle and Grisdale at Naworth Castle; the Earl of Southesk's, the Marquess of Anglesey's, at Beaudesert in Staffordshire, and Lord Lovatt's tricolours; the lemon and whites of the Earl of Seafield; the milk-whites of Llanidloes and the black and tans (and tricolours) of Gordon Castle, to the black and whites of Lort of Kings Norton. In Ireland, O'Keefe and Baker of Tipperary favoured the white and reds (as the Irish called them), Capt. Butler of County Kerry went for the black and whites, whilst the reds were promoted by the Marquess of Ely, Lord Farnham, Redmond in County Dublin and the Cavendish family of County Cork. Lord Ossulton in Northumberland, Lord Hume of Tweedside, Harry Rothwell in Westmoreland and an English clergyman, who wrote under the nom de plume of 'Sixtyone' and rented the whole shootings of Lewis and Harris in the nineteenth century, each favoured the all-black setter, renowned for its glossy waterproof coats and 'stout feet'.

'A field dog, for taking birds' was the caption for an illustration which resembled a prototypal setter in Dr Caius' well known treatise of 1576 entitled *Of English Dogs*. Caius described the action of the Setter or Index with these words: 'When he hath found the bird, he keepeth sure and fast silence, he stayeth his steps and will proceed no further; and with a close, covert, watching eye, layeth his belly to the ground, and so creepeth forward like a worm.' Half a millennium later, we still seek a comparable performance from our setters. They are remarkable dogs which have survived every challenge so far; we must do our very best to perpetuate them. Enjoying the work of setters in the open air has long been regarded as a special treat:

The scent of an autumn morning,
The tang of the moorland air,
The russet and gold of the branches,
So soon to be stricken and bare,
The deep purple line of the far-away hills,
The springy turf under your feet,
The call of the curlews, the voice of the wind
And a Setter – so life is complete.

From *Dogs Life,* August 1965

Those words straightaway provide the frame for any word picture being painted of the setters. They were the shooting companions of those with land or access to it and a life of ease, often dominated by country sports. James I addressed the landed gentry of his time with these words: 'Gentlemen, at London you are like ships at sea, which show like nothing; but in your country villages you are like ships in a river which look like great things.' The passion of such men for country sports not only shaped the English countryside but gave us our hounds, gundogs and terriers.

Studies of English Setters, lithographs by Leon Danchin (1887–1939).

Lost Breeds

One of the sadnesses with gundogs lies in the loss of old breeds, either through a lack of recognition or simply indifference to their fate. The English Water Spaniel once featured in the Kennel Club Stud Book, but is now lost to us. A number of distinct forms of setter were never perpetuated. The milk-white, curly-coated Llanidloes Setter would have provided a most distinctive element in our list of native setter breeds, had it survived. 'Stonehenge', writing at the end of the nineteenth century, described them as Welsh Setters, stating that their coats 'would resist the wet and cold of the mountains in a marvellous manner'. Is there not some proud Welsh patriot-sportsman out there who would be willing to re-create this lost breed? We have English, Irish and the Gordon Setter from Scotland, where is the Welsh representative?

Less likely to be restored is the Russian Setter, described by a number of authors in the nineteenth century. Lang wrote in the *Sporting Review* of 1839: 'Then, for the first time for many years, I had my dogs, English setters, beaten hollow. His [ie his sporting host's] breed was from pure Russian setters, crossed by an English setter dog which some years ago made a sensation in the sporting world from his

extraordinary performances…'. Not many sportsmen nowadays would dream of crossing two setter breeds, however good the blood, such is the dogma of purebreeding. In his book on the setter of 1872, the great breeder Edward Laverack remarks that he had only ever seen one *pure* specimen of Russian Setter, owned by Lord Grantley in Perthshire.

Laverack mentions another old Welsh strain of setter, similar to the Llanidloes, but jet-black, stating that: 'In their own country they cannot be beaten, being exactly what is required for the steep hill-sides.' He also mentions the liver and white setters favoured in Cumberland and Northumberland, and the jet-black breed kept by the Earl of Tankerville. Interestingly, Laverack writes that the Duke of Gordon preferred black, *white* and tans in his setters, but kept black and tans too. As discussed below, you would not guess what the Duke's preference was from glancing at today's show rings for Gordon Setters. The breed standard of this breed states: 'Very small white spot on chest permissible. No other colour permissible.' A few years back the best grouse dog in the country was a mainly white Gordon Setter. It would be wrong, however, to give the Laverack and the Llewellin Setters the sole credit for the development of the English Setter as a breed. In his *The American Hunting Dog* of 1918, published in New York, Warren H. Miller, former editor of *Field and Stream*, wrote:

There are hundreds of thousands of setters today who owe their descent to neither the Laverack nor the Llewellin strain. True, Mr Laverack did get up a happy nick that gave him dogs which could sweep all before them at the English field trials, and so were in demand, but he did not, in the nature of things, produce from his two dogs Ponto and Old Moll, more than a very small percentage of all the English setters in 'blighty'.

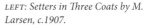

LEFT: *Setters in Three Coats by M. Larsen, c.1907.*

BELOW: *Setter in a Landscape by J. Boultbee (1753–1812). A Llanidloes Setter?*

The English Setter

> If one had to pick a dog, not a foxhound, as typical of English country life and the English country gentleman who lived it in the nineteenth century, then that dog would be the English Setter.
>
> *Champion Dogs of the World* by Sir Richard Glyn (1967)

It was three non-conformists, Edward Laverack, Richard Purcell Llewellin and William Humphrey, who contributed the most to the development of the working setter. Laverack's work was so admired by both American and British setter fanciers that they erected a monument to him in Ash churchyard near Whitchurch, Shropshire. Sadly, Llewellin's grave in Stapleton graveyard, also in Shropshire, soon became overgrown. Fittingly for a working setter man, Humphrey's ashes were scattered over the Shropshire hills where so many of his dogs had worked and been trained. Their work, spanning well over a hundred years, ensured the quality in our setters that we benefit from today.

Laverack (1798–1877) bought his first setters, both blue Beltons, in 1825 from a pure strain of strongly constructed family estate dogs, carefully bred over thirty-five years. With an established line to perpetuate, Laverack continued this work for fifty-two years, giving a total of eighty-seven years of skilful line-breeding. To him must go the credit for coordinating the best strains of setter of his time and for producing both handsome show dogs and sound workers. He is known to have used both Irish and Gordon Setter blood, with his curly-coated specimens probably having an infusion of the old Welsh Setter. Despite his age when dog shows became organized, he made up two show champions, and in the period from 1861 to 1892, eleven champions were 100 per cent Laverack-bred, with only three out of twenty-five champions made up having no Laverack breeding behind them.

The first dual champion, Countess, and her brilliant field trial winning sister Nellie, both bred by Laverack, formed the nucleus of what became known as the Llewellin Setter. The son of a great all-round Welsh sportsman, Llewellin established in his strain of setters the greatest field trial-winning record of all breeds of pointing dogs in the eighty years from 1880 to 1960. His dogs were first of all a mixture of Gordon, probably Llanidloes Setter, a big milk-white curly-coated variety, and the powerfully made Old English Setter, a black and white variety rather like the Stabyhoun, the Friesland Setter from Holland. Later he used Irish Red and White Setter bitches, eventually modifying the resulting progeny with pure Laveracks. Proud and meticulous, he never sold stock here or abroad unless he considered it near perfect. How many of today's breeders can claim that?

When Llewellin died in 1925 he left his dogs to his housekeeper, from whom William Humphrey subsequently bought them. Humphrey saw his first

Laverack's English Setter Dash of 1872.

field trial as a boy of nine in 1892 and won his first stakes two years later at the age of eleven. Winning his last stake in 1963, he set up the longest record of field trial successes since such trials started in 1865. He so approved the Llewellin strain that over fifty-five years he imported from the United States thirty-three dogs and bitches previously exported. His 'Wind'em' setters were so revered that when I was in Norway thirty years ago, my hosts were still recalling them.

Humphrey ran a winning dog in Norway at the age of sixty-seven. (He was famed for his Pointers too, and at one time he ran a kennel of 1,200 dogs!) In recent years, the importation of the Norwegian sire FT Ch Storeskars G'Snorre into Ireland by John Geoghegan led to John's impressive record of six open stake wins out of seven grouse trials and a second place in the seventh, proving the wisdom of introducing sound Scandinavian blood in this breed.

LEFT: *Llewellin Setter in the USA – note the distinctive tail carriage when alert to scent.*

BELOW: *Laverack's English Setter Fred – 4th of 1872.*

Breed Failings

The Americans still recognize the Llewellin Setter as a separate breed. They consider that the breed comes from three lines, each bred to Laveracks. One of these lines, from Rhoebe, the greatest field trial winner-producing dam of all time, passes on the blood of her sire, who was the great grandson of a Gordon Setter and a dam which was half Gordon and half Southesk Setter, a strapping tricolour strain from Forfarshire. A most knowledgeable American sportsman, Joseph Graham, wrote in his informative *The Sporting Dog* in 1904 that 'they [the claimants of the Llewellin as a separate breed] would as well go further and drop the 'pure' idea altogether, letting Llewellin blood stand for what it is – an influential but not separate element in English setter breeding'. In Britain we have long held that view.

Joseph Graham also states in his book that: 'Purity of race is a good thing when it is good. Sometimes it is a misnamed conglomeration, and sometimes it needs breaking up and disturbance'. Are we going to persevere with purity of breeds when it is 'not good'? Here are some critiques in recent years on our setters in the show ring: Gordons: 'Unless something is done quickly by the top breeders, I see no hope for the breed, because the puppies were so bad.' Irish Setters: 'I found quality in depth lacking, and the movement was on the whole very bad.' Irish Setter dogs: 'One of my main observations is the weakening of the overall body shape, the breed is losing genuine spring of rib and becoming too slab-sided.' Gordons: 'I was however rather shocked to find a lot of poor angulation front and rear, upright shoulders predominated…also too many straight stifles.' English Setters: 'Poor mouths and movement were the chief faults but straight stifles and heavy shoulders were to be found.'

Edward Laverack, in his book on the setter of 1872, wrote:

> The first thing to be attended to in breeding is to consider what object the animal is intended for… One of the first objects to obtain, if possible, is **perfection of form**, as best adapted for speed, nose, and endurance. The next, and which I consider paramount, or of as much importance as physical form, is an innate disposition to hunt, and point naturally in search of game, and without which innate properties mere beauty of colour and perfection of external form

> (however desirable) are but secondary considerations to practical sportsmen, and simply valueless.

That is a very clear statement from a master breeder and not one to be overlooked. In a letter to *Dog World* of 25 May 2012, Val Isherwood of Laverstoke English Setters wrote that, 'We have only to look at historic pictures of the breed to see that it is our show lines that have actually drifted further away from the original English Setter.' She was responding to a statement that working breeders do not care about breed type. (I was recently told of a very promising novice English Setter: Laverstoke Firefly at Gaiasett, that worked well and looked truly handsome, full of breed type.) There are urgent questions to be answered by the breed elders; the gene pool is dangerously small. Should the working dogs' blood be used? Should overseas blood be utilized? Could a similar breed's blood be introduced? I would favour the latter; genetic diversity matters!

Setters were designed to work, that is why they were handed down to us in the form they were. Setters that are not capable of working, physically and mentally, represent a betrayal of everything the pioneer breeders devoted their lives to. It does not matter if they are only pets; to be the genuine article they *must* have an anatomy that could carry out setter work. Pretty, showy, flamboyant setters floating round the ring and then earning the kind of remarks from the judge set out above are unworthy of their own heritage. If we breed them without heeding the great founder-breeder's words, and his crystal-clear message about valueless dogs, we will in time put at risk a simply splendid type of dog and an important part of our sporting dog inheritance. And unless the gene pool is widened, the breed's virility is threatened.

The Gordon Setter – the Scottish Breed

> In using the name of Gordon setter for the black and tan variety we do so because it has become universal, though it is undoubtedly a misnomer, if it is meant to specify that the breed so named originated with the Duke of Gordon, or was alone and specially fostered by him. That this nobleman, who died shortly prior to the oft-mentioned sale of dogs in 1836, by no means confined himself to a special colour is an entirely wrong idea.

Today's Gordon Setter.

Those firm words from the impressive Edwardian dog writer James Watson, in his valuable *The Dog Book*, are supported by plenty of evidence.

In his wide-ranging *A Survey of Early Setters* of 1985, an admirable piece of research, Gilbert Leighton-Boyce refers to an account of a visit to the Duke of Gordon's kennel that took place in 1862. This read:

We beguiled the way by a chat with Jubb, the head keeper, whose seven-and-thirty black-and-white tans were spreading themselves… Originally the Gordon setters were all black and tan… Now all the setters in the castle kennel are entirely black and white, with a little tan on the toes, muzzle, root of the tail, and round the eyes. The Duke of Gordon liked it, as it was both gayer and not so difficult to back on the hillside as the dark-coloured… The composite colour was produced by using black-and-tan dogs to black-and-white bitches…

Mapplebeck's Gordon Setter Blossom of 1879 – much less heavily furnished.

RIGHT: Gordon Setters of 1906 – not in acceptable livery.

RIGHT: Gordon Setters of 1906 – not in acceptable livery.

BELOW RIGHT: FT Ch Freebirch Vincent – a highly successful field Gordon Setter.

Against that background the setter colours of today look rather impoverished; we have become transfixed by the aura of the pedigree. Not so the Duke of Gordon, who was described as 'not a man to confine himself to shades and fancies'; he once used a Spitz-wolf cross on deer courses. His black-and-whites may have been a result of using a brace of English Setters given to him by Captain Robert Barclay of Urie. In New Zealand, a litter of black and tans was once produced from an unplanned mating of a Blue Belton English to an Irish Setter bitch. The Duke would not have approved the setters named after him needing to possess the now mandatory black and tan jacket of the breed. Neither would the founder of the modern setter, Laverack, who wrote that a change of colour was as good as a change of blood. The advent of dog shows has brought an absurd conformity, restricted breeding programmes to the dictat of the breed standard's stipulations and led to mismarked but otherwise high-quality dogs being lost from the gene pool. Bob Truman's outstanding black and white Gordon Setter, Freebirch Vincent, so successful as a working dog, would never win in the show ring, despite his excellent conformation and field prowess.

Our Kennel Club's breed standard for the Gordon Setter makes the following stipulation on coat colour, apart from setting out the black and tan markings:

'Very small white spot on chest permissible. No other colour permissible.' The Duke must be turning in his grave! How many potentially top-class gundogs in this breed have been destroyed at birth because of the unacceptable colour of their coats, despite the revealed honesty of the gene pool? We now very sensibly recognize red and white Irish Setters; why can't we respect the gene pool of the Gordon Setter and recognize the coat colours it throws up? As many historic illustrations show, the grouse moors of Scotland had more non-black and tan setters than today's restricted Gordon Setter type.

Would a variety of colours threaten breed type or increase diversity? This a fine breed, but with a narrowing of the breeding stock on colour grounds, far too heavy a coat and persistent anatomical faults, its breeders have much to ponder. The Crufts 2010 judge for this breed reported: 'Shortly before the show I was reminded by the Kennel Club about the need to avoid excessive coat and excessive hind angulation, overlong hip to hock and sickle hocks… I do feel that excessive coats are not really typical of the Gordon…' I doubt if the Duke would have lent his name to gundogs dripping with coat and displaying unsound hindquarters; are they truly fit for purpose? Retain the breed's name and rightly so, but associating the current breed closely with the Duke is unwise.

In America, in the nineteenth century, according to Joseph Graham in his book *The Sporting Dog* of 1904, 'the common assertion and belief are that white, black and tan is the correct and typical Llewellin colour'. Llewellin, as famous a setter man as Laverack, is stated by Graham to have strenuously objected to the drawing of a colour line but pointed out that a decided majority of his best setters were either blue belton or lemon belton. Nowadays coat colour just about decides the setter breeds, certainly for the general public, and gene pools are firmly closed. This was never the policy of our sporting ancestors who passed these illustrious setter breeds down to us for our safekeeping. It is good to hear of a potentially outstanding setter winning the Open Stake at the Gordon Setter's FT Society's 2012 meet: Denis Longworth's Breachan An Tsil of Bringwood, bred by Will Brush; I am told that the old setter men would have loved him. It's good to know of Jean Collins's success with the first dual champion for many years from her Amscot kennel and of Jane Osbourne's Boyers affix field record over a number of years.

The Setters of Ireland

> When first he sees the red setter go out gaily ranging, when the easy gait through the heather suddenly checks and stiffens, and a friendly arm – after how breathless an interval! – waves the dog forward and inward; there is gathered for him then into that short space the sum and the meaning complete of shooting as a sport of the hills for boys and men. He is out, free and a hunter…
>
> *Shooting Days* by Eric Parker (1932)

Away from the working stock, far too many of our native bird dogs are criticized for being too slab-sided and too weak in the hindquarters, and all too often have upright shoulders and short upper arms. Of course, any and every breed receives criticism and this is hardly new. A correspondent to *The Kennel Gazette* of February 1890 wrote:

Today's Irish Red and White Setter.

Today's working Irish Setter.

I have read Mr Serjeantson's remarks on Irish Red Setters in your number for this month, and probably he may be pleased to learn that very many of the most experienced breeders in Ireland fully endorse his opinions, that latterly breeders of the Irish Red Setter for show purposes have sacrificed the grand old powerful big-boned animal for the sake of beauty, chiefly in colour, coat, and feathering, and have thereby produced the many present-day weedy successors of the old type – no doubt beautiful, but weedy in bone.

A correspondent to the November issue of that year's *Gazette* wrote:

In conclusion, I must say that there is no breed of setters that could improve the best strains of Irish. Of course there are, I regret to say, men who keep Irish setters almost exclusively for show, and I could mention one or two well-known Irish setters that live half their time on the bench. Why cannot such men confine themselves to pugs or poodles?

Against that background it is easy to see how and why any setter breed divided into show and working arenas. But is it good for any bird dog to have an anatomy that would handicap it if it worked? A working dog doesn't need a super-dog structure, just a sound one. Just over thirty years ago I saw a fine specimen of the breed: Sh Ch Scarletti Cockney Rebel, full of desirable breed points but a sound gundog too.

Function Demands Respect
No doubt the died-in-the-wool gundog men will say, with a sigh, let the two worlds, show and working, get on and do their own thing. But what does that do to the *breed*? We are losing breed type in many working gundog strains and sound construction in many show strains. That cannot be good for the long-term future of any breed; should the two worlds always be totally apart? In some hound breeds the show people involve those who work their dogs – in Otterhounds, Beagles and Bassets, for example. Some sighthound breeds are tested on the racing track, but I doubt if such a sure test of sound construction is a factor in most show dog-breeding plans. For me the survival of a worker like the Korthals griffon *and* the survival of a sound show-bred setter or pointer are equally important. We have inherited these splendid dogs from devoted pioneer breeders who dedicated their whole lives to the production of *functional* animals.

On the Moors, from Shooting Days by Eric Parker, 1918.

Gordon Setter retrieving a shot fox, 1903.

It may be naive to expect the divisions between the show and the working worlds to become blurred, for the benefit of the breed concerned. But it is entirely reasonable to expect show fanciers to go and watch their breed at work and then understand what the drafters of the breed standard had in mind. Even the Kennel Club is promoting the concept of 'fit for purpose' in our pedigree breeds. It is understandable for a breed to become favoured either in the field or, quite separately, in the ring but to what gain *for the breed*?

A row developed in 2012 over the Irish KC's decision to register a red and white bred to a red setter on their Red and White Setter list, in an effort to obtain greater genetic diversity in the Irish Setter with a red and white coat (and recognized unwisely as a separate breed). Our KC is honour-bound to accept such a ruling by the mother KC, but surely any step taken to enhance a gene pool in a breed with a small genetic base and a small population too is worthy. When are pedigree dog breeders going to accept that purebreeding, for its own sake, has limitations? Show type isn't threatened by working type; it is reinforced by it. Would it not actually be good for *all* setters if breed colours were to be abolished and inter-breeding between the setter breeds permitted – just as the gifted pioneer breeders did in creating superb field dogs?

Let's have done with that nonsense one has heard for so long about the 'ruin' of the Irish Setter. Field trial

people discarded him as from now almost a century ago, and for their part he could have become extinct as has the Llewellin strain that superseded him. The show people set high store by his beauty, and **liked** his active waving tail. They sheltered, fed, bred and showed him. Most importantly of all, they preserved him as a recognizable breed, admired all over the world. He lives!

The Truth About Sporting Dogs by C. Bede Maxwell (1972)

Retrievers: The Fetchers and Carriers

Demanding Role

'A glorious breed of dog is the retriever, useful alike for sporting and for domestic purposes; his sagacity, good temper, and intelligence endear him to all lovers of the canine race.' Those few words by Webb in his quaintly entitled *Dogs: their points, whims, instincts, and peculiarities* (1883), give an instant snapshot of this ever-popular type of gundog. Retrievers are uniquely British and reflect the way in which British sportsmen have chosen to operate in the shooting field in the last century or so. Sporting writers down the years have always found something nice to say about the retrievers. Stern taskmasters driven mad by the waywardness of cockers, the selective deafness of bassets and the wildness of hunt terriers have rarely

RIGHT: *Chesapeake Bay Retriever by Reuben Ward Binks (1880–1950).*

BELOW: *Golden Retriever by Reuben Ward Binks.*

rubbished the retrievers. Quite the reverse; their prose on this subject has frequently been inspired. And yet the field role of the working retriever is a demanding one. I didn't agree with the distinguished gundog writer, Wilson Stephens, when he once described the task of retrieving shot game as 'a simple act of porterage'. The recall needed for marking falling game, the nosework required for game-finding and the softness of mouth to retrieve to hand calls for a variety of skills. Picking up in a gale-force wind or sitting in a freezing estuary on a December dawn is not a job for the faint-hearted. Retrievers have to have *character*.

A descriptive noun usually comes quickly to mind when a dog fancier conjures up a mind image of a group of dogs. For me, the sighthounds have elegance, the mastiff group stoicism, the terriers tenacity, the scenthounds single-mindedness and the spaniels merriment. So many Toy dogs have a certain coquettishness about them. The Bull Terriers always seem to have a glint in their eye. The retrievers, as British as terriers, I always connect with charm. So many of them are simply delightful, captivating and easily attracting admiration. Seeing the eternally waving tails of Golden Retrievers always gives me pleasure. All the retriever breeds charm their owners and back that with wide-ranging usefulness.

Origins

There have been claims in modern books on retrievers, published unsurprisingly in North America, that the Newfoundland, sometimes called the Father of the Retriever, was developed in North America from local stock, existing before Europeans arrived there. Such claims link early types of this breed with big draught dogs, of spitz type, used by the native Indians, and themselves originating from the other side of the continent, near the Bering Straits. The use of the blood of the Tibetan Mastiff has been claimed by these theorists, as well as that of the Pyrenean Mountain Dog, a similarly sized breed.

Before the days of purebreeding, man bred good dog to good dog, dogs excelling in the function desired. I have already covered the extensive use of ships dogs/fishing dogs along the eastern seaboard of North America in times past and refer to it again at the end of this section. If, as a fisherman or seafarer, you needed a better ships' dog or an improved

draught dog, and one able to cope with extreme climatic conditions, you would have brought in the blood of suitable local dogs, but never at the expense of the primary function. French ships would have carried dogs like the Barbet; Portuguese ships would have had dogs like their Cao de Agua; English ships would have had dogs from ports like Plymouth and Poole, with perhaps those from Scotland having a type like the Tweed Water Dog. Out of this mix came the dogs taken back to Britain to enhance our native types, used as retrievers.

Sixty or seventy years ago there was a considerable trade between Poole, in Dorsetshire, and Labrador; and it is a fact that it was by these trading vessels that the first Labrador dogs were brought to this country; and that excellent sportsman, the then Earl of Malmesbury, became the possessor of some of them. So highly was he pleased with their work, especially in water, that he kept the breed up to his death. About the same time, or perhaps a little later, the late Duke of Buccleuch, the Earl of Home (who died in 1841), and Lord John Scott, imported some of the variety from Labrador. They were kept pure for many years, but the difficulty of getting fresh blood arose, so they became crossed in and out with other breeds, especially with the flat-coated retrievers and Tweed water spaniels. There are even at present few retrievers on the borders of England and Scotland that have not a dash of Labrador in them.

J. Kerss, head gamekeeper to the Duke of Buccleuch, writing in *The Field* magazine (1902)

In the last century when I first remember Retrievers… a few well known sportsmen owned a number of black dogs imported from Newfoundland which were known as the short coated Newfoundland Retrievers. Of these owners, the best known were the Duke of Buccleuch, Lord Malmesbury, Lord Wimborne and a few others including my Father. When and why these dogs began to be called Labradors I could never find out. But on visiting the coasts of Labrador and Newfoundland many years ago I was surprised to be laughed at when asking to be shown a Labrador Retriever, which was unknown in that country.

Major C.E. Radcliffe, writing in *The Field* (1941)

Ships' Dogs

I have previously quoted from General Hutchinson's *Dog Breaking* of 1909, when giving the origin of our modern retrievers; he gave this opinion: 'it is usually allowed that, as a general rule, the best land retrievers are bred from a cross between the Setter and the Newfoundland, or the strong Spaniel and the Newfoundland...the far slighter dog reared by the settlers on the coast, a dog that is quite as fond of water as of land...'. This 'far slighter dog' indicates the variety of type found in the early imports from Newfoundland and it was the lighter-coated, lighter-built dog that caught the eye of the 2nd and 3rd Earls of Malmesbury, the 5th and 6th Dukes of Buccleuch and the 11th and 12th Earls of Home, who had the vision to see the sporting potential of the Labrador retriever, now our most popular breed of dog. The Earls of Malmesbury lived at Heron's Court, only four miles from Poole, where the ships came in from Newfoundland. They soon realized the value of the black, biddable seal-coated ships' dogs that came ashore there. But were we merely importing a British export, the black, smooth-coated ships' dog from Devon? The American gundog expert Richard Wolters certainly thought so.

The Labrador Dog from Devon

In his intriguing book *The Labrador Retriever – The History...The People* (1981), Wolters describes the settlement of Avalon, a peninsula in Newfoundland, which even in the sixteenth century had 250 ships and around 10,000 fishermen eventually employed there, who came, with their dogs – out of Devonshire. He is supported by Scott and Middleton's *The Labrador Dog – Its Home and History* (1936), which states: 'there is good reason for supposing that one of the earlier ancestors must have been the hunting dog of the Devon fishermen...of greater antiquity than the large Newfoundland dog', and points out that the settlement on the Avalon peninsula expanded over the next two centuries and the strong, black, all-purpose dogs spread outwards too. These dogs were used in a wide variety of ways, pulling fishmongers' carts, hauling fishing nets up beaches and retrieving lost ships' lines, just as they were in Devon. But then, as I discuss below, another North American breed, the Chesapeake Bay Retriever may well have come from the county of Norfolk. European seafarers certainly took useful dogs to the New World.

TOP: *Last of the old Newfoundland Water Dogs (aged 13). Photo: R.A. Wolters.*

BOTTOM: *Castro Laboreiro – a Portuguese Breed, used as utility farm dog, mainly with cattle.*

Sir John Nepthorpe out Shooting by George Stubbs, 1776.

Portuguese Look-Alike

Thirty years ago, whilst visiting a more remote part of Minho province in northern Portugal, I came across what I felt sure was a Labrador Retriever but was assured by my local hosts was a native breed – the Cao de Castro Laboreiro, used there as a cattle dog. There were several of them, black with brindled legs (as featured by some of our own retrievers), quite remarkably Labrador-like, even to the otter tail! They reminded me of the progeny produced by American breeder and vet, Leon Whitney, over half a century ago, by crossing a Newfoundland with a hound. I saw the Portuguese breed some years later at the World Dog Show in Porto and was again struck by the similarity between the two breeds. Portuguese ships were very active around the early settlements of Newfoundland and the use of the word Laboreiro in their breed's title also arouses interest. In his *Working Dogs of the World* of 1947, Clifford Hubbard provided an illustration of this breed, which I reproduce, with the otter tail very much in evidence. In 1776, George Stubbs entitled a painting *Sir John Nepthorpe Out Shooting*, which depicts a mainly white Pointer, with a docked tail, and what may well be a black Pointer but has a distinct Labrador look to it. We should always keep open minds when discussing the origins of our gundogs!

The Labrador Retriever

It is fair I believe to describe the Labrador Retriever, as I have earlier, as the sporting dog of the twentieth century, since its development as a breed, popularity and prowess is undisputed – and it continues. In 2012, it is so pleasing to hear such good accounts of them; in the field, for example, Keith Broomfield's successes with his Labradors Maverick's Goose and then Kaliture Black Spruce are excellent advertisements for the breed and the sport. At Crufts 2012, the Best of Breed Show Champion (and American and Canadian Champion) Salty Dog of Tampa Bay, a top-quality yellow, full of type and strongly built without coarseness, really impressed. In the Gamekeeper classes, the winner of the Gilbert & Page Trophy, Champion Warringah's Gundaroo typified the breed's character and was shown in commendably hard condition. The Labrador needs refreshing as a breed in the field from time to time, with so many spoiled by pet ownership and no release for their latent sporting instincts.

Whether picking up or being picked as a companion dog by the dog-owning community, the Labrador is the retriever most people choose. In 1912, 281 were registered, in 1922, 916, and by the 1950s there were 4,000 registered with the KC each year. In recent years their popularity has known no bounds: 25,000 a year in the early 1990s and over 45,000 subsequently. Being the nation's most popular breed has not been all joy but their wide use outside the show ring indicates their versatility and skill. I have used them as tracking dogs in the jungle and overseen their use as explosives detectors and body seekers; they have rarely disappointed me. This is a breed that wants to work and yet so many are purchased by people who just want a pet and seem unembarrassed by a bored, unhappy dog. It's a breed, too, that has the good fortune to attract extremely knowledgeable breeders. When making a commercial video on the breed I was immensely impressed by the informed input from breed experts such as Gwen Broadley, Jo Coulson and Carole Coode; their knowledge and the range of their expertise was inspiring.

Labrador versus Flat-coat
In the shooting field the Lab rules the roost. In 1908, of the 106 dogs entered for field trials, 62 were Flat-coats, 39 Labradors, 3 Curlies and 2 were inter-bred retrievers. The Flat-coats won 2 firsts, 5 seconds, 8 thirds and 3 fourths; the Labradors won 6 firsts, 2 seconds, one third and one fourth. Three years later, the Flat-coats won 2 firsts, 5 seconds, one third and 2 fourths; Labradors won 13 firsts, 11 seconds, 13 thirds and 6 fourths. Two years after that, Labradors won 20 firsts, 17 seconds, 19 thirds and 10 fourths, whereas Flat-coats won one first, 2 seconds, 3 thirds and one fourth, a quite astonishing performance in a field where change is not welcome. Even the popular press picked up this astonishing rise to fame. *The Daily Mail* in February 1928 stating: 'Flat-coated Retrievers, which, in the early years of this century seemed to be invulnerable, have been side-tracked latterly, Labradors having eclipsed them completely alike on the show bench and at Field Trials.'

In *The Field* magazine of December 1909, an experienced sportsman of that time gave a view of the various merits of two retriever breeds:

> Labradors – Quicker to retrieve and go out, hardier; stand exposure or heat better; short coat does not pick up mud or wet; a better dog for certain work, such as picking up after grouse or partridge drive, or stand at covert shoot; excellent companion to owner, but essentially a one-man dog; good nose and mouth as a rule, but often inclined to use eyes too much and cast

Gwen Broadley with three show champions: Lawnwoods Hot Chocolate owned by M. Satterthwaite, Sandylands Mercy and Sandylands Storm-Along.

> forward if scent weak, instead of puzzling it out – at times with great success, but it is a fault to my mind. Flat-coated – Excellent mouth as a rule; in style slow, inclined to potter; nose good; inclined to be slack on a hot day in heather; very friendly and affectionate with master and everyone else; not keen on thick fences as a rule, though some keepers' dogs are excellent at it. Given a good scent, I notice the Labrador easily beats the Flat-coated and has birds quicker. Given a bad scent, the Flat-coated will equal the Labrador, and probably beat him.

This is a valuable opinion from an experienced shooting man at a time when such a man would spend day after day in the shooting field.

Colour Variations
Studying the Yellow Labradors going through a working test a few years ago, their action in pursuit of

ground scent reminded me of another breed at work but I couldn't place it. Then it dawned on me that they were working the cover exactly as a foxhound would. I believe that Foxhound blood was used with Labradors in the north of England in the 1940s, not to improve scenting but appearance. The head of the Labrador is more hound-like than the other retriever breeds. I have heard it argued that the higher tail carriage of the hound is often accompanied by an un-Labrador-like aggression. In his *The Dog* of 1880, the knowledgeable 'Idstone' wrote that the smooth-coated retriever 'tracked his game like a Bloodhound'. 'Stonehenge', writing in 1860, referred to a famous retriever of Lord Fitzwilliam which was by a

bloodhound out of a mastiff. I see many hound-like actions in the Labrador at work in the field, perhaps because I am now looking out for it. But it is interesting that a few years ago, Bill Williamson of Staffordshire bred two black and tan Labrador pups from a yellow/black mating, with DNA proof of purebreeding. A Swedish breeder has reported mismarked pups in a purebred litter; some being black with fawn, some with brindling and some chocolate and tan. The gene pool never lies!

In an article in *The Field* in 1941, Major C.E. Radcliffe described not just yellow Labrador pups occurring in litters but pure white whelps in Labradors *and* Wavy-coated Retrievers too, with a Mr Austin Mackenzie of Carridale actually starting a breed of pure white Labradors 'which were very handsome dogs'. I have never seen a 'Hailstone' Labrador, a black coated dog with 'reverse Dalmatian' white spotting. They were associated with an old strain of water retrievers on the Solway, one even appearing at Crufts, shown by a keeper and approved by the distinguished judge, Lady Howe, as a true colour for the breed. It is worth noting that the first *registered* yellow Labrador came from two black-coated parents. Most yellows can be traced back to Major Radcliffe's dog Neptune – Major Radcliffe, with Major and Mrs Wormald, making the greatest contribution to the development

Purebred black and tan Labrador. Photo: Nick Ridley.

Hailstone Labradors, from the ancient breed of the Solway.

of the yellows between the two World Wars. But whether yellow or black, this breed is a triumph of performance over preference and shows no sign of losing its remarkable range of skills.

The Flat-coated Retriever

The Flat-coated Retriever I have long admired and when I was younger mourned its absence from the shooting field. It has been good to see a small renaissance of the breed's working qualities. They were once every gamekeeper's first choice. Combining handsomeness with intelligence, they have never been spoiled by over-popularity. Writing in his *The Dog* of 1880, 'Idstone', who was a gundog authority in his day, described one with these words:

> He was as black as a raven – blue-black – not a very large dog, but wide over the back and loins, with limbs like a lion, and a thick, glossy, long, silky coat which parted down the back, a long sagacious head, full of character, and clean as a setter's in the manner of coat. His ears were small, and so close to his head that they were hidden in his feathered neck. His *eye* was neither more nor less than a human one. I never saw a bad expression in it.

An enchanting description, richly deserved.

FT Champion Werrion Redwing of Collyers with the Hon Mrs Amelia Jessel.

Flat-coat Champion Shargleam Blackcap. Photo: David Dalton

James Wentworth Day, a demanding dog man if there ever was one, referred to a Flat-coat in his *The Dog in Sport* of 1938 with these words: 'But Black Bess…was my father's dog, a magnificent flat-coat who shone in the sun like a raven's wing, who walked the grass with the gait of a queen. She was all good looks, good breeding and good heart.' These words came back to me some years ago, firstly when watching the late Pat Chapman's Shargleam Blackcap win Best in Show at Crufts, and again when seeing FT Ch Werrion Redwing of Collyers at work in the field. Here were two happy, handsome dogs in contrasting circumstances, really 'selling' their breed. In 2007, Phil Bruton owned and trialled the only Flat-coat to be made up to Field Trial Champion in twenty-six years, his liver bitch, Shirlett Sweetheart. He had another very promising young dog a few years later, Shirlett Skylark, that showed great promise.

We hear little nowadays of the extremely mixed origin of the retriever, the huge amount of crossbreeding conducted in the early nineteenth century (and inter-breeding of Labradors and Flat-coats in the field trial world, as the KC Stud Book reveals, between 1914 and 1945) and the emergence at various times of golden-coated puppies in purebred Flat-coat litters, as well as black and liver ones. The longer head is forever linked to the setter blood and the input of Borzoi blood rarely mentioned, although Harding Cox did dub the resultant progeny from this input 'coffin-heads'. It would be strange indeed if in retriever litters, the odd throwback didn't crop up; those with knowledge of the breed's gene pool and history will smile tolerantly, the not so well informed will shout 'alien blood'. Genetic diversity is a breed's strongpoint, not a weakness.

Drawback to Dual Purpose
In her informative *A Review of the Flat-coated Retriever* of 1980, breed expert and sportswoman Nancy Laughton writes:

> One sportsman maintains that the chief stumbling block in breeding towards perfection of working stock in gundogs has been the obsession for the 'sacred cow' of 'dual purpose' by a majority of breeders. I am forced to agree with this now and believe that unless penal field faults are eliminated in Flat-coats and breeding is directed towards biddability, less excitability and the

preservation of good temperament, we will lose that working reliability in the field for which the Flat-coat was renowned in the past.

The early Labradors certainly benefited from not featuring either at field trials or the show bench, becoming the sportsman's dog rather than the fancier's or the top trainer's dog. We all admire a handsome dog; we all admire a field trial winner's prowess; but most sportsmen require a dog with fundamental skills and a sound physique. To be called a retriever, every show dog should be physically capable of acting as one in the field – even if not required to do so. The KC's 'fitness for function' campaign, now being strongly promoted, will perhaps achieve progress on this issue. I was very impressed by full champion Deep River Walk of Downstream when winning Group 3 at the National Gundog Show a few years ago.

New Name Proposed
The breed owes a great deal to early pedigree breeders like the Shirley family of Ettington Park, H. Reginald Cooke (who 'collected' Flat-coats from gamekeepers at an unprecedented rate), the Phizaklea family and Dr Nancy Laughton with her 'Claverdon' kennel. They have left us with a handsome but essentially utility breed. For me, in looks, companionability and sheer willingness, this breed is the supreme retriever. I would like to see him renamed as 'the English Retriever' and placed at the head of our rightfully revered retriever breeds – our national breed. I sincerely believe he has the qualities and the history to justify such a distinctive title. This breed has never been spoiled by over-popularity, has a healthier genotype than some gundog breeds and has every right to be regarded as solely born here, developed here and fashioned here. We are not very consistent over claiming our native breeds; we have the English Setter, we have an English spaniel breed. Unlike the Germans we do not claim our Pointer by name. We credit an overseas location in our Labrador's title, but elect to describe our other retrievers by coat texture or colour. But retrievers are a British invention and the Flat-coat is the soul of their development here; let's celebrate that.

The Curly-coated Retriever
It is probably just as fair to describe the Curly-coated Retriever as the oldest and most underrated breed

*Curly-coated Retriever by
Reuben Ward Binks.*

of retriever. Their qualities are well known to their owners but are usually untapped by the majority of shooting men. Yet there is something very masculine about the curly; they are a fussless breed and a very individual one, protected from 'mongrelization' by their astrakhan coats. I once spent a happy day judging working tests just for this breed and found much to admire in their character. A number of knowledgeable writers of times past have become seriously confused by the Curly. Youatt scarcely mentions the breed. The much-quoted 'Stonehenge' wrote that:

Little or nothing seems to be known of the history of this dog…there is no getting at the exact source of the breed… I am led to think that some non-sporting dog, such as the poodle has been used… The general belief is that the water spaniel and small Newfoundland have been used in establishing the breed, and there is little doubt of the truth of this theory.

This is quite astonishing ignorance for a writer of his standing. Dalziel, usually so reliable, attributes the curly coat to the 'old close-curled English Water Spaniel' and states that many think the Irish Water Spaniel is behind the breed.

H. Reginald Cooke's Flat-coat Ch Grouse of Riverside (from Maud Earl painting).

Rawdon Lee did the breed no favours, writing in 1906 that: 'He is inclined to be hard-mouthed… His temper too is decidedly unreliable, especially with strangers…'. Lee was a prolific writer and more of a gossip than a real dog man. At this time the Labrador was being promoted strongly and rival retrievers played down. I don't know of any evidence of a breed being hard-mouthed, that is damaging the shot game being carried in the dog's mouth. I have never come across a whole breed possessing an unreliable temper; I like my dogs to be suspicious of strangers. The Curly is the best guard dog of the gundog breeds and grows out of puppyhood rather better than some retrievers.

Even Rawdon Lee felt compelled to record that:

> We must however look to the curly-coated retrievers as the hardiest of their race, and perhaps the best animals to use as assistants for wildfowl shooting… He is a faithful and useful dog to follow the keeper who makes a companion of him, for, in addition to being very steady and easy to command, he possesses a good nose if the scent be not too stale…

'Idstone', himself a great promoter of the Labrador, wrote of one Curly: 'I don't know any dog which I coveted more, or which has produced better offspring.' The breed standard of the 1890s gave the general appearance of the breed as: 'A strong, smart dog, moderately low on leg, active, lively, beaming

with intelligence and expression.' Rawdon Lee was happy to publish these words.

James Wentworth Day, who expected a great deal from his retrievers, being a renowned wildfowler, had enormous regard for the Curly. In his compelling *The Dog in Sport* (1938), a superb read for any youngster starting out in dogs, he wrote:

> Then there was Bruno, the curly-coat… He was a good-looker from nose to tail. He stood well and moved well. He would face any tide and sniffed at the cold. I remember sitting for three and a half hours one winter afternoon in a sunken barrel by the side of the fleet on a marsh at Salcott, snow falling and a north-easterly half a gale blowing. Bruno scarcely moved the whole time, and never whimpered.

It is that fussless stoicism and supportive loyalty that makes a Curly the retriever breed for me. I warmed to the breed, too, when Wentworth Day described how when he shamefully shot a moorhen, Bruno swam out and retrieved it, placed it at his owner's feet – then pointedly raised his leg and urinated over it, showing his contempt. I doubt if his owner transgressed again! In his classic *Dog Breaking* of 1909, General W.N. Hutchinson relates how one sportsman:

> …had a famous retriever whose build, close curly hair, and aquatic propensities showed his close affinity

Curly-coated Retriever today.

to the water spaniel… He retrieved with singular zeal and pertinacity. Indeed his superiority over all competitors in his neighbourhood was so generally admitted that his master was hardly ever asked to shoot at any place without a special invitation being sent to 'Ben'.

Unique Coat

The unique astrakhan coat of the Curly, like the coat colours of the Vizsla, the Weimaraner and the Dalmatian, provides an inbuilt protection against crossbreeding; if the astrakhan coat isn't there, neither is the breed! This distinction is reinforced by the fact that this is the tallest retriever, with a silhouette all his own. Bede Maxwell, in her very forthright *The Truth About Sporting Dogs* of 1972, wrote on the Curly that: 'He is a sober customer in the main, sometimes dour, and with a mind of his own, but a magnificent dog to own… He should not (maybe could not) look like a Labrador in outline, nor a Golden, nor a Flat-Coated. He is all his own dog!'

Against these compliments can be placed the words of 'Pathfinder' and Hugh Dalziel in their *Breaking and Training Dogs* of 1906: 'I do not like Curlies of any colour. As far as my experience goes, the more the coat curls the more bounce and impetuosity in the dog and the harder his mouth.' The author's experience with the breed is not revealed but his comments on

coat texture are clearly absurd and if curly-coated dogs are harder-mouthed than others, medieval sportsmen would have noticed it and it would have been recorded and acted upon. It is therefore worth being mindful of the references we do have of curly-coated water-dogs in medieval times.

Despite the long history of the water dogs, we in England have lost both our English Water Spaniel and our Tweed Water Spaniel. We have failed to acknowledge the ancient origins of our Curly mainly through the ignorance of Victorian dog writers, who so often speculated about an origin for the breed involving crosses between the Newfoundland and the Setter. The much-quoted 'Stonehenge', writing in 1877, described Lloyd-Price's retriever Devil as 'a curly liver-coloured dog, apparently a cross between the Irish Water Spaniel and the Poodle…showing great perseverance in hunting, with a good nose.' The Curly-coated Retriever shares a common ancestry with these two breeds but as a type is as old as either. In connection with coat colour, it's worth noting that only a century ago, Brigadier Lance of Saluki fame, had a kennel of *golden* Curly-coated Retrievers, but they did not find favour with other sportsmen.

The revised breed standard for the Curly, under 'General Appearance', gives a description of: 'Strong, upstanding dog with a degree of elegance. Distinctive coat.' The general appearance in any standard should tell you what the dog looks like. This general appearance wording could refer to a Dalmatian. Breed standards must surely be written in such a way that the general public can visualize what the breed should be. It would be a major step forward if the Kennel Club were to stop drafting breed standards by way of a committee and hand the task over to a professor of English! This particular breed standard, under 'Movement', demands: 'Parallel movement. At speed, legs tend to converge'. The word 'converge' means 'tend to meet in a point; come together as if to meet or join'. How on earth can any breed function with such foolish requirements?

British Water Dog
This breed has medium-size ears: the standard demands rather small ears. The standard calls for large eyes but the breed displays quite small eyes. Ears and eyes can typify a breed; the standard should establish breed type. The American Kennel Club standard for the breed is just as misleading on these two aspects but is quite excellent on gait and temperament. A breed standard may not be a blueprint in the true sense of that word, but it should still act as the construction plan for a breed. The KC breed standard does no justice at all to this distinguished breed and needs a radical rewrite – despite its recent review. Whether undersold in its breed standard or underused by today's sportsmen, this is a breed we should be proud of; it is our contribution to the water dogs of the world. L.P.C. Astley, in Gordon Stables' *Our Friend is the Dog* (Dean & Son, 1907), likened the Curly's coat to the close-fitting, tightly curled beautiful head of hair of many native African people, stating that this was the only 'true and proper one… of which every knot is solid and inseparable. A coat of this quality is not capable of improvement by any methods of grooming, for the simple reason that its natural condition is itself perfect.' If you don't lust after the labour of grooming, this is the breed for you!

Whilst I would not wish too much popularity on any breed, this one deserves wider patronage. Whilst we are welcoming new breeds of gundog here in each decade, this native breed of gundog goes underrated and largely unappreciated. It was gratifying to see, at the World Dog Show in Helsinki, that our water dog was there in greater numbers than any other. The American standard describes the breed as: 'Self-confident, steadfast and proud, this active, intelligent dog is a charming and gentle family companion and a determined, durable hunter. The Curly is alert, biddable and responsive to family and friends, whether at home or in the field. Of independent nature and discerning intelligence…' Perhaps this distinctive breed of ours is better appreciated abroad. If so, that is not unique in a British product and shame on us for it.

The Golden Retriever

The Willing Charmer
Golden Retriever owners could make a fair claim to possess the dog breed with the greatest charm, the nicest nature and one free of any kind of malice. Stimulating great affection from the general public and attracting the admiration of those advertising all things canine has, however, brought what is to me an undesirable excess of popularity, with the relegation of far too many of the breed to the hearth. But the breed undoubtedly comes from impeccable working stock, bred by the most skilful and knowledgeable of men, with an enviable blend of blood behind the breed when utilized in the shooting field.

Origins
In *The Golden Retriever Handbook* of 1953, Elma Stonex established the beginnings of this breed, discounting all the fanciful stories of circus dogs, Russian imports and other romantic fantasies that strangely continue to this day. Mercifully, this breed has been spared an origin from dogs swimming ashore from shipwrecks, as several pedigree breeds' historians still claim. The truth is that this popular, attractive, appealing breed developed from black to black matings (one of which had to possess the gene for the golden coat), with input from local dogs like the Tweed Water Spaniel along with some Bloodhound blood. Very occasionally, a golden-coated dog crops up in Flat-coated litters; the Flat-coat expert Nancy Laughton had one in a 1968 litter and some more were whelped in the 1980s both here and in Australia.

Thankfully, no breed historian of this breed in the early days had seen a golden-coated Hovawart from Germany. When working there and visiting a remote farm, my astonishment at seeing what I was temporarily convinced was a pair of Golden

RIGHT: Golden Retriever of 1896 by Thomas Blinks.

BELOW RIGHT: Hovawart – German flock guarding breed.

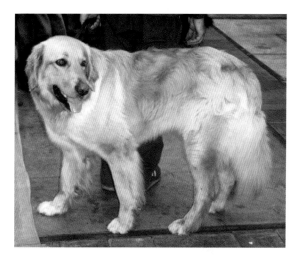

Retrievers, was soon banished by seeing their registration papers. Since then I have seen golden Hovawarts at World Dog Shows and again been immediately struck by their close similarities with our gundog breed. It is never wise to attribute origin to physical likeness. Victorian dog writers had extremely limited knowledge of foreign breeds, and when they did see one, conjectured at once on the composite breeds likely to have contributed to its make-up. The Golden Retriever was developed here from British stock. We have every reason to be proud of this native gundog breed.

Conformation

In her valuable short book *Golden Retrievers* of 1952, W.M. Charlesworth writes a quite admirable summary of the anatomy desired in the breed:

> The build of all gun-dogs runs on much the same lines as does that of a hunter and a Foxhound. They should be built for pace, endurance, and, in the case of hunters and Retrievers, to carry weight and jump with it. Hence the necessity for muscular necks (so that the Golden can lift, carry and jump with a 9lb hare when occasion arises), for long-bladed, clean-cut shoulders, sound big bone and good feet; and, above all, for short-coupled backs, strong loins, muscular quarters and second thighs, and straight, strong hocks, without which there can be propelling nor jumping power.

In 1908, she bred from Culham Brass and in 1910 from Culham Copper, each time to her Noranby

Beauty; these two litters laid the foundation of the breed, via Noranby Balfour, the sire of the excellent Heydown strain. She dedicated this book to the Countess of Ilchester, whose family became owners of the founding Guisachan dogs and kept the breed going as a sporting breed.

Yellow and Gold

Once, when assisting Sally Ancrum, the field-trial judge, to judge a working test at the annual Gamekeepers' Fair some years ago, I was reminded again of how different our retrievers are, one from another. We tend to overlook, when thinking of retrievers, that different breeds are behind each of them and that they each have quite different breed characteristics. Their function may be the same but the wise owner or trainer would benefit from reminding himself, as I was able to, of their essential differences, breed for breed, and from acknowledging how sensible it is to have this in mind when training a young dog as a retriever.

On this occasion, the most handsome breed was the Golden Retriever; the dogs running being red-gold, the real colour of the breed. How refreshing to see genuine working dogs in this lovely breed: keen but biddable, not too heavy-coated or over-furnished on the legs and tail and full of dash and drive. Red-coated hunting dogs were prized by the ancient Greeks and Egyptians; red-coated Bloodhounds were often found to have the best scenting powers. I suspect too that our own 'ginger 'coy dog' (or red decoy dog) of the Middle Ages, probably now perpetuated in the Nova Scotia Duck-tolling Retriever, has contributed to our contemporary breed of Golden Retriever. This red-gold coloration in dogs has long had genetic significance. Golden-coloured pups have cropped up in Flat-coat litters, creating the predictable cries of outside blood. But the much respected Flat-coat breeder Dr Nancy Laughton had one in a 1968 litter, with other examples occurring in Australia in the early 1980s. Black coats and golden coats are present in the same gene pool in a number of breeds; has a possible Flat-coat origin for the Goldie been intentionally suppressed?

The Chesapeake Bay Retriever

Impression of Power
The renowned Norfolk sportsman James Wentworth Day greatly admired the character of the Chesapeake Bay Retriever, as these words from his *The Dog in Sport* of 1938, illustrate: 'Their impression of power is quite remarkable. They give one the feeling of immense resources of energy, of great reservoirs of knowledge, of tolerance of disposition, obstinacy of purpose, and tenacity of principle. They are responsive, and they have a lot of quiet good sense.' They would certainly be my first choice as a wildfowling companion. In his *Dog Breaking* of 1915, 'Wildfowler', a much-respected gundog authority, spelled out the requirements for a successful wildfowling dog:

> …the dog has to learn so many more things than other breeds of dogs. He must stay ready for flighting,

remain still in a punt, he must never open under the strongest temptation, never jump up, never be excited, obey signs implicitly, hunt when told and keep to heel when ordered…be tender-mouthed, very keen-nosed, strong-constitutioned, plucky, swim for ever, and stand hard winters with equanimity. A dog who does all these things well clearly is a valuable dog.

Clearly! List the dogs you would prefer *not* to share a punt with!

Origins: Link with Norfolk
In his book *British Dogs* of 1888, Hugh Dalziel, kennel editor of *The Country Magazine*, exhibitor and judge, produced a chapter on the Norfolk Retriever. He largely relied on the knowledge of 'Saxon', a Norfolk sportsman, who provided the text. Dalziel acknowledged that 'although Retrievers answering this description may be more plentiful in Norfolk than elsewhere, they are met with often enough in all parts of the country'. 'Saxon' describes the coat colour of this retriever as 'more often brown than black, and the shade of brown rather light than dark – a sort of sandy brown, in fact'. He goes on to describe the coat as looking 'rusty', inclined to be coarse, feeling harsh to the touch, curly but not as close and crisp as in the Curly-coated Retriever of the show ring, tending to be open and woolly. He describes a saddle of straight, short hair across the back. Gamekeepers usually docked their tails which made them appear to some sporting writers as spaniels, despite their stature.

These dogs were the wildfowlers' retrievers, used 'on broad, river, sea-coast and estuary'. It was alleged that the Pointer was not hard enough for such work, the water spaniel too impetuous but the Norfolk Retriever 'will face a rough sea well, and they are strong swimmers, persevering, and not easily daunted in their search for a dead or wounded fowl'. 'Saxon' claimed that Norfolk was outside 'the magic circle of shows' and so the 'improvement' of them had not taken place. He makes it quite clear that this Norfolk dog is different from a spaniel (and appreciably larger) and from the Curly-coated, Flat-coated and Labrador Retrievers. The occasional long coat crops up in Chessie litters, causing discussion on origin, but coat variations can occur in most gundog breeds, illustrating a mixed origin, not a pure one, and that's good.

Chesapeake Bay Retriever Ch Barnum (born 1883), the breed's first recorded champion.

If you tried to find the contemporary retriever breed to fit closest to the description of the Norfolk Retriever, then the Chesapeake Bay Retriever would be my choice. The breed standard of the latter describes the coat as 'harsh…hairs having a tendency to wave on neck, shoulders, back and loins…straw/bracken coloured, red-gold (sedge) or any shade of brown… White spots on chest, toes and belly permissible. The smaller the spot the better.' The Norfolk Retriever featured white in the form of a spot on the chest. 'Saxon' stated that the most distinctive features of the Norfolk Retriever were its unique coat and its quite remarkable hardiness. The first sentence of the Chesapeake's standard mentions its distinctive coat and lists two of its characteristics as courageous with a great love of water.

Newfoundland Links
Some authorities have claimed that the Chesapeake Bay Retriever was developed from two shipwrecked so-called 'Newfoundlands' (one black, one red, which were never mated together; the red one only threw blacks) and others from 'Red Winchester' water dogs out of Ireland. The American writer Bede Maxwell, in her forthright *The Truth about Sporting Dogs* of 1972, thought this link might be with a fisheries patrol vessel HMS *Winchester* which sailed out of Cork to the eastern American seaboard, with officers taking their Irish Water Spaniels with them. But Newfoundlands

and Irish Water Spaniels have distinct anatomical differences from Chesapeakes. And, just as I suspect that the Nova Scotia Duck-tolling Retriever was taken to Canada as the red decoy dog of England, especially from the East Anglia part of England, so too could the Norfolk Retriever have been. Perhaps some diligent breed researcher could look at the records in Norfolk, Virginia, at the entrance to Chesapeake Bay itself.

Norfolk's Loss
If my theory is correct then the great sporting county of Norfolk has missed out in several ways concerning the titles of sporting gundogs. For just as the Norfolk Retriever could be behind the Chesapeake Bay Retriever and renamed in its new country, so too could the English Springer Spaniel have been named the Norfolk Spaniel and the Nova Scotia Duck-tolling Retriever called the Red Norfolk Decoy Dog. In Britain, we respected the backgrounds of both the Newfoundland, which could so easily have become the Landseer Retriever, and the Labrador, which could so easily have become the Malmesbury Retriever, from its early development in England. We lost our Tweed Water Spaniel and English Water Spaniel; the Americans still have their Boykin Spaniel and American Water Spaniel.

In his *The Illustrated Book of the Dog* of 1880, Vero Shaw felt obliged to mention the Norfolk Retriever and wrote: 'It is claimed for this breed…that it is

peculiarly adapted for the pursuit of wild birds in the low-lying districts of Norfolk, and that few, if any other varieties of dog, could be found to endure the hard work equally well.' In his *Breaking and Training Dogs* of 1906, 'Pathfinder' wrote of retrievers: 'I have known livers in Norfolk dignified with that prefix, just as it was usual at one time to speak of the English Springer when met there as the Norfolk Spaniel.' In his *The Sporting Dog*, published in New York in 1904, the American writer Joseph A. Graham stated that: 'The Chesapeake is not so peculiar or distinct. In fact, he is of rather common appearance. Stout and strong, sedge or rusty brown in colour, the coat dense and close, he is not a beauty.'

So we have a rusty-coloured, broken-coated, retriever-sized dog in Norfolk, England and subsequently an identical dog near Norfolk, Virginia, at the mouth of Chesapeake Bay. The dog in England is not recognized as a breed, Vero Shaw hinting that it was too nondescript for that to happen. Joseph Graham describes the dog in America as 'of rather common appearance' but it becomes recognized as a breed nevertheless. In his *The Dog* of 1880, the respected 'Idstone' wrote: 'Liver and sandy Retrievers have a few partisans. They are the sort which "always were kept", people tell you, "in our family"... I know of no family priding itself on this coloured species just now, but I have heard that they are not uncommon in Norfolk.' It may be far too late to have the Labrador renamed the Devon Retriever. But how worthwhile a

venture it would be to find rusty-coloured, broken-coated retrievers 'not uncommon in Norfolk', however nondescript, once again recognized, and this time registered, as a Norfolk gundog breed. Abroad or at home, it is so encouraging to learn of the Penrose and Arnac Bay dogs doing well in the field, with Penrose Jack Tar a full champion in the UK and Sweden and Penrose Nomad and Arnac Bay Winota becoming the first full champions in both the UK and Eire.

Preserving Character

The popularity of the Golden and Labrador Retrievers has, however, not been without its drawbacks. We seem to be losing that appealing 'soft' eye in the Labrador and the striking red-gold coat of the Golden. I see more overweight Labradors than any other breed and far too many with untypical, often Rottweiler-like heads with 'hard' eyes. There are worryingly frequent instances of unacceptable temperament in both these distinguished breeds. I am disappointed in the quality of coat on specimens I see at shows. A dense, waterproof coat is simply essential in such a breed. I think back to the worries of Wentworth Day on the Chesapeake:

It will take many generations of stupid women in Bayswater and suede-footed young men in Kensington to ruin the character of this eminently sensible working dog. He has all the dignity, the native aristocracy, the quiet good sense and the instinctive judgement of the British working man… If you have two or three Chesapeakes in the kennel there will never be any disturbances in your shooting routine – none of that hoity-toity flightiness of the Gordon Setter, the kiss-me-quick slobberings of the spaniel or the mental whimperings of the Golden Retriever. Do not imagine for a moment that I dislike any of these three excellent breeds of sporting dog. But I mourn for individuals among them. The show-bench and the drawing-room have made fools of them… I doubt if you could ever do that with the Chesapeake. He will probably bite someone finally, just as a protest and then walk out of the house, a dog in search of a man for a master.

This strongly worded tribute to the Chesapeake Bay Retriever may not appeal to everyone but the sentiments apply to all the retriever breeds and should be heeded by all who love their particular breed and care about their spiritual happiness and well-being.

The retriever breeds must be retained as working breeds and their conformation, character and commitment perpetuated with that in mind, ahead of rosette-winning and fashion of the day. These breeds were developed in a hard school and their precious physical and mental qualities handed on to us to be safeguarded in our lifetime as a matter of honour. We owe it to this charming and valuable group of breeds that those who come after us will respect our contribution to their best long-term interests. Such a contribution is richly deserved. Long may we enjoy our reliable retrievers!

A retriever is, to our mind, the king of all sporting dogs. He has none of the heaviness (or stupidity) of the pointer, or the fawning adulation for his master shown by the setter or spaniel. His mien is dignified, his actions show the height of animal intelligence, and he is affectionate and companionable as is no other dog used for shooting… His actions do not run in a groove, as do those of the pointer, setter or spaniel, for he often has to act, and on the moment judge for himself, what is correct behaviour on his part, and what is not; and if well broken his thoughtful sagacity rarely fails him, though he be out of sight and hearing of his trainer.

From *Shooting*, The Badminton Library (1886)

I know of a sportsman's saying he felt certain that the hare his retriever was *coursing* over the moors must have been struck, although the only person who had fired stoutly maintained that the shot was a regular miss. The owner of the dog, however, averred that this was impossible, as he never could get the discerning animal to follow any kind of unwounded game; and, on the other hand, that no rating would make him quit the pursuit of *injured* running feather or fur. The retriever's speedy return with puss, conveniently balanced between his jaws, bore satisfactory testimony to the accuracy of both his own and his master's judgement.

Dog Breaking by General W.N. Hutchinson (1909)

A mixture of retriever and colley blood has been tried, but this serves no good end; a cross between a small retriever and a large Irish water-spaniel, however, gives a very good dog. A retriever, to be useful, should have legs short and as straight as darts, firm and strong; a full-sized head (a dog with a too small head is rarely a clever worker), a tail that does not curl over his back, but is borne high and light, good loins, a shaggy and yet glossy coat, small ears, large feet with well-planted toes that do not splay outwards, and a deep well-formed chest, which does not imply a broad massive one – the latter is a disadvantage, as it means a slow and heavy dog, especially in covert; lastly, a coat as black as you can get it. A curly-coated dog is, we have usually found, harder to break than a smooth-coated one, but, on the other hand, is generally the quicker and more dashing of the two, as well as being, in our experience the cleverest.

From *Shooting,* The Badminton Library (1886)

That the Labrador was not more generally popular in the 1904 days is strange. True, until 1903 the Kennel Club did not recognize the breed, but in about 1837 the Earl of Malmesbury of that day had a kennel which was at its maximum about 1870, while Sir Richard Graham had a kennel at Netherby in 1860. The Duke of Buccleuch and the Hon. A. Holland Hibbert also had large kennels in the 1880–84 days, and there were other owners. The breed seems to date its popularity from the days of 'Peter of Faskally', handled by that incomparable handler, the late Captain A.E. Butter. The writer's 'Flapper' was also one of the pioneers, his great sagacity and game-

Labradors: Peter of Faskally, carrying a cock pheasant, with Dungavel Jet by Maud Earl. 1912. Two outstanding early specimens.

finding ability helping to bring credit to the breed. These two dogs were used extensively at stud and are responsible for a very large percentage of the Field Trial Labradors of today.

Major Maurice Portal, in the Lonsdale Library's *Shooting by Moor, Field and Shore* (1929)

Now every shooter should possess a retriever. He may have a dozen, but by **a** retriever we mean one particular dog of his own that is entirely subservient to his wishes. It is no hard thing to own a fairly good retriever, but to own a perfect one is another affair. A perfect retriever is rarely, very rarely, seen working for his master – usually it is for a keeper, and it may pretty safely be asserted that in the British Islands there are not a score perfectly broken retrievers that work only for and with their masters out shooting.

From *Shooting*, The Badminton Library (1886)

Most of the keepers had their own retriever. Old John was considered to be one of the finest trainers of a gundog. He would make it do anything bar talk. He was proud of his dogs, and like the other keepers would be offered a big sum of money by some gentlemen who saw them at work. They'd never sell. The retriever is a one man dog.

Gamekeeper – Memories of a Country Childhood by Leslie Rawlings (1977)

The Spaniel Breeds

Spaniels of both descriptions are brought into a kind of general use and domestic estimation. Their neat and uniform shape, their beautiful coats, their cleanly habits, their insinuating attention, incessant attendance, and faithful obedience insure them universal favour; but the sportsman feeling a double and superlative interest in their attachment and affection, loves them for their intrinsic merit, bestows the greatest pains and assiduity in training them for the field, and, when properly broke, and completely educated, he considers himself amply gratified by their ready services and indefatigable exertions in surmounting every difficulty that occurs in beating the various copses, brakes, covers, ditches, swamps, &c. in the pursuit of game. In addition to which accumulation of perfection, they seem to possess a degree of sagacity, sincerity, patience, fidelity, and gratitude, beyond any other of the species.

From *The Sportsman's Cabinet*, 1803.

Origins

It's the commonly held view that spaniels originated in Spain, mainly due to their name, allegedly a corruption of Espagne (French for Spain) or *espagnol*. Perhaps this is just lazy thinking; there are many references to spaniels being imported *into* Spain in early times but not much on their export. Rather than linking the word spaniel with Spain, I suspect that it may well have come from the ancient French verb *espanir*, to crouch or flatten, rather like the Italian word *spianare*, to flatten. The latter could be behind the breed name Spinone, with the French setters becoming known as epagneuls. In the Middle Ages, spaniels were usually used as hawking dogs (hounds for the hawk) and used with the net. There is an old Italian verb *spaniare*, to get out of a trap or net. Turberville, writing in 1575, often quotes Master Francesco Sforzino Vicentino, Gentleman Falconer of Italy, on the subject of 'spanels'. It has been claimed that the spaniel family ranges from the large St Bernard (the Alpine Spaniel) right down to the small companion dogs, as favoured by our own King Charles. There is a distinct similarity of coat colour and coat texture right across this range, including the French epagneuls, described later. The trade in sporting dogs between Britain and France has long been a feature and I suspect that our spaniel, like our Pointer, originated there.

The English Springer Spaniel

Speaking of the Spaniels is to bring forward very useful single-handed dogs as every pot-hunting shooting man knows. It is from the Clumber, down to the tiny little Cocker, that good sport can be obtained, but let it be well said that the best gun dog in Spanieldom is unquestionably the English Springer Spaniel, whose instinct for questing both fur and feather has been handed down to it for centuries. It is, in short, the Springer's legacy – usually a good one, but not always.

Our Dogs and All About Them by Frank Townend Barton MRCVS (1938)

Hare Shooting 1807, engraving by Godby & Merke after Samuel Howitt.

Land Spaniel, late 18th century.

Supreme Spaniel

Few would dispute the supremacy of the English Springer Spaniel at spaniel work in the twentieth/twenty-first century. With the Labrador Retriever, the springer has dominated gundog work since the First World War; these two breeds having, on sheer field merit, ruled the roost in the working gundog world. The astounding rise in popularity here of the hunt-point-retrieve breeds from mainland Europe in the last fifty years may in time change the whole emphasis of dogwork in the shooting field, but, of our native breeds, the fondness of sportsmen for these two gundog breeds continues without check.

Breed Identity

If asked to describe their breed, most working springer owners would respond on the lines of 'liver and white spaniel, foot and a half high and a real goer'!

Spaniel with Teal by Henry Wilkinson, born 1921.

The Kennel Club would opt for their descriptive if not particularly accurate 400-odd-word breed standard. But for the latter to state that this breed is 'of ancient and pure origin, oldest of sporting gundogs' with a gait or movement 'strictly his own' withstands no serious scrutiny. And phrases in this authorized breed standard like 'skull of medium length', 'eyes medium', 'nicely feathered ears', 'jaws strong', 'body neither too long nor too short', 'hind legs well let down' and 'ears lobular, good length and width' offer precious little help with their vagueness. But there has long been vagueness about breed identity.

Blaine, writing in 1870, stated that: 'The variety of Spaniels are numerous. A popular distinction made between them by many writers is into Springers, Cockers, and Water Spaniels. Conventionally this distinction is understood, but critically it will not bear examination, particularly as regards the first two divisions.' This is supported by the fact that the Welsh Springer has been called the Welsh Cocker for much of its history. Another authority of that time wrote that: 'The true English Spaniel differs but little in figure from the Setter except in size.' That great expert C.A. Phillips wrote early in the twentieth century that: 'strictly speaking, all the different varieties of Spaniels are "Springers", the name originally having been used in contradistinction to "Setters"...'

False Provenance

The Kennel Club-authorized breed standard states that the English Springer is the 'highest on leg and raciest in build of all British Land Spaniels', going on to the claim about ancient and pure origin. Gervase Markham, however, was writing in the seventeenth century: 'It is reasonable that people should cross Land Spaniels and Water Spaniels, and the Mungrells between these, and the Mungrells of either with the Shallow Flew'd Hound, the Tumbler, the Lurcher and the small bastard Mastiff...all of which are yet inferior to the truebred Land Spaniel – if one could still find one of those.' Not much support for the 'pure origin' claims of the KC there! What is abundantly clear, however, to any admirer of the breed who studies dogs and prizes breed characteristics is that the English Springer has simply lost its essential type. Broadly speaking, the show type looks like a docked setter whilst the working dog resembles a liver and white Cocker. Gundog men don't always care about appearance, quite naturally, more about performance. But you can lose a breed with that simplistic, narrow, almost self-centred approach.

Loss of Type

The springers that I see working in the field are anything but high on the leg and racy in build, as the KC also insists they must be. One day a pedantic,

Springer Spaniels on a Moor by John Emms 1903.

dissatisfied purchaser of a springer pup might invoke the Trades Descriptions Act! What is the difference between these springers and a sprocker? A cross between the springer and the cocker, the sprocker is preferred by a number of experienced, knowledgeable shooting men. The pedigree dog world loathes crossbreeds, forgetting that every pure breed was initiated from varied stock, but stock chosen on merit. Functional dogs have to *function*, that is what they are *for*! The 'pure origin' of the breed, claimed by the Kennel Club but disputed by countless authoritative writers, has not been improved in the last hundred years or so by the introduction of pointer, Irish Setter and black and tan Field Spaniel blood, as the much respected Frank Warner Hill has testified. In their book *The Sporting Spaniel* of 1924, C.A. Phillips and R. Claude Cane write, on the English Springer: 'he is expected to do every kind of work, hunt, retrieve, and go to water, so that it is rather a remarkable fact that there are so very few well-known strains of this exceedingly useful variety of Spaniel, that is to say, so few kennels where its is known that the breed has been kept pure'. What is the value of a 'pure origin' if it has not lasted?

Outside Blood

I am never against the introduction of outside blood to revitalize any purebred strain and I don't believe that small size variations or colour matter at all. But type does matter, it is a sign that the real blood is present. I don't mind whether a springer is 16in or 22in at the withers. I can see no reason to object to a lemon and white, orange and white or even a mahogany red and white springer, if it can work. But a lack of true type is much more worrying. I see English Springers which look more like Cavalier King Charles spaniels than a small setter; some feature an almost Afghan hound-like skull or an excessively curly coat like the old English Water Spaniel.

The renowned O'Vara springers, like FT champions Spy, Spurt, Spark and Sarkie were considerably smaller than say the Sandylands' springers bred by Gwen Broadley. But all of them had the essential type so necessary if this breed is to retain its identity beyond coat colour. I don't believe this 'typiness' comes from any idiosyncrasies of gait, as the breed standard hints, although their manner of hunting can be most distinctive.

Springer Colour

Colour is not much of a guide either in identifying a real English Springer. The KC nowadays decrees that their colour should be liver and white, black and white, or either of these colours with tan markings. Around 1807, Captain Brown, regarded as 'a very creditable authority' described them as red, yellow

ABOVE: *English Springer Spaniel Ch Inveresk Coronation, 1916.*

LEFT: *English Springer doing what it does best.*

or liver colour and white. Eighty years ago the breed standard itself specified: black and tan; liver and tan; black; liver; black, tan and white; liver and white; liver, tan and white; lemon and white, roans and so on. Whatever happened to the lemon and whites? Are they springers no longer? This edition of the standard incidentally put the weight of the dog at about 40lb. Forty years later it was 50lb. On the question of colour, the standard of forty years ago stated that: 'any recognized Land Spaniel colour is acceptable'; did this mean that whole-coloured jet black was acceptable? For this is a land spaniel colour.

Writing in 1906, Rawdon Lee stated that the breed could be of 'any hue, barring orange and white, which is now the acknowledged colour of the Welsh springer or cocker'. One hundred years before this, they could be 'red' – the Welsh Springer colour. So in this breed, prized for its ancient origin, the ancient colours are no longer desired! The American KC insists that 'off' colours such as lemon, red or orange should be penalized and their possessors not placed. Yet they also insist that those dogs in the breed lacking true English Springer type should be penalized. The true type in their country of origin contained red and yellow in 1807 and lemon in 1907. The real purpose behind the American wording is given away in the preamble to the AKC breed standard: 'Unquestionably the present standard has helped to make the Springer more uniform as a breed.' In other words, uniformity is seen as having more merit than traditional variety. This is breeding to suit the breeders, not the dog. The result of such thinking in this country has been to remove the rich variety in coat colours in the breed – that is, its ancient heritage. Yet today we have a breed that is anything but uniform.

Essential Type

Two hundred years ago, Richard Lawrence, a veterinary surgeon of great experience with dogs, was writing in *The Complete Farrier* that: 'The true English springer differs but little in figure from the setter, except in size; varying only in a small degree, if any, from a red yellow or liver colour, which seems to be the invariable external standard of this breed.' So our knowledgeable, more distant ancestors considered the breed to be setter-like; contemporary experts have ruled out all mention of this in the extant blueprint for the breed. For me, the essential type in springers is revealed in the overall appearance of a small setter, the shape of the head, the eager look in the eye and the ratio of body length to body height. Officially, the correct English Springer body has the same measurement from the withers to the ground as from the withers to the root of the tail. This ratio allegedly produces a thoroughly functional dog, is supposed to develop the best drive and allow a balanced symmetrical physique. If this ratio is respected, cloddy, short-legged dogs or bassetized long-backed ones are ruled out, but in a working dog greater length of back is essential. This does not matter in the show ring, it seems.

In this attractive breed, I rate highly the eager look in the eye; I see too many lazy springers that lack any strong desire to work. This cannot augur well for the future of this distinguished sporting breed. It is the desire to work, keenness to hunt, willingness to give service, backed by good construction and sound movement that makes any working dog. In 1790 this type of spaniel was described rather neatly with these words: '…is lively, active and pleasant; an unwearied pursuer of its game; and very expert in raising woodcocks and snipes from their haunts in woods and marshes, through which it ranges with amazing perseverance' (Thomas Berwick, *A General History of Quadrupeds*). Perhaps these are the only words a sensible breed standard really needs, for they tell us what an English Springer is designed to do – work!

One of the chief pleasures in shooting to spaniels is to watch a spaniel hunt in your immediate presence, but never more than forty yards away from the gun. You will be able to observe his almost every move – his dash and fearlessness in negotiating thorns, brambles and any kind of rough and dense cover – such cover as the pointer, setter, retriever or any other of the larger gundogs will not be so eager to negotiate. The size of the big dogs will prevent them from going through and hunting, in quick time the kind of cover that is usually described as *'spaniel country'* which cannot be properly or thoroughly hunted, in the fast time the springer spaniels or larger cocker spaniels can manage it.

All Spaniels: their breeding, rearing and training, bench show points and characteristics, by Freeman Lloyd (1930)

The Norfolk Spaniel

It creates no surprize with the observant traveller to hear in Ireland, the pointer almost invariably called an English spaniel, as this, with a sportsman of that country might be considered only a slight deviation from the custom of this; but in the northern counties of England, where the shooting is so good, and the breed of dogs so excellent, it is not without considerable astonishment we hear pointers distinguished by the name of smooth spaniels, and setters by the denomination of rough spaniels. The real springing spaniel is with them termed a cocker, as the woodcock is there the only bird for which they are brought into use, consequently, but rarely to be seen in those districts; as, for instance, in some of the northern country-towns, where from thirty to forty brace of setters and pointers are kept in good state and proper condition, not one brace of well-bred and well-broke springing spaniels are to be found.

From *The Sportsman's Cabinet*, 1803. Breed researchers beware!

County not the Duke

Inadequate research into the association of the sporting spaniel with the word 'Norfolk' has not helped the English Springer Spaniel's breed history; again and again, breed historians link this name with the *Duke* of Norfolk. The poet Southey's collection contains references to the Duke of Norfolk and his spaniels. These were not sporting spaniels, however, but Toy spaniels, being described as 'King James's', black and tan, and 'solely' in his possession. In his valuable and authoritative *The Dog Book* of 1906, James Watson comments: 'even the usually trustworthy Dalziel is found surmising that this was the Duke of Norfolk's breed, hence the name. [Rawdon] Lee follows suit and quotes Youatt as to the Duke getting the black and tan by crossing with the terrier.' But the link is with the *county* rather than the duke.

A number of writers have denied the existence of Norfolk spaniels but authors such as Vero Shaw, 'Idstone', 'Stonehenge' and Stables describe them fully under that name and virtually as English springers. Bede Maxwell, in her powerfully argued and forthrightly written *The Truth about Sporting Dogs*, does get nearer to the truth when she writes: 'My thought is that the name could be purely geographical'. She then suggests a link between the Norfolk spaniel,

ABOVE: *Norfolk Spaniel c. 1910.*

LEFT: *Norfolk Spaniel c.1903.*

liver and white and bigger than other spaniel breeds, and the Coke family of Holkham Hall in Norfolk in the very early part of the nineteenth century. She quotes 'Idstone's' reference to the fact that 'Mr. Coke and the Duke [of Gordon] bred from the same stock' – Gordon setters in this case – as clear evidence of Coke's possession of high-quality gundogs.

Coke's Spaniels

Leighton-Boyce and Gompertz, the justly well-respected breed historians of setter breeds, both acknowledge that Alexander, 4th Duke of Gordon (1743–1827), obtained his original setters from Thomas William Coke (1754–1842), later Earl of Leicester, around 1815. Coke also favoured pointers, as Reinagle's portrait of him in 1815 indicates. Coke would have needed dogs for spaniel work too. They too would have been bred to his standards and therefore coveted.

Thornhill describes Coke as 'a man of fortune, surrounded with gamekeepers…pointers, setters, etc, without number…' (*The Shooting Directory*, 1804). Coke is nationally famous as an agricultural innovator and an acknowledged breeder of farm animals, but also as a superlative shot and sporting landowner. But any link between this celebrated sportsman and a particular type of sporting spaniel is best illustrated in three separate portraits of him. For the two major portraits of Coke on display at his family home to feature spaniels indicates to me the value he placed on them. The third painting shows Coke as a youth, but also features a brown and white spaniel and again confirms his partiality for this type of dog.

There would have been no shortage of spaniel work in Norfolk when Thomas Coke and his neighbours were shooting. His estate comprised 40,000 acres, with the first game records starting in 1789. From Elveden Hall on Breckland Heath up on the Suffolk border across to the Sandringham estate, there was Lord Walsingham's Merton, Lord Henniker's Thornton, Lord Abemarle's Quidenham, the Duke of Grafton's Euston, as well as Holkham, with Lord Kensington's Heydon Hall, Lord Orford's Houghton and the Windhams' Felbrigg not far away. Walked-up shooting on estates such as these would have demanded the support of spaniels by the hundred. The nearby fens and the needs of the wildfowlers would have substantially increased that demand.

Thomas Coke, Earl of Leicester at Holkham Hall, 1776.

There is a delightful picture, by William Redmore Bigg in 1803, of a shooting party at Felbrigg Hall that depicts the Norfolk type of spaniel. There is another painting, *A Big Shoot at Sandringham in 1867* by Thomas Jones Barker, which also portrays perfectly the liver and white spaniels in use in Norfolk in those times.

Coke's Fame

Before the days of driven game, pheasants were quite often shot by a man on his own in covert with a 'bobbery' pack of spaniels. Shooting in the fens was conducted using a pointer or a springer. In *The Banville Diaries – Journals of a Norfolk Gamekeeper, 1822–44* there is a charming colour print of snipe shooting in the early nineteenth century showing a Springer and a Pointer working together. Coke

LEFT: *The Shooting Party at Felbrigg Hall by W.R. Biggs, 1803 (courtesy National Trust Photographic Library).*

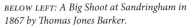

BELOW LEFT: *A Big Shoot at Sandringham in 1867 by Thomas Jones Barker.*

in 1837) and the social standing that enabled him to turn down a royal request to shoot on his estate. As a successful breeder of Foxhounds, a renowned breeder of farm animals and a respected breeder of setters, he would have had top-class spaniels. If the Duke of Gordon wanted to own Coke's setters, wouldn't his spaniels have been prized too?

Water Dog Capability

The Norfolk spaniel featured the liver colour (inherited from the water dog, as the surviving water spaniels and some retriever breeds illustrate today) and a coat inclined to curl (associated, too, with the water spaniels and also inherited from the ancient water dogs, as the Barbet of France, the Wetterhoun of Holland, the Portuguese and Spanish dogs demonstrate to this day). Spaniels in a county such as Norfolk, with its fens, lengthy coastline and long wildfowling heritage, would need to be good in water. If Coke's spaniels were anywhere near as good as his other livestock, they would not have been confined to Norfolk for very long.

Vero Shaw described the Norfolk spaniel as like a thick-made English setter, liver and white, heavily flecked, with a blaze of white up the forehead. He gave this spaniel more height than the Clumber or Sussex and less bone, but stated that frequent crosses had been made between these breeds. Dalziel describes the

supplied gundogs – setters, pointers and spaniels to his fellow sportsmen. He was a highly respected breeder of farm animals (successful with cattle breeds and the Suffolk breed of pig) and maintained his own pack of foxhounds.

At the turn of the century Coke was acknowledged as just about the best exponent of shooting flying. In 1797, within a circumference of a mile, he is reported to have shot forty brace in ninety-three shots in eight hours; each bird was apparently shot singly. Colonel Peter Hawker in Hampshire was his main rival as a shot. Coke had lived and studied abroad, was a leading Whig politician who revitalized his estate's finances. This was a man who had the individuality to twice reject a title (finally accepting an earldom

ABOVE: *The Wetterhoun of Holland: Amsterdam Winner in 1982.*

RIGHT: *Today's Springer. Photo: Kate Watson*

Norfolk as belonging to the springer family, liver and white and leggy. 'Stonehenge' says the breed should stand 17 to 18in and Youatt states that the Norfolk of his day was larger, stouter, and stauncher than the 'common Springer'. Across the sea from Norfolk lies Holland, with traditional trade routes between the two. Holland was once famous for its hawking and its hawking dogs, as well as its decoy dogs (the Kooikerhondje surviving to this day) and water dogs (the Wetterhoun also remaining). The Wetterhoun is remarkably similar to our (now extinct) English Water Spaniel: curly-coated, liver and white, 21in at the withers.

Springer's Heritage

In nineteenth-century Norfolk, dark reddish-brown springer spaniels, retrievers and water spaniels were frequently inter-bred, good dog to good dog, performance rated above purity as usual in past times. At Aqualate, Shropshire, the Boughey family kept a stud book from 1813 onwards for their 'springer' spaniels, introducing the blood of a French poodle at one stage for 'extra sagacity'. The Bougheys' Mop 1 and Velox Powder are an important part of the

pedigree English Springer's heritage. A century ago, there was a small barrel-chested wildfowling dog in Cambridgeshire known locally as the Fen Spaniel, renowned for its resistance to the cold and wet, and, in time no doubt, subsumed into the other spaniel breeds. Perhaps another example of the lost sporting dogs of East Anglia.

For a century, the English Springer Spaniel has been our most successful sporting spaniel. The topknots and curly coats have been mainly bred out, although they still crop up from time to time. But the Norfolk influence has lasting significance. Men like Coke of Norfolk and Boughey of Aqualate bred for excellence in the field, not handsomeness of appearance. They have left us an outstanding breed to provide both an efficient service in the shooting field and great companionship at the hearth. The prowess of working springers in Norfolk in past centuries should never be devalued by being blurred with the Toy dogs of a Duke, wherever his dukedom is located.

The Norfolk spaniel is still be found scattered throughout the country, and is generally of a liver and white colour, sometimes black and white, and rarely lemon and white; usually a good deal ticked with colour in the white. Higher on the leg than the Clumber or the Sussex, he is generally more active than either, sometimes almost rivalling the setter in lightness of frame; his ears are long, lobular, and heavily feathered, and he is a very useful dog when thoroughly broken…but he is so intermixed with other breeds that it is impossible to select any particular specimen as the true type.

The Dogs of the British Islands by 'Stonehenge' (1878)

The Welsh Springer Spaniel

The late Mr. A.T. Williams was a great believer in the employment of teams of spaniels to flush the game instead of having beaters, and always had Welsh springers or red and white Welsh cockers, at times having as many as seven teams of four or even five out and working under the keepers in line, and affording a sight which one will probably not see again. It is, of course, easier to break and work a team of non-

retrieving spaniels, as the jealousy created to be allowed to retrieve is eliminated. Of all Mr Williams' many Welsh springers, one, 'Rover of Gwern', was the most outstanding type, red and white in colour and the sire of 'Roverson of Gwern' (out of an English springer 'Belle of Gwern') who, many will remember, won so many Spaniel Trials under T. Gaunt in the 1911 days and became Field Trial champion.

Major Maurice Portal, writing in the Lonsdale Library's *Shooting by Moor, Field and Shore* (1929)

Welsh Input

In his well-researched book on the Welsh Springer Spaniel of 1975, the American gundog authority William Pferd III wrote:

By the early 1800s the varieties we now know as Clumber, English, Welsh, Field, Cocker, Norfolk, and Sussex, with all their different colors, were well along in development and were all being used to spring the game across the fields and woods of England and

Ch Rover of Gwern, Welsh Springer Spaniel, 1909.

Today's Welsh Springer.

Sporting Dogs by Edwin Frederick Holt 1854, with two Welsh Springers (right rear) of that time.

Wales. Distinct strains were appearing through very careful breeding and stud records were conceived as a necessary means to keep track of events and the results of the matings… It was in 1902 that the secretary of the Kennel Club was finally instructed to register into the Sporting division such dogs as the English Springers and the Welsh Springers (Red and White). After many years of relative obscurity during the 1800s, this red and white spaniel of most ancient origin was finally recognized as a distinct type, and thereby, sanctioned a condition that was obvious to most people who lived with and used springer spaniels as a way of life outside of the sphere of the show world.

Every gundog breed came to the show bench from the shooting field and this must always be foremost in their design, robustness and spiritual needs.

It was interesting to note that the American Kennel Club amended their breed standard in 1989 so that, under 'Size, Proportion and Substance', it read: 'Length of body from the withers to the base of the tail is very slightly greater than the distance from the withers to the ground. This body length may be the same as the height but never shorter, thus preserving the rectangular silhouette…'. Our own KC's standard for the breed states that the length of body should be proportionate to length of leg, which may not provide very precise guidance to judges and breeders. The

soundest, best-moving specimens that I see in this breed have noticeably longer backs than their height at the withers; too cobby a dog may look smarter in the show ring but is handicapped in the field. It was significant for me that in 1970, a British-sired, French-bred Welsh Springer, Quetzal des Fretillants, was judged to be the best spaniel of all breeds at the top championship show in Paris – discernibly more rectangular than the others!

The sporting spaniels of Wales, *their* springers, gladden my heart whenever I see them. They are so handsome, with their rich red jackets, alert looking-for-work expression and their wholly unexaggerated anatomies. There is nothing overdone in this breed; symmetrically built, not over-coated, neither aggressive nor nervous and lacking any faddy undesirable breed features, they deserve wider use in the field and a stronger breeding base. This is not a spaniel breed under threat but still one deserving greater recognition by sportsmen. Linked by some with the Irish Red and White Setter and the Brittany, the Welsh Springer's head is a main distinguishing feature. One eminent breeder from the past, Mr H.C. Payne of Monmouthshire, used to argue: 'Cut off a Welshie's head and all you've got left is just another spaniel.' Unless this splendid ancient breed is supported, Wales could lose a distinctive, worthy breed. Unless, in England, we value our Fields, Clumbers and Sussex Spaniels, they go too.

The Cocker Spaniel

There is no doubt the Cocker has changed more quickly in appearance and requirements than any other of the spaniel family, but this is chiefly by reason of the changed methods of shooting. For this reason he has developed from the smaller unit of a team to the larger-sized 'dog of all work', thereby adding to his popularity – but we cannot have it both ways. If he is to fulfil the requirements of today as a working dog, he must be of such a build, and such a size, to meet these altered conditions.

C.A. Phillips of the famous Rivington kennel, writing in the Introduction to the first edition of *The Cocker Spaniel* by H.S. Lloyd (1924). (The first field trial champion ever, Rivington Sam, was a first-cross Springer/Cocker Spaniel.)

Mixed Origins
Devon Cockers, Welsh Cockers, Black or Lutterworth Cockers – the modern breed can boast a very mixed origin. In his *The Sporting Spaniel* of 1924 (written with Claude Cane), C.A. Phillips described shooting with local spaniels in Devonshire, writing:

> At that time pretty nearly every hamlet along the coast from Dartmouth to Plymouth had its Spaniel of sorts running about…no covert was too thick or forbidding for them to face… Most of them were bred anyhow, but a few sportsmen kept their own strains, and it was wonderful how well they kept to type, and although some were a bit inclined to be curly in coat, and had their ears set on higher than we care for, many were quite typical cockers… They were pretty noisy when on their quarry, and very few would retrieve…'

He has described how a type survived casual breeding, as well as the training challenge presented by such gundogs.

ABOVE LEFT: *FT Ch Dan of Avondale by Reuben Ward Binks 1923.*

LEFT: *FT Ch Rivington Sam (born 1911), renowned dual-purpose dog.*

Trainers' Challenge

The spaniel, in my opinion, is the most difficult of all dogs to break in a scientific manner, and this for one reason only, simply because his work takes him very frequently out of your sight in thick cover. You may say that he is naturally of a wilder nature than most sporting dogs...his duty being for the most part to 'roust out' his quarry...

Those words from *The Scientific Education of Dogs for the Gun*, by 'H.H.', of 1920, give an instant impression of the task facing spaniel trainers, as well as indicating their time-honoured role. Sportsman, writer and breeder, the late Brian Plummer would no doubt have crossed a spaniel with a working sheepdog to obtain that measure of human control needed! I have long been surprised at how tolerant of a lack of steadiness many gundog men are of their spaniels. Half a millennium ago, in his informative *The Master of Game*, Edward, Duke of York was writing: 'a spaniel, if he see geese or kine, or horses, or hens, or oxen or other beasts, he will run anon and begin to bark at them', going on to accuse them of 'so many other evil habits'. I have known experienced gundog men reduced to hair-tearing exasperation whilst striving to educate a wayward Cocker. In many ways they are the terriers of the gundog tribe. But their advance in the early trials world was praiseworthy.

The American spaniel expert, Carl P. Wood, in his *Sporting Dogs* of 1985, wrote:

Cocker Spaniels are excitable and emotional and should be handled with sensitivity and gentleness during training. They seem to know immediately when play stops and the boss gets serious. An act or motion that would not matter at all in play or roughhousing with a Cocker, if done at a 'serious' time, will cause emotional difficulty with many Cockers.

This is a subtle point and a perceptive one, but innate hot-headedness, allied to great sensitivity, in any breed, really tests the trainer, despite being rooted in an eagerness to perform. C.A. Phillips wrote on this aspect:

A really good working Cocker is quite the merriest and most delightful companion a sportsman can have, and if taken in hand early is almost as easily trained as any other breed of Spaniel... I find that if stopped early in life from chasing rabbits and hares, a Cocker is never so wilful and headstrong when he is taken in hand later on...

Breed Progression
Isaac Sharpe made history for the breed when his Cocker Stylish Pride won the spaniel stake at the

Spaniels waiting to be called forward, by Reuben Ward Binks.

A Shooting Party by F.C. Turner (1795–1846).

first field trial run for spaniels at Sutton Scarsdale in 1889. The first Cocker Field Trial Champion was Walhampton Judy, owned by Colonel Heseltone, in 1905. In 1920, only four Cockers competed at trials. Five years on and the figure had progressed to forty-one. In 1930, sixty-three participated, with the peak number of seventy-three being reached five years later. In the show ring, in 1909, the breed had an uplift when Phillips' Rivington Robena won her working certificate as well as winning three show challenge certificates, making her a full champion.

General Hutchinson, in his valuable *Dog Breaking* of 1909, wrote that 'even good spaniels, however well bred, if they have not had great experience, generally road too fast. Undeniably they are difficult animals to educate…' The late Keith Erlandson once wrote that 'a good Springer should have the qualities of the Spanish fighting bull and the Zulu warrior' – some combination! But he did describe Cockers as 'inveterate belly crawlers and the sight of one pulling himself forward by his elbows, hind legs stretched straight out behind him causes me such amusement, with a resulting breakdown in concentration…' Sounds like a dog literally pushing its luck to me! Erlandson also wrote:

> A good Cocker reminds me of a combination between a Corsican bandit and a seven-year-old dog fox. Basically, the Cocker needs more game to get it going than the Springer requires. Their attitudes

are so different. Order the Zulu to charge a line of machine guns and he would charge without question. The Corsican would decline and take the guns by night attack.

Winning Ways

Erlandson handled the outstanding working Cocker FT Champion Speckle of Ardoon to an unprecedented trio of championship wins from 1972 to 1974, without ever being involved in a run-off. At a Game Fair Spaniel Test at Raby Castle, on a seriously testing hot day, she ran the opposing Springers into the ground. Cocker Spaniels *can* excel! The breed may have declined in the 1950s but the 1980s was a decade of great progress for the working breed. Handlers like Denis Douglas and Jack Windle ensured that the breed reached for and attained the highest standards. The breed has long had distinguished handlers and kennels producing a distinct type: the Ware and Falconers alongside the Colinwoods, the Treetops and the Broomleafs. The Lochranza blacks showed

The less common sable Cocker.

up with their remarkable uniformity, with the quite striking Craigleith parti-colours producing such high-quality bitches in the 1960s.

Perils of Popularity
After the First World War, the breed really came into its own: in 1914 only 400 were registered, but by 1939 the figure reached well over 5,000 and in 1947, 27,000 were registered. The Cocker was most popular breed from 1936 to 1953. In 1956 there were just over 7,000 registrations. In 1971, there were still over 6,800. In 1980, there were well over 9,000 registrations, in 1990 nearly 13,000 and in 2000 well over 13,000 again. By 2010, over 23,000 were being registered, with recent royal approval likely to swell that figure. In the field, too, a revival has taken place. In the last quarter century, the Cocker has steadily replaced the English Springer in the field.

But the show dogs, for all their handsomeness, display worrying faults. The strange pursuit of the 'swan neck' in the 1990s and early 2000s has spoiled the compactness of the breed. The 2009 Crufts judge reported: 'Forequarters are still a problem, with too many upright shoulders and short upper arms.' These are serious anatomical faults in a working breed and it is depressing to think such faults still allowed the bearers to qualify for the top show. A championship show judge reported that same year: 'a lot of them were very thin and had no substance, body or muscle up to the upper thigh, some with vast amounts of hair left on the back legs trying to conceal extremely poor hind action and some were far too small.' Were the exhibitors of these dogs so ill-informed that they seriously thought such dogs could win? If not, why enter?

Reckless Registration System
The KC Breed Records Supplements show that over a twelve-month period one single Cocker Spaniel breeder was allowed to register fifteen litters – totalling 108 puppies. It also revealed that in their lifetime, these dams had so far whelped 230 pups. None of the sires and dams in this puppy-farming exercise had been health tested. Inherited defects are also a source of worry in this breed. Gough and Thomas list over five pages of breed-disposed health problems in the breed, some not breed specific but some potentially crippling. Honourable breeders can now avail themselves of two DNA tests: for prcd PRA (Progressive Retinal Atrophy) and FN (Familial Nephropathy), both hereditary diseases which are carried as simple recessives, so that the outcome of matings could be predicted. It is known that Cockers can be afflicted by entropion, PPM (Persistent Pupillary Membrane), distichiasis, slipping patella, HD and dilated cardiomyopathy, but without mandatory testing of breeding stock or a faithful recording system, who knows the incidence rate?

Spaniels and Wildfowl by J.J. Perring (early 20th century).

LEFT: Woodcock Shooting by H. Merke, after Samuel Howitt.

BELOW: Two 'of Ware' Cockers by Reuben Ward Binks c.1946.

The Cocker Spaniel, the working type especially, is not, despite this list, more susceptible to inherited defects than many other pedigree breeds but urgent action is needed to monitor the breed's genetic health. Now more popular than the English Springer, this is an admirable native gundog breed that merits our very best care.

Working Base

A couple of decades ago, the breeding base of the working Cocker was worrying narrow; FT champions such as Templebar Blackie, Monnow Mayfly, Ardnamurchan Mac, Speckle of Ardoon and Carswell Zero each had a deep developmental influence on today's dogs, as indeed did the Jordieland

'CUDDLESOME of Ware'

'NINETTE of Ware'

Cockers of Jack Windle. In the show world the overuse of certificate-winning sires can narrow the gene pool too. The large number of Cockers registered each year diverts attention from the fact that nearly every Cocker goes back to Bebb, a famous winner from 1867 to 1873 and an even more famous stud dog.

The lack of interplay between show stock and working dogs as far as breeding is concerned is an enormous pity. Cynics may say that show people are seeking beauty queens whilst sporting owners are only interested in performance – well ahead of physical perfection. Yet when virility and vigour are desired ahead of beauty of form, then the health of the whole breed should come first. Gundog men sometimes describe the show dogs as over-furnished and gormless; show exhibitors say that the working specimens lack breed type and can be too headstrong. Perhaps the Kennel Club's recent mandatory requirement for show judges of gundogs to attend a field trial at Open Stake level or an Open Gundog Working Test for the relevant gundog sub-group, before being considered for a Challenge Certificate, will bring the two gundog worlds closer together. It would be good to see a working Cocker with the sheer handsomeness of the 'of Ware' show dogs.

Recent winners at the Kennel Club's Cocker Spaniel Championships indicate a new arrival of talent in the breed: Ben Randall's FT Ch Heolybwich Fatty's two wins, 2011 and 2012, Joe Shotton's FT Ch Chyknell Iris, Nigel Partiss' FT Ch Winhocklin Single Star of Tiptopjack, Janet Menzies' FT Ch Gourneycourt Ginger, Will Clulee's FT Ch Poolgreen Farlow Ben and Derek Lee's FT Ch Lockslane Archibald all impressed, continuing a breed revival that is so pleasing to see. With genetic diversity being sought and inbreeding coefficients being scrutinized, it was interesting to read in *The Countryman's Weekly* of 21 March 2012, Derek Robinson, himself a Cocker enthusiast, expressing his delight with the field performance of a Lab-Cocker cross: 'The hunting ability and nose is far better than any Lab while his coat is dense and coarse, drying so much quicker than spaniel's.' Gundogs developed and were bred from because of their *performance* not their pure blood.

Gundog writers have expressed conflicting views on this breed. In his book *Gundog Sense and Sensibility* of 1982, Wilson Stephens wrote:

Ben Randall and FT Ch Heolybwitch Fatty.

The Cocker, by nature a realist, is inclined to pessimism when things are not to his liking. In face of a known difficulty, a Cocker has the heart of a lion, but he is no enthusiast for forlorn hopes, and if asked to beat out a gameless piece of country is apt to treat the proposition with the contempt it deserves.

In contrast, the eminent working Cocker Spaniel man of that time, Peter Moxon, once wrote: 'The Cockers are the anarchists, the Freedom Fighters of the gundog world. One day they will liberate a city, next day they sack a town and go on a drunken binge. They are unique. May they never conform.' I'll drink to that!

That there is a meaning in the term Cocker few will deny; nevertheless, to argue that in this breed we must go back to the form of Cocker used a 100 years

American Cocker Spaniel at Bath Dog Show 2004.

The American Cocker Spaniel

The Americans have developed their own brand of Cocker Spaniel but in some ways the new breed would have been better named the American Land Spaniel or something without the word 'Cocker' in its title. They are established here, with over 300 being registered with our KC annually – far more than several of our native spaniel breeds.

Just over a foot high, with long ears, a long coat and deep stop, I find it difficult to accept them as a working gundog breed, although I know that the late Bill Ironside used them in the field as working dogs from his Belcrum Tavirosh kennel. Sportsmen can do without the grooming challenge presented by this breed after field use; vets argue against such a deep stop in a dog's skull and in the show ring it's not easy to find an exhibit within the ear length laid down in the breed standard. Once departures from the stipulations of the breed standard are condoned by show ring judges, you are well on the way to an exaggerated dog. In my magazine articles, I have expressed my concern over excessive coats in setter breeds, and if gundog breeds are to remain in the Gundog group then their ability to pass the KC's desire for 'fitness for function' may one day come under far greater focus.

A heavily coated Yankee starts off with a lovely, level topline in the water; then the dead weight of the coat begins to tell and soon he is swimming in the perpendicular and getting no forward propulsion from his back legs. The choice is to get in after him or let him drown.

Bill Ironside, writing in *Our Dogs*, June 1999

ago is, in my opinion, most absurd; surely we have made some progress, done something to improve this variety of spaniel as well as many others during the existence of dog shows… Of course, people can be found (as with other classes of sporting dog) to argue that the Cocker of today is not so suitable as a cocker built on the lines of the 'Cocker' of a quarter century or more ago, but I know better. I have used the two varieties, and many times on some of the best woodcock ground to be found in the East of England.

James F. Farrow, the renowned spaniel man, writing in *The Kennel Gazette*, April 1890

We have seen other breeds rapidly burst into favour, reach high water mark, and often as quickly recede; but in the case of the Cocker Spaniel it has been otherwise…if we take the number of Cockers registered in 1906 they amount to 485, whereas the number registered in 1926 was 3,997, or approximately nearly ten times the number…the answer will be found in the fact of the Cocker having two strings to its bow – that is, one in the sportsman, and the other in the showman.

The Sporting Spaniel by C.A. Phillips and R. Claude Cane (1924)

Overlooked Spaniels: The Minor Breeds

As time went on, they were subdivided into three separate varieties, the water spaniel and the two land spaniels, ie the springer and the cocker. Shortly before the beginning of last century the numbers were increased by Clumbers, and afterwards came the Sussex. The field spaniel as we know it is an outcome of modern times, although the term has been in use for a longer period. After the show era set in, the classification for spaniels underwent a good many variations. At the Crystal Palace Show of 1871 there were classes for Clumbers, water spaniels, both Irish and others, and the rest were divided by weight.

Sporting Dogs by Arthur Croxton Smith
(1938)

Loss of Minor Breeds

If you glanced at the annual registrations of spaniels with the Kennel Club you would be impressed by the sheer number being bred each year: some 38,000. But if you then take away the totals for two particular breeds, the English Springer and the Cocker, you would be left with less than a thousand registrations from all the other sporting spaniel breeds. Of four of the land spaniel breeds, the Welsh Springer can reach around 500 each year, but the remaining three give cause for serious concern. For the Clumber, with only around 200 registrations a year, the outlook is worrying. For the Sussex, with just over fifty, and the Field, with around seventy-five, the outlook is dire. These two old British gundog breeds deserve our support.

In 1908 over 280 Field Spaniels were registered with the KC, against less than fifty English Springers; the Sussex Spaniel was a dying breed even then. Just after the Great War, the Field Spaniel was out-crossed to the English Springer Spaniel, led by Mr R.R. Kelland with his Black Prince and Mr G. Mortimer-Smith's renowned Wribbenhall strain. In due course, the Field Spaniel Society, formed in 1923, was able to organize field trials, where Major Beaumont's Strouds kennel became highly successful.

In 1945, there were only four Field Spaniel bitches left to breed from and they were all by the same dog. In that year too, there were only six purebred Sussex Spaniels left, all owned by the same breeder and all closely related. In 1964 the Clumber Spaniel Thornville Snowstorm was mated to the Sussex Spaniel Weiden Jhansi of Patmyn. In 1978 there was at least one Sussex Spaniel owner still breeding this line. If such a course of action has actually strengthened the breed's gene pool and breed type has survived I see little to complain about in this sort of breeding diversion. Nowadays in the shooting field the English Springers and the Cockers rule the roost. But I see so much to admire in the handsome springer from Wales, the distinctive spaniel from Sussex and the fussless Fields.

(From top) Clumber, Sussex and Field Spaniels.

The Field Spaniel

It is not always easy to recommend a breed of gundog to an individual, what with differences of terrain, temperament, quarry and handler capability. But when the country being shot over calls for the resolute *flushing* of game, then give me one of the old-fashioned spaniel breeds, ideally a Field Spaniel of say Rhiwlas breeding. I once spent a day on a Welsh hillside with part-time gamekeeper Clive Rowlands watching his Rhiwlas Field Spaniels work the undergrowth like little tanks (and later going on

when the Kildare hounds were drawing the new gorse at Castletown and finding it most difficult to work, with no foxes prepared to bolt for them. Colonel Claude Cane, from his adjoining property, teased the Master and said his spaniels would shift them. Invited by the Master to attend next time, Colonel Cane did so with six spaniels, four of them being black Fields, all well-known show winners, one of them Champion Celbridge Chloe. With hounds and field gathered together some distance away, the spaniels were sent in. A good deal of ribald comment came from the hunting people, but, in only a few minutes, out came not just pheasants, rabbits and the odd hare, but no fewer than six foxes, and a grateful hunting field set off in pursuit.

ABOVE LEFT: Field Spaniel Shillingford Rona by Arthur Wardle, 1906.

LEFT: Mortimer Smith's Ch Wribbenhall Whitewash, a Field Spaniel, born 1928.

to call on the admirable Jack Tallant, who developed this line). A combination of low-growing bramble and bracken or thick gorse is more than a match for a fast, whippety field-trials dog, whose instinct may be to try to go over dense, prickly undergrowth rather than get his head right down and bore his own trail. A sturdy Field Spaniel with a powerful low drive is the breed for such a task.

In making a plea to the shooting fraternity to utilize this admirable breed more, my mind goes back to a story told by that great spaniel fancier, C.A. Phillips. He was recalling an occasion in Ireland in the 1920s

The Field Spaniel may well be the truest model for all our modern English breeds of land spaniels. This breed is the sturdy, active contemporary version of the old sporting spaniel. To avoid confusion between Field (the name of the breed) and field spaniels (spaniels used in the field) it might have been preferable to have named this breed the 'English Land Spaniel'. The present title is rather a nondescript name for a breed that is anything but nondescript. Today's lively, well-proportioned, fine looking breed certainly merits a suitably distinctive name. Field Spaniels have made enormous strides in physical

conformation since the antics of their fanciers of the 1890–1900 period, the peak of the 'bassetized era', in which a needlessly low stature was favoured. Then, exhibitors could be seen at shows actually aiming to impress the breed judge with the sheer length of their entry – to claim, on one occasion, that Rother Queen was half an inch longer in the back than Undeniable, as a point of merit in a working gundog! Sometimes the greatest threat to a breed's well-being comes from its own fanciers.

The Sussex Spaniel
The Field Spaniel comes in a variety of colours: black, liver or roan, with the liver and whites revealing the approved outcross to the English Springer. Two inches lower at the withers, in a richer golden liver only, comes the Sussex Spaniel. If the Field is a little tank in heavy cover, the Sussex is a little bulldozer. The latter is employed to find and flush game, can give tongue when hunting and can be slow-maturing and strong-willed, not the gundog for the impatient or short-tempered. For me, this breed can be handicapped by its own breed standard: who seeks a rolling gait in their sporting dog? Who wants a frowning dog? Who, in these days of obese dogs, desires a gundog without a waistline? I am pleased that the Kennel Club has recently removed the word 'massive' from the general appearance section and the word 'much' from the phrase 'not

showing much haw'. A rolling gait can put extra stress on the hindquarters; a frown can soon become an overlapping fold which hampers vision. Does the presence of a waistline indicate a shelly, lightweight spaniel incapable of smashing through heavy cover? A balanced symmetrical build is sought in most sporting spaniels; why not in this one? Balance should be a top goal in breeding Sussex Spaniels.

LEFT: Sussex Spaniels by Arthur Wardle 1907.

BELOW LEFT: Sussex Spaniel of today.

The history of the breed standard of the Sussex Spaniel tells you a great deal about show gundog fanciers. The standard in use in 1879 didn't include words like massive, brows and haw or mention a rolling gait. In 1890, in came 'fairly heavy brows', a 'rather massive' appearance and 'not showing the haw overmuch'. In the 1920s, in came 'brows frowning', a 'massive' appearance and 'no sign of waistiness' in the body. These words were approved by the KC, the ratifier of all breed standards. In 1890 the breed's neck had to be 'rather short'; from the 1920s it had to have a long neck – in the same breed! The need for this breed to walk with a rolling gait is, relative to the long history of this admirable little gundog breed, relatively recent. Here is a breed of sporting spaniel, developed by real gundog men, which subsequently, with the connivance of the KC, has been altered to

suit show dog people, most of whom never work their dogs. It is a sorry tale, with echoes in other breeds.

The so-called 'Chocolate Drop' spaniels of Richard and Jenny Mace have their admirers in the field. Originating in a cross between a working Cocker and a Sussex Spaniel, they are seriously effective working spaniels – strong, biddable and determined. Over the last fifteen years, over 100 of these 'chocdrops' have been bred, always from working stock that had been eye and hip tested. The aim was always to produce working spaniels, not a designer dog or to make the Sussex breed less pure. I can see nothing but merit in that.

In the last ten years, pedigree Sussex Spaniels have only been registered in these numbers: 89, 98, 70, 82, 68, 79, 77, 74, 61 and most recently 56. What would you want? A dying breed prized for its unique rolling gait, characteristic frown and waistline-free torso? Or a proven worker benefiting from a blend of blood? Gundog breeds which lose their working role soon lose their working ability and then the patronage of the shooting fraternity. There is worry, too, over the scale of inbreeding, with some Sussex Spaniels having a coefficient of inbreeding of over 25 per cent, the highest of the gundog breeds. I see much to admire in the Sussex Spaniel and long for a wider employment for them in the field. I was very taken with a Sussex Spaniel at a show a couple of years back: Jubilwell Thor, a very sound specimen and good breeding material. I was also impressed by the entry at Crufts in 2012, an encouraging collection of admirable spaniels.

DOGS USED FOR COCK-SHOOTING… The Sussex spaniel is the best I have ever seen, being hardy, and capable of bearing wet with impunity. His nose is also wonderfully good… They are bred so much for hunting cocks that they own the scent very easily, and seem to delight and revel in it, giving generally a very joyous note on touching upon their trail. The true Sussex may easily be kept strictly to feather, and though they will readily hunt fur when nothing else is to be had, they do not prefer it, as most other dogs do.

Manual of British Rural Sports by 'Stonehenge'
(1856)

The Clumber Spaniel: Breed under Threat

At the third International Clumber Spaniel Symposium in Sweden in 1993, Dr Sungren, a leading Swedish geneticist stated that 'the breed may not survive more than thirty years' and recommended an early outcross. In one of the weekly dog papers in December last year a leading Clumber Spaniel breeder rather patronizingly described the working Clumbers as 'the Springer type dogs belonging to those who solely use them for working'. I doubt whether the working Clumbers will need an early outcross, the ones I see are eminently sound dogs. But the dogs I see in the show rings, even at Crufts, have faults, inbuilt faults, which any gundog breed

Field Spaniel of today.

could well do without. For me, the so-called 'Springer type dogs belonging to those who solely use them for working' are more like the original Clumbers than any dog I see in the show ring masquerading as a sporting spaniel. Who needs an 80lb spaniel?

I hope and pray that the Clumber Spaniel does survive more than thirty years; it is a distinctive

The Weston Family exercising their spaniels by Ben Marshall, 1818.

LEFT: *Duke of Northumberland's Clumber Spaniel 'Charles' by J. Quinton, 1893.*

BELOW LEFT: *King George V's Clumber Spaniels at Sandringham by Reuben Ward Binks.*

Health Issues

But what do the experts say about health in this breed? The Weston-Blower survey for this breed found that 61 per cent of Clumber bitches suffer birth problems, 36 per cent from entropion and 38 per cent from hip dysplasia. Clark and Stainer's *Medical and Genetic Aspects of Purebred Dogs* (1994) lists undershot and wry mouths, missing adult teeth, hip dysplasia and disc problems attributable to its low, long, heavy build as reported problems. Entropion is the most common hereditary defect, with ectropion and 'diamond eye' other health problems. The mean hip score in the breed is 40, worryingly high, the second worst breed mean score in the BVA/KC scheme as at October 2001. The breed standard actually demands slightly sunken eyes with some haw showing. I see dogs in the ring with excessive haw, the red-rimmed socket looking sore and not a desirable feature in any sporting spaniel breed. When I have complained of this in magazine articles, I've received muted abuse from breed activists. But at Crufts 2012, the Clumber winning Best of Breed was denied access to the group judging because of veterinary concerns over its degree of haw. This was otherwise a fine specimen, from Croatia, and an international winner. Fanciers of this breed really have to take outside advice seriously for a change.

Standard Failures

The breed standard has required the breed to have a massive head, a heavy muzzle and weigh in at an ideal weight of 80lb for dogs, well over twice the weight of a Cocker. What benefit to any gundog is a massive head? A show-ring judge reported in a show critique in 2008:

> Soundness has always been a problem in the breed and it is still a problem today. It also surprises me to find bad mouths and some of these have been winning! There were some who were undershot and a handful who looked like they had had teeth thrown in for good measure as an after thought.

breed well worth saving and very much part of our sporting dog heritage. Would the Duke of Newcastle have tolerated spaniels at Clumber Park weighing 80lb, with serious eye problems, whelping difficulties and 'slipping kneecaps'? If he had, we would not have the breed of Clumber spaniel with us today. If we do, then we are betraying a trust, the belief that we too would care for such dogs and perpetuate them in their own mould. The show-ring Clumber is not being perpetuated in its own mould, but in a form a misguided group of fanciers have decided is better for their purposes. This is not breed loyalty but breed dishonesty.

The Crufts Clumber judge in 2006 reported: 'Truly I was disappointed by the number of unsound exhibits and by the number of incorrect mouths.' And these were the best dogs in the breed, on parade at the top show. Thankfully, the KC is at long last amending harmful word descriptions in their breed standards, but it is not pleasing to read of the hostile response from Clumber purists to the denial of group progression to a Clumber Spaniel by an examining vet at Crufts in 2012. The working Clumbers have eyes free of haw, the latter being a handicap in the field.

Working Prowess
But how are the despised 'Springer types' doing on the working side? Dogs like James Darley's Sedgehurst Maxim Venaticus, John Zurich's Sedgehurst Tormentum, David Wood's Julchris Bob, Mrs S Ruffles' Lliojaschar Digby and Bill Cadwell's Greencourt Mistic Meg of Jubiwell have all won trials. These dogs are usually the lighter type, the type promoted by James Farrow, the great pioneer breeder of Clumbers. He found that the original Clumbers were around 25–30lb, less than half the weight of today's show-ring specimens. His information came from the Duke of Newcastle's kennelman. Why breed away from a breed's history? Farrow also records how the showing of haw in the dogs' eyes was discouraged at the turn of the century but show breeders overruled those who worked their dogs and the toleration of

haw in the eye remained. Incidentally, he linked their origin with the Blenheim Spaniel, in a lemon and white coat.

Need for Support
With the Kennel Club's campaign for healthier dogs underway, the desire for massive heads, sunken eyes and eyes showing haw is likely to be curtailed, and not before time. It shouldn't take an outside body to instruct breed clubs how to breed healthier dogs but clearly the need is there and not just in this breed. I am full of admiration for working Clumber fanciers like James Darley and the Zurichs. This is not a popular breed, with 146 registered with the KC in 1906, 143 eighty years later and, encouragingly, 223 in 2007. The triumph of the English Springers in the field and the sustained popularity of the Cocker show what can be attained by unexaggerated spaniels. With the Fields and Sussex Spaniels also struggling (only just over sixty registered for each of these breeds in 2007) the minor spaniels need support.

The perhaps predictable response from the show breeders to any criticism is to fault the basis on which any such critical comments are made. The Weston-Blower survey is alleged to be founded on the wrong methodology, the hip score rating was run by a man who isn't an expert on the breed, no Clumber

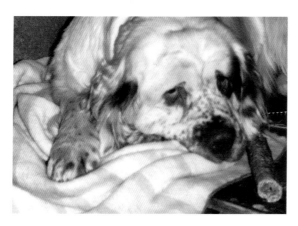

ABOVE: *Red-rimmed eyes on show ring Clumber.*

RIGHT: *A sound Australian Clumber – Ch Erinveine Crackerjack.*
Photo: *J. Irving*

Bred for Work

Over the last quarter-century, the movement to re-establish the breed as a sound and effective working spaniel has been headed by The Working Clumber Spaniel Society. Its aims include: the restoration of physical soundness and working qualities, the promotion and encouragement of training for work and the breeding from sound, work-proven dogs, and resistance to moves to alter type that may damage utility. These aims alone indicate serious concerns about the departure of the modern pedigree breed from its true type. This society has already reawakened awareness of the breed's special characteristics, revived and run the minor breeds' field trial, highlighted the

ABOVE LEFT: *Working Clumbers – the Zuricks's dogs.*

LEFT: *James Darley's working Clumber.*

weighing 80lb is allegedly ever seen in the show ring (where the entries are never weighed), there are Clumbers being exhibited without a display of haw so the problem doesn't exist, and so on. It doesn't seem to occur to them that real breed lovers *welcome* criticism – they want problems to be faced, and to learn lessons that will benefit their breed. The closed mind so often goes with closed gene pools; the best 'Clumber' I've ever seen was a Springer-Clumber cross, full of breed type and a sounder gundog than so many Clumbers exhibited in the ring. Breed purity in so many pedigree breeds is considered more important than inbreeding coefficients, which is precisely why those breeds are having inheritable defects.

importance of soundness and purpose-breeding for field work and developed its own unique breeding commendation scheme, rooted in hip-scoring, eye tests and a working capability assessment. This is quite admirable work.

Every breed of gundog came to us designed by function. The Duke of Newcastle's white spaniels didn't need to weigh 80lb, have a massive skull and a rolling gait or show haw or be heavily boned dogs, as today's breed standard dictates; the need for the breed to display a rolling gait was thankfully removed in 2010. (The 2012 registrations for the breed showed a decrease of a third, not good news.) These are show-breeder inflictions. Every real gundog man should give support to the admirable Working Clumber Spaniel Society and applaud its work. The sneered-at 'Springer types' are the genuine Clumbers; the breed of Clumber Spaniel now depends on James Darley and his Society members. They will be helped by the KC's 'fit for purpose' clause, now being applied to such breeds. In the end, they will succeed and all credit to them; they will have saved the breed.

Working the Minors
Spaniels were designed for work, whatever their modern misuse by man as a house dog, walking companion, hearthrug or model on the Crufts catwalk. It was heartening therefore to once see a group of devotees of the minor spaniel breeds assemble on the Shugborough estate, near Stafford, which I managed for fourteen years, for a working test organized by the admirable Field Spaniel Society. I had the pleasure of assisting Geoff Nicholls, gamekeeper and field-trial judge, on the day. The ground used offered good spaniel-testing country: bracken, bramble, long grass and fallen branches, but not too impenetrable to daunt young and inexperienced entries.

Organized by Clive Rowlands, generously sponsored by Dodson and Horrell, the day will not be remembered so much for impressive spaniel work as for the encouragement it offered to well-intentioned owners anxious to keep working instincts alive. The schedule attracted Field Spaniels (mostly), Clumbers, Welsh Springers, Sussex and Irish water spaniels (that is, any variety except Cockers and English Springers) and spanned novice, open and puppy classes.

The Kennel Club gundog working test regulations, introduced this year, state that 'a spaniel's first task in the shooting field is to find game and flush within range of the handler...credit points – natural ability, nose, drive, marking ability, style, control, quickness in gathering retrieve, quietness in handling, retrieving and delivery'. Listed faults include: 'running in and chasing...out of control'. At the risk of offending many, I must say how I wished some of these minor breed spaniels on that day had chased and run, out of control or not!

For here we had a collection of willing owners, very commendably trying to work their dogs, driving a long way on a hot day to do so, giving up their valuable time, really striving to keep the minor breed flag flying, only to find that with one or two exceptions, their spaniels would not hunt. I say

'would not', but perhaps 'could not' is more accurate. At first I wondered about the scenting conditions on the day but then we sniffed fox, saw recent signs of deer and rabbit, and I know that pheasant abound in that area of mixed woodland. Yet here were sporting dogs, whose first task is to find game in the shooting field, displaying no excitement ahead of their noses, no enthusiasm for game-finding, no keenness to work, no interest in their breed's role in life.

Unless a spaniel, of any breed, is excited by game scent, wants to *hunt* and is self-motivated, how can any trainer, skilled or novice, bring him on? These spaniels had excellent temperament, no obvious physical impediments, no apparent distractions, no excuses. They simply would or could not hunt. Not one of them got under the bramble and 'made it move' as Geoff Nicholls put it. The basic element in any working dog simply wasn't there. A number of these spaniels retrieved quite capably, walked to heel and stayed on command. But so can so many breeds, not necessarily gundog breeds.

Lack of Zeal
For me the biggest shock of the day was this fundamental unwillingness of these spaniels to seek game, with zeal – and tails frantically working. As a direct result of this concern, both Geoff and I in the judges' critique at the end of the test, felt compelled to propose the unthinkable (nowadays): the use of outside blood to get the hunting instinct rekindled. I was in favour of an out-cross (for the fields) to a working English Springer. This has happened before; pre-war Icy Kiss was produced from a field bitch, Wardleworth Libby, and an English Springer dog Dismal Desmond (of field trial breeding) and, post-war, Lady Lambe's Whaddon Chase Duke was bred to show champion Teffont Lalange.

But Geoff Nicholls proposed inter-breeding with a liver Cocker and, not surprisingly, knew just where to go for one. This raises an issue which, whilst making lurcher and working terrier enthusiasts laugh out loud, has to be faced by all sportsmen who value dogs for what they can do rather than what they look like. The question is: are dogs valued for their pedigree or their prowess? Over the last 150 years breeding for the pedigree and show-ring certificates has ruined breed after breed. 'Got a pedigree long as your arm' has been used ingenuously as an excuse for non-

LEFT: *Silver Firs at Osberton by John Ferneley Snr (1835) showing unexaggerated dogs.*

BELOW: *Portraits of Dogs by D. Lepiniere, c.1775 – there is a distinct 'Clumber' look to the four spaniels in the foreground.*

performance for far too long. Yet spaniels of all the gundog types have been inter-bred, out-crossed and reclassified the most.

These minor breed spaniels, owned and handled by a most likeable and admirably intentioned bunch of devotees, could not work! Some lacked confidence; some retrieved soundly, one (a field spaniel of Clive Rowlands' breeding) might make progress if worked with a really keen young English Springer for a while. Perhaps we should look again at how we mark spaniels at working tests, giving the highest marks for hunting ability, encouraging raw material with essential spaniel characteristics and not worry quite so much about the finer points of dummy-carrying. Not one of these spaniels went *under* cover; most went round it altogether.

Of course, in the gundog world, there are plenty of fine working dogs: Cockers, English Springers, Irish Setters, Pointers, Labradors and, increasingly, the hunt-point-retrieve breeds. But the minor breeds of spaniel are part of our national sporting heritage, with genetic importance too. Much as I admire a top-class field trial Labrador or Cocker, I just as much want to see the separate idiosyncrasies of the less popular breeds conserved. A crossbred spaniel that can really work is a much more valuable animal to me than any statuesque show-ring poseur with no working capability. As Wilson Stephens, doyen of contemporary gundog writers, once drily wrote: 'They didn't send male models to recapture the Falklands!'

Those involved in the future of our minor breeds of spaniel have much to think about.

In judging it may perhaps be said that 80% of good spaniel work lies in finding game and showing the desire and ability to do so under all conditions which entail nose, brains, steadiness and control, while about 20% of the value of work done rests in style of work and the retrieve. A spaniel is expected to quarter its ground with method and to range within gunshot, to search out any thick clumps it may meet, whether old thorns or brambles, etc., to be steady to shot or wing, to push out a rabbit from its seat and not pounce on it, and not to run the line which has moved on.

Major Maurice Portal, writing in the Lonsdale Library's *Shooting by Moor, Field and Shore* (1929)

Restoring our Water Spaniel

In no one time since the Sussex Spaniel has been recognized and classes made for him at the principal exhibitions has he been so strong as today. The Cocker is also looking up a bit… Good and typical Clumbers are almost shorter in numbers than ever; and that useful and hard looking variety of Spaniel, the English Water Spaniel is now almost extinct, and no specimen has been recorded in the Kennel Club stud book for several years.

'Thornbush', writing in *The Kennel Gazette*, January 1893.

Flacker Shooting by Henry Alken, 1820.

Disappearing Breeds

The multiple talents of the English Springer Spaniel may well have ended the employment and seen the demise of a once-recognized English gundog breed: the English Water Spaniel. This mirrors how the supremacy of the Border Collie in the working field saw off the Rough (Scottish) Collie, now purely a show dog. The blood of the Tweed Water Spaniel is prized in the Golden Retriever and, in Holland, their water specialist, the Frisian Water Dog or Wetterhoun, is being faithfully protected, and their small black spaniel, the Markiesje, has also recently been saved. McCarthy saved the Irish Water Spaniel and it usually requires one utterly determined enthusiast to achieve such a task. We British are remarkably fickle about our native breeds, gundogs especially; the little Devon Cocker, the solid black setter, the milk-white Llanidloes Setter and the rusty-coated Norfolk Retriever were also allowed to disappear.

Like the extinct English White Terrier, the English Water Spaniel was allowed by the Kennel Club to vanish from their lists. The majority of breeds now recognized by that body originated overseas. Whatever the merits of foreign dogs – and the patronage of exceptional dogs will always transcend national boundaries – the KC's current interest in preserving vulnerable native breeds such as the Skye, Dandie Dinmont and Sealyham terriers, is novel. The Belgian Mastiff has been saved but only through the lifelong devotion of one fancier, Alfons Bertels. One of Poland's oldest hound breeds, the Gonczy Polsky, has now been rescued from obscurity by a bunch of enthusiasts from the southeastern part of Poland. If such breeds are only conserved by individuals acting unilaterally, what really is the point of national kennel clubs taking it upon themselves to oversee breed status?

Historic Water Dogs

It would be good to see an English Water Spaniel featuring in our sporting scene once more. Establishing its identity with so much variation in the working English Springer might, however, be difficult. I see the latter ranging from curly-coated to flat-coated specimens, standing 16in at the shoulder or almost 2ft, featuring small smooth ears or judges' wigs for ears. Is there another sporting breed with so much variation in its appearance? The water dog breeds of Europe now being favoured here, whether from Italy, Spain, Portugal or France (the Barbet, not the Poodle), each display a clear identity, as do our other native sporting spaniels, like the Field, the Sussex and the Clumber.

The newly restored Dutch breed, the Markiesje (courtesy of Dutch KC).

ABOVE: *Water Spaniel at work.*

RIGHT: *The Water Spaniel of 1809.*

We must be careful too that our precious English Springer doesn't become 'any variety sporting spaniel', embracing a host of shapes and sizes.

But what should an English Water Spaniel look like? The curly coat, more open than the tight curls of the water dog breeds, would be the first characteristic, followed by shorter ears than the Springer, and a set size of around 18in at the shoulder. The Irish Water Spaniel should be just under 2ft but I see some giants, far bigger than their role demands. Depictions of the English Water Spaniel of a century ago usually show a parti-coloured dog, as portrayals of Lucky Shot reveal. But a self-coloured dog, rather like the Curly-coated Retriever, our water dog, would be more distinctive. Reinagle's depiction of *Fid, the faithful dog of Sir Gilbert Heathcote* shows a whole black, wavy-coated, really workmanlike specimen. Jessica, which won at Birmingham in 1904, exhibits the same phenotype. What do the gundog sages of a century or so ago say about this long-lost breed?

Water Dogs and Water Spaniels

In his *The Early Life and Training of a Gundog* of 1931, the knowledgeable dog-trainer Lt Col G.H. Badcock described the English Water Spaniels that he trained for the Earl of Devon as being fascinating and attractive dogs, eighteen inches at the shoulder, with a short curly coat, a very beautiful neck and shoulder, with an exaggerated 'crouch' in the hindquarters. He thought they had been in use in the West Country from about 1850 onwards. I don't believe that

English Water Spaniel 'Lucky Shot'.

'Fid', the Water Spaniel of Sir Gilbert Heathcote.

Rawdon Lee, in his *Modern Dogs – Sporting Division* (1906), was right when he stated that the old water dog and the English Water Spaniel were identical. Water dogs have a distinct tight close astrakhan curl to their coats, while water spaniels have a more open curliness in the texture of theirs.

The American Water Spaniel, rescued by Dr Pfeifer and used as a 'jump-shooting' retriever in northern Minnesota, solid liver or dark chocolate, has this marcelled texture, so aptly conveyed by Herring's *Water Spaniel beside a River* of 1829. *The Sportsman's Cabinet* recorded that 'the black is the best and hardiest; the spotted or pied the quickest of scent and the liver-

coloured the most rapid in swimming and the most eager in pursuit'. *The Sportsman's Repository* (1820) described a strong and sturdy dog, with 'hooped' ribs. The breed standard published in Phillips and Cane's *The Sporting Spaniel* (1924) gave the coat as covered in crisp curls but leaving the face smooth.

'Idstone' writes that they 'may be seen by the sides of most canals, and in the gaudy kennels of most barges' but I don't believe he is correct in stating that English Water Spaniels are simply crosses and modifications of the 'Irish race'. In *Our Friend the Dog* (1907) Gordon Stables quotes the more knowledgeable gundog men Lort and Shirley in stating that 'this is the

The English Water Spaniel depicted in France in 1934.

only spaniel which is allowed to be curly…excellent
water dogs, combining as they do, the qualities of the
Spaniel proper with that of the Retriever'. Rawdon
Lee described a bright chestnut-red dog, with a coat
'dense but silky in texture, the curl of which was not
so close or crisp as we like in an Irish Water Spaniel'.
He considered this the right texture for water work.
I once had a working sheepdog with this marcelled
coat; his coat often got wet, his skin never did.

ABOVE: *'Jessica', winning English Water Spaniel at Birmingham,
1904.*

RIGHT: *'Bob', the celebrated water spaniel of the 'Eira'.*

RIGHT: *Water Spaniel Beside a River, by
J.F. Herring , 1829.*

Foreign Breeds Introduced

Each year more and more foreign water dogs enter the KC's lists, each year many of our revered native breeds lose ground. Writing on the loss of the English Water Spaniel, W.D. Drury in his *British Dogs*, of 1903, gave this robust pronouncement:

This does not seem a very creditable performance on the part of a body of men possessing the great power and influence of the Kennel Club, the avowed object of which is the encouragement and improvement of every breed of dog. The reason is not far to seek. But surely a dog club occupying the position of a national institution, whether self-assumed or not, ought to encourage the indigenous and long-established breeds of dog of Britain; and the Water Spaniel has a title to be included in the list superior to many that are made much of whilst it is neglected.

I couldn't have put it better myself! Come on, you patriotic gundog men of England, let's get our water spaniel back at work.

The best dog for hunting these birds in the brooks is the old English water-spaniel... There is little very difficulty in entering these dogs to wildfowl, as they seem to have a natural bias that way...the desiderata in a water-dog are – a liver colour, without white – black and white being alike conspicuous; an extraordinary nose, to make out waterfowl, whose scent is not remarkably strong; a strong woolly and oily coat, to resist the water...he should also be mute, as his tongue is never required, and would disturb distant waterfowl. All these qualities are scarce, and should be highly prized when they are united in one, which they seldom are.

Manual of British Rural Sports by 'Stonehenge' (1856)

ABOVE LEFT: *Welsh Spaniel of 1890, of the water dog type.*

LEFT: *An English Water Spaniel depicted in 1908.*

CHAPTER 3

THE ALL-ROUNDERS

Creating a British HPR

In 1815 there was a famous pointer called Don, the property of Jasper Bates of Parnshurst, Sussex. On two occasions this dog performed the remarkable feat of pointing a pheasant while in the act of returning with another pheasant in his mouth which had been shot by his master.

Dogs and Guns by R.V. Garton (1964)

National Preferences

Just over fifty years ago, the distinguished gundog writer Frank Warner Hill revived the old pointer-retriever concept in his weekly column for the dog press. One reader responded with: 'Nothing spoils the manner and style of a young pointer or setter quicker than being allowed to retrieve... Every retrieving pointer I have seen had a mouth like rat-trap.' Another, Mrs C.S. Darley of the well-known Watermill setters, wrote in with: 'I well know that pointer and setter style is lost when you use one of these breeds for general purposes. These purposes must include hedge-hunting and that is the end of your setter setting and your pointer pointing.' (I was working in Germany when I read this, seeing the local gundogs excelling at indicating and later retrieving game, and found it all rather sad!) Against such entrenched views it is scarcely surprising that sportsmen here seeking all-rounders have had to go abroad. Rather puckishly, Warner Hill ended this controversial issue by stating that the best gundog he ever saw on a grouse moor was a cross retriever-pointer, looking exactly like a black Pointer; it was owned by Tom Simpson when he was on Longshawe for the Duke of Devonshire.

Continental Preferences

Did our ancestors at the end of the eighteenth century not prize style and seek soft-mouthed pointing dogs that could retrieve? Continental breeders have never

Conradijn Cunaeus's painting of Danish gundogs, c.1880.

hesitated to crossbreed or outcross when seeking excellence in the field, whether in hounds or gundogs. The great sporting dog fancier Alban de Lamothe once advised:

> The breeding of the wire-haired pointer and its enormous success in the field should be a lesson to those who regard the secondary and conventional characteristics as immutable dogma. They are in danger of forgetting that our hunting dogs belong to the working breeds, not the category of domestic pets.

From such a background and attitude did the top-class all-rounders have their creation. Behind the Hungarian Vizsla, for example, lies the blood of the Balkan Hound, the Bloodhound, the Pannonian Hound, the Roumanian Hound and the German pointers. Here, on the other hand, the *purebred* dog, a twentieth-century phenomenon, ruled the roost and shame on our sportsmen for tolerating it.

National Prejudice

Sportsmen in Victorian times usually saw less merit in foreign gundog breeds and, when they saw one they couldn't identify as a breed, immediately linked it with the British breed most closely resembling it. Art historians tend to do the same. Conradijn Cunaeus' fine painting of a Danish Braque and a Danish setter is always described as portraying an English Pointer and Setter. The German artist Toni Aron's depiction of a Langhaar is forever captioned 'An English Setter'. A fine painting of a gundog bitch and her litter by the Danish artist Ejnar Vindfeldt is always captioned as an 'English Setter and her Pups'. Abraham Cooper's portrayal of Lord Townshend's sporting dogs is always described as just that, never as a depiction of a French Braque, a Llanidloes Setter and a water spaniel, as it so easily could be – with immediate interest for gundog breed historians. National pride is admirable, but seeing value only in native livestock is prejudice. There has long been prejudice here, too, against pointers and setters that could retrieve, even when they excelled in such a task. That is blind prejudice.

British Need

I would like to see a British breeder develop a hunt-point-retrieve gundog from native stock. We have proven stock in each specialist area – is it really beyond the modern generation to produce a native all-rounder? If the noble families have failed to retain their historic interest, surely the BASC or a game-food/dog-food manufacturer would show interest in such a challenge. The Kennel Club may not recognize a new native breed very readily but it is never slow to chase more registration fees, as the fairly recent recognition of the water dogs from Italy, Spain and Portugal, a retriever from Canada, a decoy dog from Holland and an HPR from Slovakia indicates.

Toni Aron's 1897 portrayal of bird-dog.

RIGHT: Ejnar Vindfeldt's 1944 painting of a Danish bird-dog with her pups.

BELOW LEFT: Sporting Dogs belonging to Lord Townshend by A. Cooper, 1787–1868.

BELOW RIGHT: English Setter retrieving a partridge by Richard Ansdell, 1862.

Economic change, sporting style and the type of ground shot over have combined to contribute to the ever more frequent choice of a Continental all-round gundog by British sportsmen. But if we know what we want from foreign gundogs, why not produce our own all-rounder? It would not be difficult to draw up the blueprint. By this I don't mean a description of what such a gundog should look like. I admire a handsome dog but I respect a dog for what it can *do*. I would be seeking a functional word picture, not a detailed list of cosmetic breed points. *All* breeds of sporting dog came into being for what they could do, not what they might look like.

An English Pointer being used as a retriever – abroad!

Colin Carvel's Black Labrador – Weimaraner cross.

Harrier cross Flat-coat Retriever.

We often overlook that, of the gundog breeds, only the retrievers were specifically developed to work with the gun. The technical advance that provided the breech-loader created the retriever. Sporting dogs worked traditionally with the falcon, the net, the bolt and the arrow and with hounds in some countries. They have had to adapt to every change, whether technical or otherwise. Our ancestors developed the best gundogs in the world, breeds valued far beyond the shooting field. Are we now saying that we can breed retrievers, setters, pointers and spaniels for the demands of times past but only the Germans, the Hungarians, the Slovakians or the French can produce the type of dog favoured today?

Influence of Shooting Style

Our native breeds of gundog were developed in response to the needs of man when hunting game. Thus the water dog would retrieve arrows, bolts and shot duck from ponds, the decoy dog would entice wildfowl within range of the hunter's guns, the pointing and setting breeds would indicate feathered game hiding in cover, the spaniels would flush or spring it and retrievers would pick up shot game on battue shoots.

New, different blood was introduced into an established gundog breed in order to modify that breed to suit particular styles and methods of the sport. To style and method you could usefully add country, for the terrain, cover and going over which game is shot has played a crucial role in the

English Springer–Labrador cross. Photo: Nicola Flynn.

Irish Water Spaniel crossed with a Large Munsterlander.

development of gundog breeds. From these three considerations our specialist pointers and setters were produced, retrievers introduced and the various spaniel breeds emerged in the last century or so. So too were the 'all-rounders' from mainland Europe.

Fondness for the Exotic

The quite astonishing increase in the popularity here of the breeds that hunt, point and retrieve over the last fifty years, of which, from my own personal dislike of 'battue' shooting, I thoroughly approve, must however have some harmful effects on our native breeds. This preference for novelty breeds from abroad though is not without precedent. Four hundred years ago the much-quoted Cambridge scholar Dr Caius was writing of spaniels in England with these words: 'There is also at this day among us a new kinde Brought out of Fraunce (for we Englishe men are Marvaious greedy gaping gluttons after novelties, And covetous covrorauntes of things that be seldom, Rare, straunge, and hard to get.)'

But there is nothing rare or hard to get about gundog breeds from the Continent nowadays. The Kennel Club registrations for such breeds for 2009 reveal at a glance their current popularity: over 1,200 German Short-haired Pointers, 1,500 Hungarian Vizslas and nearly 2,000 Weimaraners, quite apart from Spinoni, Large Munsterlanders, German Wire-haired pointers and Brittanys. Forty years ago the position was very different: 100 more of our Pointers than GSPs,

LEFT: English Pointer crossed with a French Braque.

BELOW LEFT: A 'Dalmaraner': a Dalmatian–Weimaraner cross.

twice as many of our Pointers than Weimaraners and seven times as many of them as Vizslas. Now there are three times as many Weimaraners as there are English Pointers. Such a trend can easily be put down to changes in shooting styles as well as cost-effectiveness. But in the last 200 years, whatever the preferred style, our gundog breeders have responded by producing native breeds to fit the bill.

Native Breeds Marginalized
In this way, the Sussex, Welsh Cocker, Devon Cocker, Clumber and English Springer Spaniels emerged to suit the needs of sportsmen in different localities, as did various strains of setter: the Earl of Seafield's, Lord Ossulton's, the Earl of Southesk's, Lord Lovat's,

the Earl of Carlisle's and Lord Wallace's. The break-up of many great estates and the loss of a large number of ancestral homes are often cited as the reasons for the lack of noble patronage for our native breeds today. But if you research the real history of our great houses and big estates down the centuries, such changes are entirely in keeping with previous trends, not a contemporary phenomenon. I suspect that lack of noble patronage today comes from lack of interest more than anything else.

The patronage of the setter by the aristocracy can be matched in other gundog breeds too: the Clumber by the Dukes of Newcastle; the Pointer by the Duke of Kingston, Lords Derby and Sefton, Sir Richard Garth and the Earl of Arran; the Labrador by the Earl of Malmesbury, the Duke of Buccleuch, the Earl of Home, Lord Knutsford and Countess Howe; and the English Springer by Sir Francis Boughey, Lady Portal and the Duke of Hamilton. The current scene is so very different and this to me is a most important change from a hundred years ago.

Undeserved Reverence
Another key element has been the almost absurd reverence for the pedigree since the advent of the conformation dog show. Nowadays the pedigree is often considered more important than the dog. I believe it is fair to say that our modern pedigree breeds evolved because of our ancestors' *irreverence* for the pedigree.

English Pointer (of 1832) thrilled by a retrieve.

Time and time again when you are researching a famous breed you come across out-crosses or the use of outside blood to infuse quality or certain desirable characteristics. Once a breed is stabilized it is easy to appreciate a subsequent reliance on purebreeding, but when a wider or changed function is required, then new blood is needed. The sanctity of a gene pool in changing times is surely challengeable. A gundog should be bred to the demands of the day, not those of yesterday. I have seen some extremely handsome and talented crossbred gundogs in the shooting field here, from combinations of our native breeds, and they were impressive.

Traditionalists will understandably point out the problems of Foxhound blood manifesting itself in the Pointer, of setter blood coming through too strongly in the Flat-coat or of Tweed Water Spaniel blood influencing the search pattern of the Golden Retriever. But this serves to play down the admirable desirable qualities passed on by these ancestor breeds. There is quite often, too, as wide a difference within a breed as between breeds. With a closed gene pool in modern pedigree breeds, the most powerful genetic influences will inevitably gain the ascendancy, however gradually.

Loss of Classic Type

This trend can be seen in the increasingly hound-like Labrador, the Greyhound phenotype coming through in the Pointer and the setter-like appearance of the show English Springer. Beyond the gundog breeds this tendency is also revealing itself in other breeds: the St Bernard increasingly displays Mastiff blood, the show Collie Borzoi blood, the Bedlington Terrier Whippet blood and the Irish Wolfhound Great Dane blood. Breeding for type in a dog breed is a perpetual search, not a one-time achievement.

As C.J. Davies wrote in his very informative *The Theory and Practice of Breeding to Type*: 'The key to success in breeding to type lies in the one point – SELECTION. Everything else is subordinate to it… Inbreeding creates nothing new. It merely ensures the perpetuation of qualities already present.' Selection within a closed gene pool would not be the best way to obtain new or varied qualities in a gundog breed. But if you select a superb retriever and a pointer that excels, once you get the *blend* of qualities correctly attuned, then a good pointer-retriever is within reach. The attainment of this blend is the skill of the master-breeder. There is no country in the world to rival the British record in producing high-quality pedigree breeds of dog. Have we lost the skill? I don't think so, just the will. Around eighty years ago, a bunch of enthusiasts tried to recreate the 'old English sporting spaniel', their product very much resembling the German Kleine (Small) Munsterlander, a hunt-point-retrieve breed. It can be done!

Seeking the 'Hunter'

In *The Countryman's Weekly* of 18 April 2012, there was a report of sportsman Adrian Simpson using a three-quarters GWHP/one-quarter lurcher hybrid in open arable country, where her hunting style is less frenetic, able to last the whole day without losing thoroughness or drive, excelling in alertness to sound and sight as well as scent. Specialization can utilize only *some* of a dog's skills; all-round hunting dogs can apply *all* their natural senses. The best all-round hunting dog I ever saw was a Collie X Greyhound lurcher, which could use air and ground scent superbly, react like lightning to movement yet retrieve to hand without marking the still-live game. Such a hunting dog is only bred by an informed breeder, rigorously selecting breeding stock according to inherited functional capability.

Our national pride should be thoroughly dented by the growing public preference for foreign hunt-point-retrieve breeds. The demand has been there for some years; the modern sportsman ever increasingly prefers an all-rounder. As our trading deficit reveals each month, the consumer gets what he wants from abroad when we cannot produce it at home. Yet I recently saw a Newfoundland-Pointer cross that was preferred by its sporting owner to all the purebreeds available, *as an all-rounder*. I believe that as far as the all-round gundog is concerned Britain could produce a world-beater. For an experienced, knowledgeable gundog breeder this would prove a most marvellous

LEFT: *An 'Old English Spaniel' re-created in the mid–20th century.*

BELOW LEFT: *Chesapeake Bay Retriever crossed with a Golden Retriever, producing the old rusty-black wildfowler's dog's dense waterproof coat.*

BELOW RIGHT: *English Pointer crossed with a Newfoundland, a preferred all-rounder.*

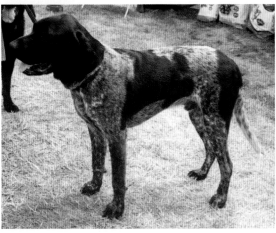

challenge. We once had the 'dropper' – a pointer-setter cross, now we're looking for the 'hunter'. What are the best ingredients from native stock to create such an all-round gundog breed? Every reader will have a view! But those who prize the skill and performance of the all-round shooting dog have reason to be grateful to German breeders and this I cover in the next section.

The All-Rounders from Germany

Just over half a century ago, the shooting fields of Britain featured British gundog breeds almost exclusively. Now the Germans have arrived! I have lived in Germany three times, each time in a different part. The local German sportsmen in each location favoured a different breed of gundog, ranging from the Langhaar and the German Wire-haired Pointer (GWHP) to the Korthals Griffon and the Small Munsterlander. If I had imported a gundog from Germany after each of these experiences, it would have been a different breed each time. Location as well as the merit of the dogs would have played a part. Some German sportsmen, too, favoured British gundogs. But I was able to assess breeds like the four varieties of German pointer, by name, including the less well-known Stichelhaar, or 'bristle-haired' pointer, *stichel* being linked to our word 'stickle', as in stickleback. I didn't see the Pudelpointer at work, but did see the German 'spaniel', the workmanlike Wachtelhund, or quail dog. I was told of a lost breed, the 'dreifarbiger Wurttemberger', a tricolour, coarse-haired pointer once favoured in the south and likely to have been subsequently subsumed by a sister gundog breed.

In Germany, like Hungary, pointing dogs were produced in smooth, coarse and long-haired varieties, to give us the pointer breeds from Germany and Vizsla varieties of today. According to Wenze, the Vizsla was known in the region of the kings of the House of Arpad (eleventh to fourteenth centuries) but was used as an all-purpose hunting dog until the late nineteenth century. At that time, the German pointer was being standardized through Hector I and Waldin, a whole-coloured brown dog. The Weimaraner, like the Vizsla, was initially used as a multi-purpose hunting dog, for tracking deer and boar for instance. Liver-roan, smooth-haired pointing dogs were not, however, confined to Germany, as the French pointers indicate; many attributing the German short-haired Pointer to a braque origin.

German sportsman supported by a Langhaar.

German Pointer takes a dive.

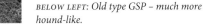

LEFT: *Wachtelhund.*

BELOW LEFT: *Old type GSP – much more hound-like.*

Undeserved Prejudice

In the 1980s there was widespread prejudice against the hunt-point-retrieve breeds (HPRs), or continental all-rounders, in Britain, led by two leading contemporary gundog writers in the foremost gundog magazine at that time. One of these writers, in an article tendentiously entitled 'The Teutons', wrote: 'I do not want an HPR… Nevertheless, I can see that the German dogs have their uses…'. Such damning with faint praise didn't prevent more open-minded British sportsmen from adopting 'The Teutons'. In 1984, 740 German Short-haired Pointers and 893 Weimaraners were registered with the KC. In 2003, 1,406 GSPs and 2,978 Weimaraners were registered here. These all-

rounders were evidently here to stay. They came on merit; they flourish because of their capability.

New Hostility

The resentment against overseas dog breeds described above is very much at odds with past attitudes. In *The Kennel Gazette* of September 1893, a more enlightened view was taken in an editorial headed 'Alien Dogs' and which contained these words:

> A glance at the Kennel Club's Registry of names reveals the printed fact that our shores are chosen as the happiest hunting ground for alien immigration; we are being peaceably invaded by a canine Foreign Legion; but…has not our own human race been improved by foreign crosses? Where would our own pedigree take us if worked out on proper canine lines? Is it not a mixture of Welsh and Old English, Scottish and Irish, Germans and hardy Great Danes…?

Since that time, two World Wars have not reduced our admiration and ownership of German breeds like the Shepherd Dog, the Rottweiler, the Dobermann and the Dachshund. Why shouldn't gundogs, so well bred there, be admired too? Pedigree dog breeding in Germany has long been better conducted than here.

New Awareness

In 1989, Tony Jackson edited a new book, *Hunter-Pointer-Retriever*, for which I wrote the first chapter, which did much to spread the word. Before that, writer-photographer and gundog expert David Layton's book *All Purpose Gundog* (1977) did much to explain the differing training needs of the HPR breeds, and they are different. The German pointers have found favour with rough-shooters here. The rough-shooter expects his dog to range wide or close according to the terrain, confirmed by the handler's signals. The dog is expected to be a ground-scenter and an air-scenter, a soft-mouthed retriever and a gamefinder. It should be capable of holding game on point until its handler is within range and then flush it. It must be able to work with equal ability in water, dense cover or in open country. British falconers prefer the German pointers and the Brittany, impressed by their passionate hunting and solid pointing, and – unlike some retrievers – they don't return with the hawk!

All-Round Skills

It is hardly surprising that a dog that has to adapt its range, head height and pace, and then find, point and retrieve shot game, is open to criticism from purist pointer users. It is unreasonable to expect such a wide repertoire to be instilled easily or perfected effortlessly in such a gundog. The all-rounders demand more time and more enlightened handling; they are *not* utility dogs for tyro sportsmen but complex dogs for knowledgeable rough-shooters. The HPR breeds show early signs of instinctive behaviour yet mature slowly. A German Short-haired Pointer at one year is very different from, say, a Labrador of that age. Professional trainers are therefore given less scope and this could result in talented amateur owner-handlers, able and willing to devote more time to their dogs, excelling with HPR breeds.

This slowness to mature must never be confused with stupidity or lack of innate ability. Here is a group of dogs that can follow wounded game or track deer and boar, work with the falcon, quarter ground close or wide, hold game on point, flush on command, mark and retrieve shot game, work in water and dense cover, withstand the cold and the wet, and yet provide companionable loyalty and affection for their owners. These highly versatile dogs were developed in

ABOVE: *German Pointer excelling at the retrieve.*

LEFT: *The Stichelhaar.*

a stern, demanding school by experienced sportsmen over several centuries. We should recognize and enjoy their special talents and their spiritual needs. Diana Durman Walters, President of the German Wire-haired Pointer Club, has owned and bred gifted falconry dogs at her Wiggmansburg kennels in Carmarthen, with her Erle vom Alten Berg, an import from Bavaria, excelling in this skill. Diana owned and bred the first GWHP to become an open field trial champion.

Working Stock

The early imports in each German pointer breed came from working stock – you could see this in their conformation and uniformity of type. Since then I suspect that the show dogs have separated from the dogs expected to work. An impressive dog from the 1960s, Holland Island Rex, was worked by a wildfowler and could hunt close rather like spaniel or wider like a bird dog. He was a compact, stocky but not over-boned dog and a proven sire, but being based in Scotland had less influence on the breed than he should have. I now see in the ring dogs with too short a back, over-boned specimens, coarse dogs with loose movement in front and, increasingly, short upper arms. The set of tail seems to vary widely and the coats in the wire-haired entry defy the breed standard, which states that the coat should lie close to the body, with the outer coat thicker and harsh. Coat colour seems to be accompanied by other genetic tendencies. In the GWHPs the solid livers and mainly blacks tend to have shorter coats than the liver and whites.

In GSPs the 'white factor' or white body, liver head and pink pads, has cropped up here as well as in the USA. The tricolours, defined as 75 per cent black, 10 per cent liver and 15 per cent white, considered highly undesirable both in GSPs and GWHPs, have been described by one coat-colour expert geneticist as 'impossible'! The colour black still excites discussion in the GSP world. In the 1920s, Christian Bode, with his Altenauer strain, became concerned

ABOVE LEFT: Weimaraner

LEFT: A brace of Stichelhaars depicted in 1908.

RIGHT: *German Pointers of the 19th century, seeking ground scent.*

BELOW LEFT: *Wire-haired Weimaraner.*

BELOW RIGHT: *Long-haired Weimaraner.*

about poor pigmentation in his stock, mainly yellow eyes and pale, faded coats. He introduced the blood of a black Pointer to rectify this, with success, although objections to this coat colour in GSPs continues today, especially in America. His dogs were once referred to as Prussian short-hairs and his methods illustrate the value of improvement in defiance of dogma, perennially needed in breeding animals but rarely seen in the world of the purebred dog today.

Colour Prejudice

Prejudice about colour influenced the emergence of the Munsterlander, especially the large variety. Originating in the ancient German province of Munsterland, stretching from the Dutch border up to Bremen in the north, this distinctive breed was born from bias against black Langhaars. The latter were often given to farmers and not favoured by sportsmen, some of whom disputed their 'pure German' blood, because they were not the more acceptable liver-brown. At one time the blue roan coats were not desired in Large Munsterlanders and solid black heads preferred. The weird world of coat colour preferences in breeds of dog will always exasperate me. Give me an outstanding dog and I'll tell you my preferred colour as an afterthought. Here, I find much to admire in dogs from the Ghyllbeck kennel of Robert and Tracey Hargreaves; they breed dual-purpose dogs, with their Ch Foxbrae Flora holding the record for FT awards, and their Sh Ch Ghyllbeck Rapax becoming the first of the breed to win a group at a UK championship show.

Here on Merit

The Langhaar is gaining ground in Britain; it may look like a setter but works as an all-rounder. In Holland it is the favoured wildfowler's dog. A Dutch Langhaar won the title of World Field Trial Champion in Spain some twenty years ago. It is an extremely handsome breed with an admirably wide range of coat colours.

Large Munsterlander.

Small Munsterlander.

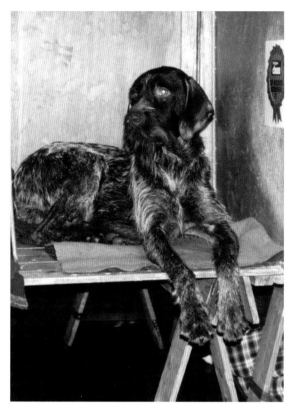

Wire-haired German Pointer.

Hans von Mulert with Pudelpointer Harras-Biebrich, born 1892, sire a Pointer, dam a Pudelpointer.

Combining handsomeness with usefulness has long been man's desire in breeds of dog. The German gundogs have always had to earn their keep and I hope British fanciers will honour this heritage. Maxine O'Connor' writing in *The Countryman's Weekly* in 2007 asserted that 'if we do not breed from correctly constructed, strong GWPs with good coats and correct mouths that are capable of working, then tragically the breed will become as Labradors and Springers – a show/working split'. Her GWHP won Crufts that year and her words apply, not just across the German gundog breeds but across gundog breeds of every country. The German gundog breeds once sneered at as 'Teutons' are here on merit and deserve to be perpetuated as highly competent working dogs – and handsome ones too.

Perfecting the Pudelpointer
Relating Need to Breed
Sportsmen have long striven to improve their gundogs and at times, especially in the late nineteenth century,

each breed has benefited from such strivings. All sporting dogs, whether they are scenthounds, terriers or gundogs, have to suit the terrain over which they hunt, the quarry they pursue and the objects of the sport itself. When function was the only decider, form was easier to shape. Stamina, robustness and ability to perform their set task, backed by perseverance, decided the stock to be used as breeding material. Nearly all our revered gundog breeds came down to us as the direct result of the dedication of pioneer breeders. Some were gifted, some inspired, a few simply fanatical, in their pursuit of the perfect gundog for their needs.

Contribution of Individuals
The contribution of Laverack and Llewellin to the setters, Arkwright to Pointers, Shirley to Flat-coats and Phillips to spaniels is well documented. The remarkable dedicated pursuit of clearly identified qualities in an all-rounder led Korthals to bequeath

us the Wire-haired Pointing Griffon that bears his name. But both the breed of Pudelpointer and its creator, despite having a long-established history, is hardly known here. Sigismund Freiherr von Zedlitz-Neukirch is not a name to be forgotten quickly or, sadly, remembered easily, but in the second half of the nineteenth century he almost single-handedly created, from Pointer and Poodle stock, the breed of Pudelpointer. He is to this day remembered as perhaps the most important pioneer in German pointing dogs. It is surprising, too, that in Germany he chose to base his breeding plans on the Pointer from Britain and the Poodle, normally linked with France. But he knew what he wanted and where to get it.

Set Criteria

Born to a noble family, a keen hunter and an innovator, von Zedlitz wished to preserve what he called 'the real German working dog'. He set out the desired qualities as: having a good nose, great

German depiction, by Sperling, of the gundogs used by them in the early 20th century.

stamina, a griffon coat in a 'forest' colour, with sound temperament. He insisted that the dog should be highly proficient in water, be extremely biddable, be bold and curious, and, unusually, give tongue when working. Surprisingly, he did not consider that the German gundogs of that time, 1870–80, possessed these qualities to his expectations, which would not have made him at all popular with his sporting peers. In an article published in 1881, he wrote what could loosely be translated as:

> We ought to try, utilizing the bloodlines of the Pointer and the Poodle, to produce top-quality working dogs that will pass on to their offspring, strongly and consistently, these stated qualities. We are seeking a leggy, rough-coated, stylish but strongly-made pointing dog. It will not resemble a Poodle, but display its cleverness and common sense.

For this breeding plan, he himself provided with a black standard Poodle bitch and persuaded a royal forester called Walter to mate her to a substantially built brown and white Pointer from the kennels of the Prince of Wales but owned by the future emperor of Germany, Friedrich III. Their first litter was born in 1881. Originally named by breed type as Hegewald (von Zedlitz's pen-name) Rauhbarten (rough beards), under the affix vom Wolfsdorf, their breeders were delighted with the results. Von Zedlitz admired the combination of the intelligence of the Poodle with the quartering, scent-seeking, stamina and obedience of the Pointer. The short, harsh coat was weatherproof and its colour blended well with their hunting grounds. A further infusion of Pointer blood was used and gradually the vom Wolfsdorf dogs became more widely known. Less adventurous and more conventional German gundog men were outraged by such imaginative thinking – and successful breeding!

Surviving Opposition

A well-known German writer of that time, Richard Strebel, a man of some influence, led the opposition, declaring, in rough translation: '…this brings nothing new, the result is a dog resembling a German pointing dog, nothing else', calling it a 'stillborn child'. But von Zedlitz ignored the scorn and abuse, and like Korthals, used his writings to expose the limited thinking of the German gundog world at that time. Unabashed, von Zedlitz founded the Society for Testing Working Dogs in the Field in 1891 and a year later, the first working test for Pudelpointers took place. Two dogs from the new breed were successfully entered by their breeder Walter. The breed prospered and between 1894 and 1899, 120 dogs were placed on the breed register. By 1934, there were over 500 Pudelpointers, but occasionally unwanted features, such as a woolly black coat, cropped up and had to be bred out.

Surviving the War
The Second World War did the breed no favours but by 2000 there were around 180 Pudelpointer breeders in Germany, some exporting their stock to neighbouring countries and to North America. Two feet high, with a harsh, weatherproof coat in a distinctive hue, they could from afar be seen to be either a Korthals or even a Wire-haired German Pointer, but when all three breeds are alongside each other, the separate breed identities soon manifest themselves. It's worth spending a thought on how the other German wire-haired and *stichelhaar* breeds were first bred and from what ingredients. Sportsmen who have used all of these in the field have reported different styles of working but none have complained about the working performance of the Pudelpointer. When working in Germany, I heard it described as the perfect rough shooter's dog: staunch and enduring, a gifted tracker, a fine retriever, especially from water, intelligent and easy to train, with a non-shedding coat. It was not considered a show dog but one brought up for the demands of fieldwork, not notably pet dog material; a dog looking for employment. I was pleased to learn that a Scottish sportsman has imported the breed and been highly impressed by them, in demanding terrain.

Remarkable Conviction
The sheer determination of an individual like von Zedlitz brings outstanding dogs into our use; his utter conviction was unusual and admirable. Who in late Victorian Britain would have had the will and the commitment to breed a totally new breed of gundog? In more enlightened times, we do come across deliberate gundog hybrids being favoured by quite experienced gundog men. How enterprising and

how admirable the self-confidence to proceed with such a non-conformist approach. Sporting dogs must always be fit for purpose; thoughtlessly perpetuated purebreeding can sometimes be the laziest of answers. Of course other continental breeders, outside Germany, developed outstanding shooting dogs and these I describe in the following sections.

Continental setters

Setter Origins
Any Briton interested in dogs who has lived on the Continent and is familiar with the art galleries, museums and libraries of Amsterdam, Brussels, Rome, Madrid, Vienna and Budapest, must find the origin of our setter breeds, as described by our Victorian writers, more than a little ill-researched. Again and again, the writers on dogs in the nineteenth century saw the excellent gundog breeds that were then being stabilized in Britain through wholly British eyes. Youatt in 1854 wrote: 'The setter is evidently the large spaniel improved to his peculiar size and beauty…', going on to repeat the old story of the Duke of Northumberland being the first man to break in systematically the setting dog in 1535.

Classic epagneul pose.

This portrayal of an English Setter by H.B. Tallman (American, 19th century) could so easily be of a Large Munsterlander or a Frisian Setter of today, so similar are all these breeds.

In 1878, the much-quoted 'Stonehenge' recorded: 'The setter is commonly supposed to be the old spaniel, either crossed with the pointer or his setting powers educated by long attention to the breed... I believe it came to pass that the English setter imitated the pointer...' Drury in 1903, closer to the mark, considered that: 'The setter is probably the oldest and certainly the most elegant and beautiful of our gundogs. The ability to "set" or "crouch" at game was one developed in certain dogs by our sporting ancestors in the days when the hawk and falcon performed the offices of the modern gun.'

Traded Dogs

If you lined up a blue Belton English setter with a Large Munsterlander, a Brittany and a Welsh Springer, a Stabyhoun and a black and white Langhaar, a Drentse Patrijshond and a Irish Red and White Setter and a solid-coloured Langhaar with a red Irish Setter, there are few observers who would not argue a common origin. I believe it is unwise and insular to think of setter breeds as coming purely from a Land Spaniel source, with added pointer, collie and hound blood, wholly in this country. The trading between Ireland and Spain, Wales and Brittany, London and Rotterdam, our south coast ports and their French counterparts over many centuries included trading in valuable hunting dogs, however different their employment.

Dogs for the Net

Espee de Selincourt, writing at the end of the seventeenth century and making early use of the generic term gundogs *(chiens de l'arquebuse)* separated the spaniels from the braques. He defined setting dogs *(chiens couchans)* as 'braques that stop at the scent *(arretant tout)* and hunt with the nose high... The spaniels are for the falcon *(oyseaux)* hunting with the nose low, and follow by the track.' But before the use of firearms in the field of hunting fur and feather, the net was the most common device, with huge nets being drawn over both setting dog and the area containing the game being indicated. The earliest sporting dogs were probably the dogs *'da rete'* (of the net) and the water dogs, which would retrieve both arrows or bolts and duck. The *'oysel'* dogs of the sixteenth century were much more setter-like than anything else. It could be that the expression *chiens d'arret,* or stop dogs, is a corruption of *'da rete'*.

The instinctive 'setting' or 'crouching' action was the essence of the meaning of the Old French verb *s'espanir*, from which I believe our word spaniel and the French noun *epagneul* comes, rather than from the word *espagnol* (Spanish), just as we use functional words like point and set. The epagneul breeds of the Continent are rather more than setters in their sporting function, but that is a result of their wider employment, rather than any separate or different

Dutch gundogs portrayed by Conradyn Cunaeus, 1828–1895.

origin from our native setters. Just as pointers and hounds of the chase were imported from France, so too were setters. And there is nothing unusual in valuable hunting dogs moving from one country to another at any stage of recorded history. The ancient Greeks, when settling in what is now Italy, came across the Tuscan, a shaggy-haired dog that would actually point to where the hare lay hidden. Wolves have been known to display this instinctive hunting skill too. Man harnessed this instinctive behaviour rather than initiated it and all over Europe, before the invention of firearms, it was greatly valued, as many old prints of netting partridges reveal.

Setting Spaniel

Although the comparatively recent introduction of pointing breeds from Germany, Italy, France and Hungary here as pedigree breeds is unusual in the gundog world, I believe they are following a traditional route, disturbed for a century or so by our preference for specialists in the shooting field, rather than hunt, point and retrieve all-rounders. The setting spaniel was known all over Europe in the Middle Ages, but then, as until quite recently in Ireland, the words referred to what we now call setters or epagneuls. Our modern breeds of setter have of course developed in their own way throughout the last two centuries, but the setting dog is an established European type of

sporting dog, evolving into separate breeds through local needs and preferences. It is dangerous to think of any breed in total isolation, whether gundog, scenthound, sighthound or shepherd dog.

Common Function

It is of interest, therefore, remembering the common function of setters and pointers, to look at the German pointer with its various coats – short, wire, *stichel* and long-haired. The short and wire-haired kinds are now well-established in Britain but the other two are largely unknown. The Langhaar is all setter in appearance and instinct. The two Dutch gundog breeds, the Drentse Patrijshond and the Stabyhoun, are also setter-like in physique and field behaviour. The Stabyhoun, or Friesland setter, is a sound, versatile, fussless working dog, staunch and biddable, robust enough to last a long day in the field and to be free of the many distressing inheritable conditions affecting gundog breeds. It resembles a small Landseer Newfoundland, whilst the Patrijshond looks more like the Irish Red and White Setter.

The Dutch Gundogs
Anglo-Dutch Trade

Dutch gundogs, in many ways, reflect their country, a land with a long history of dealing with water. Whilst German gundogs are now well established in Britain

LEFT: Stabyhoun or Friesland Setter.

BELOW: The Partridge Dog from Drentse Province.

and Italian, French and Hungarian breeds have made their mark too, the admirably workmanlike, more modest, relatively unsung gundog breeds from Holland are almost unknown here. This is despite the long association between sportsmen in our eastern counties and those of northern Holland. Friesland, too, is well known to cattle breeders but the gundogs from there are little known to potential users here. Water dogs and decoy dogs were undoubtedly traded between the Frisian Islands and East Anglia for centuries, influencing our now extinct red decoy dog and English Water Spaniel. The Dutch have retained their water dog and their decoy dog and shame on us for not doing likewise. The Kennel Club has recently recognized the American Water Spaniel but offer no incentives for a re-creation of our lost water spaniel, despite it once being recognized by them.

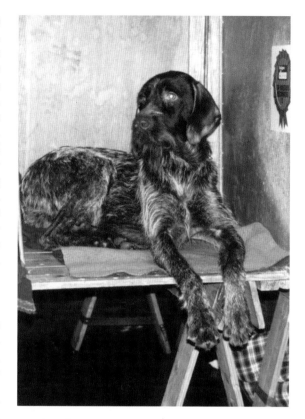

Wire-haired German Pointer.

Little Known Here

If you asked the average British sportsman if he knows of the Stabyhoun, the Drentse Patrijshond, the Kooikerhondje or the Wetterhoun, you would probably get a blank stare. Their other names give clues as to their origins: Frisian Pointing Dog, Partridge Dog from Drentse Province, Dutch Decoy Dog and Frisian Water Dog respectively. They are unspoiled breeds, unfashionable but unexaggerated – favoured mainly by true devotees of each breed, rather than fickle sportsmen or show fanciers, ever ready to move on to the next 'breed of the day'. Bred for robustness and performance, not show points or flashy coats, they are not breeds for show-offs or followers of the latest trend. Even when living on the Dutch/German border, I found it hard to get news of them. But a Dutch Decoy Dog has been working at the Boarstall Wild Duck Decoy at Brill near Aylesbury, under Jim Worgan.

Provincial Dogs

The Drentse Partridge Dog is 22–25in high (about the size of a whiptail) and white with brown or orange patches, a most handsome gundog. A bigger dog is tolerated in the breed if the symmetry is there. It looks like a miniature English Setter or Small Munsterlander. It was developed to hunt the country of the small Dutch province whose name it bears, rough terrain with plenty of heather and tall grass, often fenced by dense wooded banks. The breed is

prized for its calm temperament, strong desire for work and especially for its tracking ability in an area where game could be lost too easily. It is believed to have developed from the European group of gundogs known variously as the *epagneul* in France, the spaniel in Britain and the *spanjoel* or *spioen* in the Low Countries. It is a pointer-retriever in modern terms.

The Frisian Pointing Dog is a little smaller, at around 21in high (a shade bigger than our Springer) and in appearance resembles a long-haired parti-coloured small setter. Also known as the Stabyhoun, they were often inter-bred with the Frisian Water Dog and used as mole-hunters and polecat eradicators. Some fanciers promoted the black-headed versions, as did some Munsterlander breeders, but the Water Dog influence, seen in the curly tail, is discouraged. A wavy coat is accepted but a curly one found objectionable by the current breed club. The depiction of these dogs in old Dutch paintings leads to their being identified by 'art experts' here as English Setters or Springers, much to the fury of patriotic, more knowledgeable Dutch authorities. This is an attractive, fussless breed, unspoiled by modern trends, such as exaggerated coats and over-angulated hind legs.

The French Influence

The French gundog breeds – epagneuls, griffons and braques – are, despite the richly deserved admiration here for the Brittany, largely unknown to us but well worth a look. Just as we failed to recognize our individual varieties of spaniel, like the Norfolk, the Devon and Welsh Cockers, the Tweed and the English Water Spaniels, despite utilizing their blood in successor breeds, the French did the same with some of their ancient types. Perhaps that is the way it goes; we can't conserve every variety – some being lost through a sheer lack of patronage or simply a lack

of field prowess. But since so many contemporary gundog breeds have alarming inbreeding coefficients, and worrying rates of inherited defects, you could question the wisdom of permitting old breeds to fade away. The survival of domestic livestock breeds has demonstrated the sense of valuing long-established if not fashionable breeds. Visionaries like Joe Henson and his Rare Breeds Survival Trust provide lessons for dog breeders too.

Even French gundog men have trouble remembering minor breeds or varieties such as the Epagneul de Saint-Usuge, the Epagneul du Larsac, the Braque de Toulouse, the Braque de Tarbes, the Gascony variety of the Braque Français and the Griffon d'Arret Picard. They are of course big users of our gundog breeds. It is likely too that their native gundog breeds have received infusions of blood from ours in past centuries.

The Brittany

> The character of the Brittany is complex and contradictory. The only thing it has in common with the spaniel is its love of hunting. Actually, Brittanies have a passion for hunting, which might explain their initial indifference to retrieving…A good Brittany covers the ground at great speed, head up, sometimes whipping round on point, or leaping in the air as it catches a whiff of game, and landing on point. This makes for a very exciting dog to watch at work…
> From Angie Lewis's contribution on 'The Brittany' in
> *Hunter-Pointer-Retriever* (Ashford, 1989)

Epagneul de Saint-Usuge. Photo: Hofer

The quite astonishing rise in popularity in Britain of the gundog breeds which hunt, point and retrieve has seen their numbers advance from just over five hundred annual registrations some thirty years ago to well over 7,000 nowadays. The early registrations, however, were for just two breeds – the German Short-haired Pointer and the distinctive Weimaraner, both breeds having impressed British servicemen in Germany. The current list shows over a dozen different breeds, with the pointer-retrievers from Germany making up the bulk of those registered.

One relative newcomer in that list is the Brittany, or more accurately l'Epagneul Breton, for the continental epagneul breeds, setter-retrievers in our terminology, should never be called spaniels if they are to be fully appreciated and correctly used in Britain. Slightly smaller than an English Springer Spaniel, with a Welsh Springer look about them, Brittanys can be orange and white, liver and white, black and white, roan or tricolour. The brown roans look very much like the Small Munsterlander and the black roans like the Stabyhoun of Holland, with one significant difference: the Brittany has a short tail, an unusual feature in an epagneul breed. This may save damage to the full tail that dense cover can inflict but most other breeds of this type – Epagneul Picard, Epagneul Français and Epagneul Bleu de Picardie – feature the full tail whilst the Epagneul Pont-Audemer has a shortened tail. With the latter breed coming from Normandy, excelling on woodcock and being chestnut and white, it could well have more in common with our own more specialist springers.

Foreign Interest

These French breeds are both distinctive and individual and should never display the 'type' shown in our setter breeds. One leading American expert on the breed has compared the Brittany to 'a good riding cob, short-backed, full of fire and go, neither nervous nor high-strung, the epitome of stamina and carrying power for his size'. And it is in America that the Brittany has made the greatest advance outside its native province, mainly as a field dog. The American Brittany club, formed as long ago as 1942, dropped the noun spaniel from its title, recognizing that the misleading translation of epagneul as spaniel could bring misuse in the shooting field. (How I wish we ourselves would drop the noun spaniel from our Irish Water Spaniel breed name, for it was and always will be a water retriever.) By 1972 there were over 100 dual champions in the United States and from 7,600 registrations in 1965 their popularity grew so fast that in the next five years this total had just about doubled.

Whether established in America or just becoming appreciated in the United Kingdom, the Brittany is essentially a working dog, and as such needs the attention of one owner to develop best and regular field work to bring out its full personality and spirit. Nearly two hundred years ago the breed was known as 'le fouguere', the high-spirited one, in the Callac area of Brittany. A French breeder called Arthur Enoud is usually credited with establishing the classic orange (known as 'tabac' in France) and white colour

TOP: *Epagneul du Larzac.*

BOTTOM: *Epagneul Picard.*

LEFT: Epagneul bleu de Picardie.

BELOW LEFT: Epagneul de Pont-Audemer.

combination. The story goes that the breed originated in the middle of the last century from a highly talented hunting dog, born tailless, and so impressive in the field that visiting British sportsmen used him on their English, Irish and Gordon Setters, some of which remained in Brittany in the hands of local hunters. This is held to account for the range of colours found in the modern breed, although black is not acceptable in the United States. I am inclined to think that this range of colours existed in the setter-like gundogs on the Continent well before the middle of the last century, as the contemporary epagneul breeds display in Holland and Germany, as well as France. But there is no doubt that these tailless setters hunted the wind in great style and made their name in their own way with sportsmen willing to try them. It always pays to be open-minded about breeds of dog, whether from here or afar.

Celtic Links

I have read articles claiming a common descent for Welsh Springers and Brittanys, some theories being based on the portrayal in the Bayeux tapestry of Harold taking a red-coated hunting dog to France. On similar lines there are many who believe that the Brittany hound is really a Welsh hound taken there by Welsh colonists. There is no doubt that red-coated spaniel-like dogs were used in hawking and fowling, with the *chien oysel* of early medieval times likely to have been the forerunner of all our spaniel, setter and setter-retriever breeds. More than one breed from Brittany has developed a distinctive appearance, the chestnut basset *(fauve de Bretagne)* being very different from the other breeds of basset

RIGHT: *Brittany on point.*

BELOW RIGHT: *Epagneuls Francais. Photo: Baufle*

hound. For many centuries the Celtic and British influences were stronger in Brittany than Frankish. Brittany was, in the Middle Ages, known as Lesser Britain to distinguish it from Great Britain and this Celtic-speaking province kept its own rulers during what was only nominally Frankish rule. Politically and culturally, the cross-channel links are strong, with many centuries of trade, including the movement of useful dogs, being conducted. The first time I saw an Epagneul Pont-Audemer I thought it was an Irish Water/Sussex spaniel cross and it is forgivable to confuse a Welsh Springer with a Brittany, although the red of the former is appreciably darker and richer.

Introduced in Britain

In 1907 the Short-tailed Brittany Spaniel Club was formed in France and the breed has gone from strength to strength despite the setbacks created by two World Wars. In 1981, gundog fancier W.C. Stanley Smith imported a dog and two bitches from well-chosen, unrelated, continental stock and a year later a further young dog puppy to establish sound breeding lines in Great Britain. In Ireland, Michael Horgan and George Kingston of County Cork have also imported excellent stock from France. In March 1981, I wrote an article in *Shooting Times* on the Brittany and ended, to the scorn of the hidebound gundog writers, by saying that I could see them, once introduced, becoming immensely popular and highly successful in field trials. In that year no registrations were made here; in 1982 nine were registered and by 1988 over fifty were listed, with over 200 registered

in 2007. Angela Lewis, known previously as a Welsh Springer enthusiast, bred and handled the first Brittany field trial champion in the country, her four-year-old bitch Riscoris Fleur de Lys. Mr W. Thayne had a willing little bitch, Victoria of Talwater, running well and Bert Young, a Dorset gamekeeper, proved a successful trainer of a breed that requires a rather different approach to their training.

The breed has been criticized for being too spirited, carrying its nose too low, ranging too wide and being too small to retrieve a hare in trying country. But it has to be appreciated that this breed has a style of its own, a marked individuality and *is* different. I am pleased to learn that the Brittany Association in Great Britain has rules that closely follow those of the club in its native land. Every puppy is tattooed with a number that registers the dog with the association. Each purchaser of a puppy must sign an agreement to train and work or field trial their purchase.

LEFT: A George W. Horlor painting of c.1880, with collar inscribed Bridlington Brittany Spaniels.

BELOW LEFT: Brittany of today.

Classic Movement

As fast as any setter, the Brittany, being shorter-coupled, has however a different style of movement, which has been described as a 'short gait', appearing to flow over the ground rather than gallop. I am told that the French owners often used their dogs for poaching and therefore favoured stealthily moving dogs with a low crouch on point. American owners prefer a wide-ranging dog with greater self-reliance, depending less on the handler. In French trials the dogs are trained to lie down on the approach of the handler to the dog's point. It would be foolish for any sportsman to consider buying a Brittany without first learning about the style, instincts and idiosyncrasies of the breed. We bred out the versatility in many of our own gundog breeds, going for pointers that only point and retrievers that only retrieve. We so often forget that our pointers were originally required to retrieve too.

Bright Future Here

Brittanys have great reserves of energy, respond only to gentle handling and have gained a reputation for keeping going on the longest day in the field. Ideally they need a handler as intelligent as they are! Not over-feathered and with ears of a sensible shortness for field work, leggier than our spaniels but shorter-backed than our setters, with a smooth, fluid, light-footed gait, this is a versatile, adaptable breed for the sporting owner aware of their traditional method of operating in the field. I foresee a bright future for the Brittany in the United Kingdom. There is economic sense in having a gundog weighing only 30lb or so that can hunt, point and retrieve. All true dog men admire spirit in a working dog and harness it for good. And all true sportsmen respect real shooting as a genuine sport, demanding hunting skills and knowledge of wind, ground and game – rather than an indulgence for mere marksmen with guns waiting for the beaters to do their stuff. We have made so many of our native gundog breeds into limited specialists serving spoilt pseudo-sportsmen; perhaps hunting dogs like the Brittany can help us to find our way once more.

Limited French Entry

The French gundog breeds embrace a wide variety across a variety of functions and in very different country. We are becoming aware of the Epagneuls Breton, Français, Picard, Bleu de Picardie and de Pont-Audemer, with the latter resembling a water dog rather than the setter type. If you add to these setter-like breeds the braques, such as Saint-Germain, d'Auvergne, d'Ariege, Dupuy, du Bourbonnais and Français (in two sizes), and include the Korthals Griffon (now regarded as a French breed), our nearest Continental neighbours have plenty to choose from in the HPR family. A half century ago the Epagneul Français was getting almost St Bernard-like in build but is nowadays more like the Irish Red and White Setter and the Patrijshond. The Brittany is well established here, with 150 new registrations each year. The other French breeds are largely unknown in Britain, although the pointing griffon, the Korthals, and the Braques d'Auvergne, du Bourbonnais and de l'Ariege have their admirers.

Understanding Potential

British sportsmen are at last really beginning to understand the HPRs. Whilst we haven't always imported the best stock, or indeed the best breeds for the country we shoot over, I see little to convince me that we make the best use of the strong points of the all-rounders. The French, the Dutch and the Italians still appear so much more enlightened over their utilization and training. They seem to get wider-ranging, better-nosed, more whistle-conscious, softer-mouthed and infinitely more stylish dogs than we. I still come across British sportsmen trying to make spaniels and retrievers out of them and then complaining. A gifted sportsman like Coke of Norfolk would have had the country, the knowledge and the wit to have used them to their full potential.

Common Heritage

However misused or under-utilized, whatever their origin, instinctive behaviour or contemporary breed form and however bleak their working future, the European setters are a most distinctive sporting type. Their noble patronage, high breeding and aristocratic style bring a touch of glamour and class to the world of the working gundog. Their remarkable physical similarity to the British setter breeds hint strongly of a common heritage, their design for a different manner of shooting notwithstanding. Our Victorian writers had probably never benefited from a close study of gundog breeds from overseas; at that time the British were famous throughout the Western world as livestock breeders, especially of dogs. Whatever the origin, the future of the setter breeds, whether Continental or native, rests with today's *sportsmen*; the show breeders' obsession with rosettes and interpreting the breed standard to suit their personal whim can only lead to degeneration. This is a heavy responsibility – but as Laverack and Llewellin, the great setter breeders, and Korthals, who perfected his own Griffon, proved, such single-minded determination can lead to immortality!

The Hound-like Braques

The French Types

The short-haired, hound-like pointing dogs of France, or braques, have never found favour in Britain, despite the immense popularity of the German equivalent and the growing interest in the Bracco from Italy. But then, neither have the French epagneul or setter-like

Braque d'Auvergne.

Braques bleu d'Auvergne.

gundog breeds from France, apart from the admirable Brittany, now achieving deserved recognition here. But discerning gundog men here who favour the German Short-haired Pointer might well be inclined to look at the French braques, if only their merits were on show; it is not exactly the case that our sportsmen are set in their ways and breeds, as the astonishing rise in popularity of HPR breeds from the Continent since the Second World War amply demonstrates.

The French have a wide range of braques or pointing breeds: the Braque d'Auvergne (recently introduced into Britain), the Braque Saint-Germain, the Braque de l'Ariege, the Braque du Bourbonnais, the Braque Dupuy – with few specimens remaining – as well as the Braque Français in two sizes. (As described above, they also have a good span of what we would call setters – their epagneul breeds: Breton, Français, Picard, Pont-Audemer and Bleu de Picard.) Despite this, many French sportsmen use our breeds. Now that our sportsmen have got used to the concept of all-round gundogs or hunt-point-retrieve dogs, the French breeds might in time have the appeal of the German breeds. The Brittany is well established here and the Braque du Bourbonnais already introduced.

<small>ABOVE:</small> *Braque Saint-Germain.*

<small>LEFT:</small> *Braque Français (larger size).*

The Bourbonnais Pointer is shown at FCI shows, with over 100 registered annually, after nearly disappearing in the 1960–70s. Some are born tailless or with just a rudimentary tail. A distinctive breed, with a very individual coat colour, roan with a pattern described either 'dressed like a trout' or *'lie de vin'* (dregs of wine). I have heard this breed described as a short-haired Brittany in North America but my French colleagues dispute this. It is good to know that such a distinctive sporting breed has been saved. Sadly the Braque Charles X has been lost, perhaps subsumed into the other braque breeds.

Only two French HPRs, the Brittany and the Korthals Griffon, have so far made their mark outside France. Interest in the Braque du Bourbonnais here and in North America may be about to change that. After the Second World War only some 200 specimens of the breed existed, but now a well-

Braque Charles X by Riab 1940.

planned resurgence is in place. An ancient breed from the very centre of France, its supporters claim that it has survived, without out-crosses, for nearly 500 years. Less hound-like than, say, the Italian Bracco it reminds me, despite its coat colour, of both the Hertha pointer of Denmark and the Portuguese Perdigueiro or partridge dog. The latter has now been imported but the Hertha Pointer is struggling to survive even in its native country. Genetically, such minor breeds are very important, especially now that over-breeding and unskilled breeding have left their mark on the highly popular gundog breeds. An expensive but short-lived gundog is a poor investment both in training time and man-dog bonding terms.

The Braque Français, or French Pointer, is an ancient breed, according to the French: '...undoubtedly the oldest breed of pointer in the world. It has been the origin of nearly all the continental and British "short-haired setters"'. No concession to any Spanish origin there! The Auvergne Pointer comes from the old Pyrenean braque and the Gascony Pointer. The German Short-haired Pointer, however, is admitted to have both English and Spanish Pointer blood. In his informative booklet on the GSP, Michael Meredith Hardy points out that:

Another indication of the interchange of these dogs throughout Western Europe is the somewhat strange fact that German hunters to this day often speak to their dogs in French. I think that the tradition has an

ABOVE LEFT: *Braque du Bourbonnais.*

MIDDLE LEFT: *Braque Français – Gascony type.*

LEFT: *Braque Français (smaller type).*

historical origin, in that down the centuries dogs were constantly being imported [into Germany, that is] from the West, from France.

Today's *'vorstehhund'* is yesterday's braque.

The Hungarian Braque

The Hungarian braque, or Vizsla, has a host of admirers in Britain, an early fancier being Gay Gottlieb, who wrote in her informative book on the breed in 1985:

> The work a Vizsla is capable of doing is manifold. He can be used for all purposes of shooting, stalking and falconry. But the ideal conditions where he is seen at his best and is most productive as a bag-filler is as a rough-shooter's companion, where hunting hard for game and pointing it staunchly, is the order of the day. One must be prepared to give up time and energy to his training and have suitable ground for him to work over. Is he any better than the other breeds which hunt, point and retrieve? To those who know and love the breed he is. Why? Because to succeed in training a Vizsla brings a very close relationship between man and dog and the character of the Vizsla makes this relationship more meaningful.

ABOVE RIGHT: Outstanding Hungarian Vizsla: Cragg & Armstrong's Ch Hungargunn Bear Itn Mind; a highly successful show dog in a number of countries.

That sounds heartfelt. What is a little disturbing however is the critique of the Crufts 2011 judge of this breed, when it reads: 'The breed is still in its infancy… but I can see that already a fraction of people have begun to change what breeders have worked hard to achieve in the past over here and in their birthplace, Hungary.' When show breeders think they know better than pioneer sportsmen in a breed's homeland, bells ring for me! I was alarmed too to read in 2012 of a lack of cooperation in health schemes/research by far too many Vizsla owners, which can only be bad for the long-term interests of this fine hunting dog breed.

RIGHT: Hungarian Vizsla.

The Danish Dogs
Golden Coat

The golden braque or Hungarian Vizsla has a coat colour I have only seen rivalled by the Portuguese Partridge Dog and the Danish Hertha Pointer. The latter has been described as a variant of the English Pointer, but despite some distant infusions of Pointer blood, now has every right to be recognized as a distinct breed, mainly thanks to the ceaseless endeavours of devotees like Jytte Weiss. Its highly individual coat colour ranges from clear yellow to dark lemon to deeper orange-red, with shades of brown being discouraged. It was first seen around

1864 and from a bitch called Hertha, later Old Hertha, allegedly from the Duke of Augustenborg's kennel, which specialized in chestnut-red pointing dogs and was famed for its hunting dogs. It has a different head structure from the Pointer and characteristic white star face markings.

Old Danish Breed

The Danes also have the Old Danish Bird Dog, the Gammel or Gamle Dansk Hoensehund, a short-coated pointer with a mainly white coat, with liver or lemon markings. First recognized by the Danish Kennel Club in 1960, there were 244 registrations twenty years later. There are special hunting trials for the breed. It resembles an English Pointer with hound blood, the dewlap being unwanted in many braques. Little known outside Denmark, it is now more an all-round hunting dog rather than a specialist bird dog and already has a reputation as a tracker, benefiting from its '*blodhund*' ancestry. The breed is sometimes called, in Denmark, the Bakhund, after its saviour from extinction, the sportsman Morten Bak.

The Portuguese Dog

The Perdiguero or Portuguese Pointer is a yellow-brown or chestnut-coated, short-haired, strongly muscled dog, once known as the Perro de Mostra, and developed by the Portuguese royal family and other noble families as a hawking dog. An athletic

ABOVE LEFT: Hertha Pointer from Denmark. Photo: Jytte Weiss.

LEFT: Gammel Dansk Honsehund – an old Danish breed.

dog, moving with power and grace, with a calm and yet lively temperament, just under 22in at the withers, around 50lb in weight and stronger-headed than many breeds of this type. In adjacent Spain, the Perdiguero de Burgos and Navarro are heavier dogs, more like the Bracchi of Italy, more hound-like and with the Navarro coming in a setter coat too. Both Spanish breeds are not just bird dogs but used on four-legged quarry too, as all-round hunting dogs.

The Italian Braque

The Bracco Italiano, the most hound-like gundog breed, can be chestnut and white or chestnut roan (from the old larger, heavier Lombardy dog), orange and white (from the old lighter and smaller Piedmontese Pointer, used in the more mountainous areas) or orange roan, with a fine but dense glossy coat. A fairly large dog, weighing from 55 to 90lb and standing around 2ft at the withers, it has a distinctive head, with a shallow stop, a Roman nose and a throaty, heavy-flewed neck. Developed to work on small game, with quail and woodcock its traditional quarry, it is used also on hares and even wild boar, although not to the extent the German pointers are. In Italy they have more field trial entries than any other breed. Here they are being used as picking-up dogs, excelling on runners. It's good to read of the new breed society's working efforts, with Gunstrux

Rosa Caro at Ardenstorm, handled by John Abraham, graded 'Good' at the 2012 spring grouse pointing test held at Burncastle.

I was disappointed to read the show judge's critique on the entry at the Birmingham National Championship Show 2011:

> The first thing that comes to my mind after looking at the breed, both in the UK and in the northern parts of Europe, is that many dogs tend to get bigger in size. They are usually heavier all over than what we are used to see here in Italy. Some almost remind me more of Bloodhounds in the body than of a stylish

ABOVE RIGHT: Portuguese Partridge Dog.

RIGHT: Perro de Mostra – Spanish pointing dog.

Bracchi Italiani.

pointing dog. Many dogs have wide heavy skulls without the correct profile. We also often see dogs with too straight toplines, short flat croups and very high tail sets. The topline of the Bracco must never look anything like a Pointer or a Setter.

The breed points of a braque make up its breed identity and should be bred for by every serious breeder and respected by all breed fanciers. It is tempting always to fancy your own dogs ahead of breed features, but it's the latter that distinguish one braque from another.

Need for Recognition

The braque family of gundogs, like the pointing griffons, are either latecomers to our sporting scene or hardly known to us at all. In Victorian times, our gundog breeders had such a high reputation that our breeds ruled the sporting world, both the new world and the old. Unusually, a Monsieur Leonard, in the 1880s, was reported as having exhibited in the Strand a brace of continental pointers, one Spanish, the other 'of the French breed, called Braque. Both were sagacious brutes; but Braque, the lesser and leaner of the two, was the quicker and the more clever...' It is surely for each nation to conserve its own native breeds but gundogs from afar have a role, not only introducing new blood into inbred lines but bringing in too wider-ranging hunting skills. Like every good pointing breed – they provide 'backing'!

The Pointing Griffons

To many, the griffon is a composite mythological creature, the fabulous beast of heraldry and architectural decoration, the oldest and most common of outlandish monsters. But to gundog men, the griffon is an old and much-respected continental pointing dog of infinite variety, a composite sporting creation. Varieties of the canine griffon are found from Italy in the west to Hungary in the east, and within central Europe too. All were developed in pursuit of function by knowledgeable hunters, not for cosmetic appeal but much more hard-headedly to the level of field excellence demanded by their owners. Some authorities, not all Italian, claim that the coarse-haired pointing griffon of Italy, the Spinone, not the prettiest gundog breed, is the oldest form of this type of dog. Certainly the Spinone type was known throughout the Piedmont, in Venetia, Istria, Dalmatia and as far as the Danube, leading some to suppose that the type came from further east.

The researches of Tale tell us that well over a century ago, roan-coloured Spinoni were well known in Lombardy and Venetia, usually with longer and noticeably silkier, almost setter-like hair. The researches of Tschudy suggested that all pointing breeds originated in the Roman Empire, when Greek traders and others from the western Adriatic coast brought coarse-haired quail dogs to be developed consequently by sporting fanciers in what became southern Italy. Whatever its

origins, the Spinone has distinct similarities with the Czech coarse-haired griffon, the Cesky Fousek, the Stichelhaar and the Drahthaar, or Wire-haired German Pointer, and the Slovakian dog. The Hungarian rough-haired variety of Vizsla may have a separate origin in hunting dogs from western Turkey.

ABOVE LEFT: Italian Spinone.

*ABOVE RIGHT: Korthals Griffon –
head study.*

The Korthals Blend

When working in Germany near the Dutch border, half a century ago, I was very impressed by the Korthals Griffon, developed from a blend of Barbet, French hunting griffon and other hound blood. The skill of Korthals, who, although Dutch-born, lived in

RIGHT: Korthals Griffon.

Germany in the household of the Prince of Solms in the late 1800s, was the successful use of hound blood, a cause of temperament problems and unwanted scenting traits in other hound crosses in pointer-hound blends. Encouraged by the visionary Baron von Gingins, who founded the German kennel club, Korthals began in the early 1870s with seven well-chosen coarse-haired dogs from Germany, France and Holland. He eventually produced a number of outstanding dogs, strong physically and mentally yet still biddable, keen-eyed and resolute, hardy and waterproof-coated, with great stamina and impressive hunting skills. Soon to become known as *the* pointing griffon, their blood has been used to enhance the performance of sister-breeds, including the Drahthaar.

As a working gundog, the Korthals Griffon has gained a considerable reputation as a game-finder and is ideally suited to finding woodcock in winter and partridge in spring. The breed has a distinctive running style, with a half-rolling gallop and a head held 'hammer style', instinctively preferring to work just over 50 yards to either flank and around 30 yards ahead of its handler. Smaller than the GWHP and the Spinone, the Korthals Griffon has a jacket slightly longer than its German cousin and of a different texture from the Spinone. The Korthals Griffon has

ABOVE LEFT: Cesky Fousek at work.

LEFT: Korthals Griffon depicted by Lagarrigue in 1934.

a distinctive beard and eyebrows, and, unlike the Spinone, a level topline. It is favoured in steel-grey, with parti-coloured brown and white or orange-red and white also featuring; the coat texture is harsh and rough, like fine wire to the touch, never frizzy, curly or woolly, but with a softer, thicker undercoat beneath, providing the waterproofing its creator desired in a wildfowlers' dog.

In his *The American Hunting Dog* of 1919, Warren H. Miller, former editor of *Field and Stream,* writes:

Another breed not to be overlooked by American sportsmen is the French pointing Griffon. In 1916, for the first time, one of them ran in one of the great field trials and gave such good account of himself that one of the best Llewellins had to stretch himself to make good against him.

He went on to state that the breed was as good a pointer and bird-finder as retriever, praising the double coat, and describing the breed's appearance as looking like a cross between the Airedale and a blue belton setter – not a bad guess for an outsider. He recommended the breed for any all-round sportsman who can only afford one dog, stating that this bred solved the problem of finding the right dog for upland game and wildfowl. This has long been the great strength of this breed: their great versatility.

Boulet's Dog

Another griffon variety to be named after its creator, the Boulet griffon was developed using even more of the Barbet, in France. Emmanuel Boulet, a northern French industrialist, was advised by the great sporting authority of that time, Leon Vernier, and after ten years

Griffon Boulet.

of experimental crosses, produced two particularly talented gundogs, Marco and Myra, behind every soft-coated griffon of that name. This soft coat comes from the water-dog blood of the Barbet, possibly the original water dog of Europe. Boulet sought the 'dead-leaf' colour in the coat of his breed, to blend with the vegetation of his favourite shooting ground, the forests of Londe. Another griffon pointer with water dog blood is the Pudelpointer of Germany, described earlier, created initially from a mating between a forester's black Poodle and Kaiser Wilhelm II's best English Pointer, Tell. The desired blend was one-quarter Poodle to three-quarters pointer, but in time Drahthaar blood was introduced to produce a more determined hunter.

The Italian Griffon

The Italian Spinone is now very much part of the British gundog scene. Well over 2ft high, weighing nearly 80lb and strongly built without coarseness, the breed has been linked with the 'Tuscan' mentioned in Roman times. Breed historians have related the breed to the Bresse Griffon and established it developed in the Piedmont region of northwest Italy.

ABOVE: *Pudelpointer at work.*

LEFT: *Spinoni working in Northern Italy.*

Cesky Fousek – a Czech Champion.

I was disturbed however to read a show critique in 2012 in which the judge comments:

After nearly thirty years judging the breed this was my most challenging and frustrating appointment. The KC's commitment (quite rightly) to a 'fit for purpose, fit for life' policy and its directive to judges not to award prizes to dogs unsound in mind and body caused me much head scratching and must have confused many at the ringside, as many top winning exhibits left the ring cardless because their movement was not up to the standard expected of the breed and that of a working gundog… Hind movement is appalling and must be addressed urgently. I found many close hocks, hocks crossing over and general weakness in the hock area, as well as stilted and general lameness in the hind movement.

These are alarming criticisms from such an experienced judge and ones which must give all in the breed here a great deal to put right and soon. The faults listed are crippling in a working gundog.

The Czech Griffon
The Cesky Fousek resembles the Korthals Griffon and some say its field performance. For several centuries, a wire-haired pointing/hunting dog was used by Bohemian nobility and this breed, once called the Bohemian Wire-haired Pointing Griffon, had to be revived using German pointer blood, including that of the Stichelhaar, after the Second World War. Just over 2ft high and weighing around 70lb, the breed is gaining ground in Britain, earning the respect of experienced sportsmen.

The Hungarian Griffon

The russet-gold coat associated with the Vizsla is perpetuated in the coarse- or wire-haired variety, a rich, distinctively Hungarian gundog hue. They are a robust variety, stronger-boned than some griffon gundog breeds; I have seen them in the USA featuring both a dark red coat and an almost sandy one, with the latter invariably heavier-boned and more Spinone-like. The first wire-haired Vizsla I saw in Britain was owned by Mrs C. Appleton, Borostyanko Gulyas of Carric Temple, a handsome dog with excellent conformation. This is a gundog type well worth utilizing in the shooting field, their calm nature, weatherproof coat and eagerness to work offering much to the weekend shooting man.

Slovakian Newcomer

The Slovakian Rough-haired Pointer has only existed since 1950, created from a blend of the Bohemian roughbeard, now known as the Cesky Fousek, the GWHP and the Weimaraner (as its coat colour betrays), but is steadily gaining ground in the UK. Some 300 have now been registered here, mainly owned by the working gundog fraternity. Of the dozen or so that I have seen, the variation in coat texture has been noticeable. Commendably, these early British owners have made good use of their dogs, gaining field trial awards and success in spring pointing tests, agility and obedience tests. The Ansona and Stormdancer kennels have so far led the way.

Working Breeds not Domestic Pets

Continental breeders have never hesitated to crossbreed or out-cross in the dedicated pursuit of excellence in the field. In an earlier section, I have quoted the great sporting dog fancier, Alban de Lamothe, who once advised: 'The breeding of the wire-haired pointer and its enormous success

Wire-haired Hungarian Vizsla – strikingly coated.

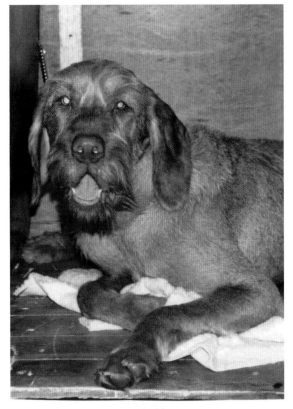

Wire-haired Hungarian Vizsla at LKA 1992.

RIGHT: *Slovakian rough-haired Pointer.*

BELOW: *Griffon d'Arret Picard, depicted in 1905 but now probably extinct as a breed.*

in the field should be a lesson to those who regard the secondary and conventional characteristics as immutable dogma. They are in danger of forgetting that our hunting dogs belong to working breeds, not the category of domestic pets.' All sportsmen who breed their own dogs should have this quote pasted over their kennels. All owners of gundogs as companion dogs too need to keep in mind the spiritual needs of their chosen pet – a gundog needs spiritual *release.*

The French hound breeds with griffon in their name have a reputation for being *'excessivement meurtier'* and, whilst not being 'murderous', the pointing griffon breeds display much more 'edge' than many of our native gundog breeds, some of which are almost too soft-natured for a hunting dog, where utter determination has its merits. The mythical griffon was depicted as having the hind parts of a lion and the head, shoulders, wings and forelegs of an eagle. The canine griffon merely combines the heart of a lion with the more symmetrical, if rather conventional, build of a really good all-round gundog. We will, however, never obtain the good all-round gundog unless we nurture the nature of the type and the best interests of the breeds; this I cover in the next chapter.

Classic Griffon pointers: a Stichelhaar and a Korthals Griffon, depicted by Richard Strebel in 1903.

CHAPTER 4

THE FUTURE – CONSERVING THE REAL GUNDOG

Scenting Success

The subtle dog scours with sagacious nose
Along the field, and snuffs each breeze that blows;
Against the wind he takes his prudent way,
While the strong gale directs him to his prey.

Now the warm scent assures the covey near;
He treads with caution, and he points with fear.
The fluttering coveys from the stubble rise,
And on swift wing divide the sounding skies;
The scatt'ring lead pursues the certain sight,
And death in thunder overtakes their flight.

Setters Seeking Air Scent by Thomas Blinks.

Pointers Searching For Scent by Thomas Blinks.

Those words of John Gay, the poet and dramatist, in his *Rural Sports* of 1711, one of the earliest mentions of wing shooting, convey neatly the sureness of sight in the human shooter and the singular skill of the gundog in locating its quarry using scent alone. Perhaps the greatest failing of man in his understanding of dog is his recurring inability to appreciate how dominant in the senses of the domestic dog is the sense of smell. For man the main detecting senses are sight and hearing; indeed I have read scientific papers claiming that our sixth sense only lapsed because of the high quality facility given to us by our eyes and ears. I have also read articles in field sports magazines extolling the superb eyesight of dogs, which I find hard to justify. I have never come across a dog with better *all-round* eyesight than man, although we will never be able to match their remarkable detection of movement. Nor will any of us ever match the quite astonishing sense of smell in dogs. If we wish to perpetuate real gundogs, we must ensure that we select for scenting power as an essential.

Nose Consciousness

The more perceptive writers on dogs have long appreciated the overriding importance of the canine sense of smell. Wilson Stephens in his quite excellent *Gundog Sense and Sensibility* has written: 'To gundogs, with centuries of nose-consciousness bred into it, noses are for serious business, eyes merely come in useful occasionally', going on to state that he had never needed to teach a dog to use its nose but usually had to teach one to mark the fall of game using its eyes.

'Wildfowler" in his *Dog Breaking* of 1915 gave his list of setter qualities in this order: 'Nose, pace, energy, style and indomitable endurance' – no doubt in his mind of the value to man of dog's sense of smell. But to limit scenting powers just to the nose is not entirely correct. In his informative *The Mind of the Dog* (1958), R.H. Smythe explained:

> Now, odours, scents or smells represent the delights of paradise to every dog…it is well known that delicate smells make the mouth water. Saliva dissolves the scent-bearing vapours and so the dog not only smells them but also tastes them. It is believed that hounds use both smell and taste, especially when the scent becomes strong, and it is believed by many that when hounds 'give tongue' they are actually savouring the delightful odour as it dissolves in their saliva.

In pursuit of this belief our ancestors utilized the 'shallow flew'd hound' to hunt by sight and scent, in that order, as a 'fleethound' and the 'deep-mouthed hound' as a specialist scenthound. No gundog should ever feature a short muzzle.

Trackers and Trailers

There is a link, too, between well-developed sinuses and the ability to track. The best trailers have the skull conformation to allow good sinus development, adequate width of nostril and good length of foreface so that there is sufficient surface between the nostrils to house the smell-sensitive lining membrane. Scenthounds, gundogs and other hunting dogs depend on the shape of their skulls for their acute smell discrimination. In pedigree breeds, the wording of the description of the skull in the breed standard can therefore directly influence the scenting prowess of the dog. The narrower skull of the terrier leads

German Short-haired Pointer tracking a hare.

it to prefer to hunt by sight and show less interest in following a trail of scent yet, through selective breeding, show enormous interest in scent coming from below ground.

Mystery of Scent

Imagine the delicacy of scent that allows a gundog, at some distance, to distinguish between a partridge and a lark, a pheasant and a woodcock. General Hutchinson, writing at the start of the twentieth century, in his classic work *Dog Breaking*, advised hunting pointers and setters together, stating on the subject of scent that, 'on certain days – in slight frost, for instance – setters will recognize it better than pointers, and, on the other hand, that the nose of the latter will prove far superior after a long continuance of dry weather…' The different breeds often display definite strengths in such a way and so too do individual dogs.

Spaniels on the Scent by C.O. de Penne 1831–1897.

Writing in his the *Arte de Ballesteria y Monteria* of 1644, Alonzo Martinez de Espinar noted, when using partridge dogs, that:

> On taking them to the field, one gets to know what they are, and whether they tend to seek the partridges by the foot-scent or by the body-scent...it must be insisted that they quest the partridges more by the body-scent than by the foot-scent, hunting them at first up-wind...that they may become body-scenters and not trackers; for there is a great difference between these two ways of seeking the birds.

He went on to list the ways in which bird dogs hunt, preferring those that point and circle as well to those that simply circle. He favoured the natural 'pointers of game' because they disturbed the game the least. He rated nose and speed the foremost qualities in his dogs. He appreciated the subtleties of scent and the scenting capabilities of his partridge dogs.

No scientist has ever been able to explain satisfactorily the mysteries of scent in the hunting and shooting field. Scent is variously affected by the direction of the wind, heavy rain, freezing fog, high humidity, different crops, baking heat and the ground temperature. But no one has confidently stipulated the conditions needed for good scenting. H.B. Pollard observed, in his masterly *The Mystery of Scent* of 1929, drawing on Budgett's *Hunting by Scent*, that 'scent is almost certain to be good between 3.30 and 4.30 after a warm October day, when the thermometer suddenly drops to near freezing point'. He then hastened to add: 'Under no other conditions would the writer care to back his opinion that scent will be good'! Not a lot of value there then! No wonder the scientists stay away! But if we do not select breeding stock on their *scenting power* as well as their other essential attributes, then we risk losing their greatest value to man.

ABOVE: *Gundogs closing in on ground game by Josef Schmitzberger (born 1851).*

RIGHT: *A Pointer in pursuit of grouse by Paul Jones (1855–1888).*

All shooting men know well that the deadly killing time for game is after 4pm. About this hour the air becomes cooler and moister; the dew commences to fall, and the birds to move; and the dogs hunt keener, because the scent lies. As a rule, the best scenting days are when *scent rises*. It is then that many dogs who generally carry their heads low will hunt high, to catch the taint which is borne and wafted away in the current of air. There is not the slightest doubt that scent rises or is depressed according to the atmospheric pressure; damp, rain, and other causes will affect it as well.

The Setter by Edward Laverack (1872)

Scent is affected by causes into the nature of which none of us can penetrate. There is a contrariety in it that ever has puzzled, and apparently ever will puzzle, the most observant sportsman (whether a lover of the chase or gun) and therefore, in ignorance of the doubtless immutable, though to us, inexplicable, laws by which it is regulated, we are contented to call it 'capricious'. Immediately before heavy rain thee frequently is none. It is undeniable that moisture will at one time destroy it, – at another bring it. That on certain days – in slight frost, for instance, – setters will recognize it better than pointers, and, on the other hand, that the nose of the latter will prove far superior after a long continuance of dry weather, and this even when the setter has been furnished with abundance of water, – which circumstance pleads in favour of hunting pointers and setters together.

Dog Breaking by General W.N. Hutchinson (1909)

A Pointer staunch on hare c.1850.

Setter transfixed by scent of game by F.W. Rogers.

All gundogs rely on their noses more than their eyes when it comes to finding and retrieving game, but none of the breeds have had developed their sense of smell to the extent that it has been refined in pointers and setters. Again, this is down to the nature of the game: bird dogs have to find game out in the open without flushing it, and this means they must locate their quarry at a sufficient distance to positively identify it before they close in to the point at which the birds decide that flight is a better alternative than concealment. And since they will be finding the quarry using scent alone – not sight, not sound, but scent only – it follows that one of the prime characteristics that the first breeders of birddogs will have selected for was scenting ability.

Working Pointers and Setters by David Hudson (2004)

The Nature of the Gundog

Mr TA Knight, in a paper addressed, some years ago, to the Royal Society, remarks: '...A young spaniel, brought up with the terriers, showed no marks of emotion at the scent of polecat, but it pursued a woodcock, the first time it saw one, with clamour and exultation; and a young pointer, whom I am certain had never seen a partridge, stood trembling with anxiety, its eyes fixed, and its muscles rigid, when conducted into the midst of a covey of these birds. Yet each of these dogs is merely a variety of the same species, and to that species none of these habits are given by nature. The peculiarities of character can, therefore, be traced to no other source than the acquired habits of the parents, which are inherited by the offspring, and become what I call *instinctive hereditary propensities.*'

From Cassell's *Popular Natural History*, 1890.

The dog-show setters are most beautiful creatures, but the points on which they win here and in America are not the points that a sportsman requires. Slack loin is only a drawback at the shows but it stops a dog in work. A long refined head is a beauty at the shows, but it holds no brains that amount to anything… To be induced to range they must be excited. Now, in the truly bred pointer or setter you may start by repressing, go on by directing, and end by many 'dressings', but you cannot weaken the hunting instinct, however hard you try.

The Complete Shot by G.T. Teasdale-Buckell (1907)

Nurturing Innate Character

Books on training dogs a hundred years ago, especially on training dogs for the gun, often contained the word 'breaking' in their title. Some of the latter included such classics as: *Dog Breaking* by General Hutchinson (1909), *Dog Breaking* by 'Wildfowler' (1915) and *Breaking and Training Dogs* by 'Pathfinder' and Dalziel, a little earlier. The trainer is called the breaker in such books and a trained dog is described as 'broken'. Although words can change their meaning over the years, I have always felt considerable distaste over the use of the verb 'to break' in dog training; it suggests training by overt bullying. In Youatt's *The Dog* of 1854, he wrote: 'The cruelties that are perpetuated on puppies during the course of the education or breaking-in, are sometimes infamous.'

I was therefore pleased to see, in the preface to the 1908 edition of Hutchinson's book, these words

Victorian gundogs of 1886 – considerate masters.

Victorian retrievers of 1886 – under calm control.

by his son: 'It is far less common than it used to be to see a dog brutally ill-treated, and I venture to think that the principles inculcated by my father in these pages have gone far to create a more intelligent sympathy between man and dog.' The harm of course had already been done, with whole generations of sportsmen and indeed ordinary dog-owners believing that the expression 'dog-breaking' meant exactly that: breaking the dog's spirit. Yet in areas of dog use where the dog is expected to excel the dog's spirit is rightly considered to be of huge importance. It is vital with gundogs to nurture their innate character.

Steady Temperament

In her most informative book *Advanced Labrador Breeding* of 1988, experienced show and field breeder Mary Roslin Williams stressed the combination of construction and temperament in gundogs for functional performance. She put build and temperament as the first things to be looked for, linking the two together, pointing out that it's no good having a dog of speedy, agile build if the mental ability and game sense is missing. She accepted the need to sacrifice some of the solidity of the show dog, whilst keeping the correct breed type, but removing all traces of lumber, or cumbersome movement. She wanted a dog to be free-moving and agile, but

essentially biddable, looking at you during training, neither feckless nor rowdy. She pointed out that the show ring can demonstrate both freedom of movement and steady temperament, if the judging is wise and enlightened. These are important features in a gundog for shooting men.

Importance of Individuality

Many books on training gundogs tell you how to train the dog for a task but rarely advise on individual dogs, dogs with great potential but a wayward reaction to being taught a skill. In his *The Scientific Education of Dogs for the Gun* of 1920, gundog training expert 'H.H.' wrote:

> You must study your pupil's disposition and general character; if he is open-hearted, bright, and has great courage, you can afford to educate highly, but if he is the least shy, sulky, or indifferent, let it alone or you will spoil him for the real business; indeed, the moment that you observe the least 'slackness' in anything, drop it at once, at all events for a time.

Most gundogs are willing, responsive and nice-natured; but it is wrong to think of every member of a gundog breed having the predictable expected temperament of that breed. Some wayward

Show dog with working skills – a champion Clumber with full champion sire and grandsire.

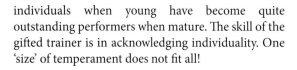

ABOVE: *A working Clumber Spaniel – but still a handsome dog.*

RIGHT: *Wild Spaniels of 1907– from General Hutchinson's book Dog Breaking.*

individuals when young have become quite outstanding performers when mature. The skill of the gifted trainer is in acknowledging individuality. One 'size' of temperament does not fit all!

Man-Dog Rapport

The same dictum applies of course to man! As Badcock wrote in his perceptive *The Early Life and Training of a Gundog* in 1931:

> Dogs vary in their natures very much like humans do. What does not change, and what so much endears them to us, is that their moods never vary. They always adapt their moods to the company they are in… It is this that makes them such charming companions, and is why incompatibility of temper between a man and his dog should never occur.

I have been out shooting with a man so soft-natured and indecisive that his dog disgraced him (and itself); it was confused and ill-directed. I have been at a working test where the behaviour of a handler disgusted everyone present; even his dog looked embarrassed! The behaviour of dogs can so often reveal the temperamental failings of their owners. The rapport between man and gundog is key. As Badcock advised: 'Only your own intelligence will help you in matters such as these. In all things remember that if a dog fails, search yourself and your own methods first before putting the blame on him…'

Bench and Field Control

It is never easy to judge a gundog's potential in the show ring, where it's controlled by collar and lead, and its field future – an environment where control is imposed on a free-running dog. Dogs over-schooled for the ring can feel lost when let off the lead – as far as control is concerned. As 'Pathfinder' and Hugh Dalziel wrote in their *Breaking and Training Dogs* of 1906:

> So far as show-rings themselves are concerned, they are useless for testing even the elements of intelligence possessed by any gundog – Retriever or other wise. Apart from the restricted area in which the judging takes place, the dogs themselves are, by Rules which are imperative, still further restricted in action by chain and handler.

Clumbers as beaters from Dog Breaking by General Hutchinson.

They went on to suggest quite separate intelligence-testing off the lead, to examine the dog's ability to think for itself. A gundog needs this capability as well as a good memory and great drive, based on sheer determination and natural zest, never linked to any sign of aggression; a gundog with unreliable temperament is more than a menace.

Problems of Aggression

In their 1994 Annual Report, the Association of Pet Behaviour Counsellors compiled a table of his cases involving dogs with serious problems of aggression. It showed that of Britain's most popular four breeds, three topped the league for unwanted aggression; two of them were gundog breeds, the Labrador and the red-gold Cocker Spaniel. But the Golden Retriever came sixth and the Irish Setter eleventh; the Dobermann came twelfth. The savage, unpredictable behaviour

found in far too many golden Cocker Spaniels has been traced back to four show champions which were extensively bred from and their offspring exported. Thirty years ago when I was researching their native breeds in Portugal, a local dog owner complained bitterly about his 'English spaniel', which had bitten his little daughter quite badly. I asked him if it had been a golden Cocker and he looked surprised at my knowing not just the breed but the coat colour involved too. The 'rage syndrome' has been known for some time in golden Cockers but not often publicly acknowledged.

As Dr Roger Mugford, the distinguished consultant in animal behaviour, has scornfully pointed out: 'Very little thought is given to the physical well-being or temperamental characteristics of pedigree dogs so long as their ears point in the right direction.' Much of the aggression found in dogs is rooted in

The expectancy of these Gundogs is palpable.

Calm handler – calm retriever.

fear – perhaps in humans too! The Germans used to label such dogs on their show benches with the warning notice 'Angstbeisser' or biter from anxiety. The honorary secretary of the British Veterinary Association once stated that: 'If the judges at dog shows, when they see a nervy, snarly dog, no matter how beautiful, said, "Sorry, we're not looking at him", that would be the end of it.' But of course show ring judges lack the moral fibre to do just that and so 'Angstbeissers' win prizes and are bred from.

The late Dr Malcolm Willis, in his time the leading canine geneticist in this country (once foolishly expelled from membership of the Kennel Club), in an article in *Our Dogs* of April 1995, wrote that 'The Kennel Club could force judges to be more careful about character but they don't. When they say they can't do anything, it means they don't *want* to do anything.' The Kennel Club expects breeders to shoulder all responsibility and impose discipline on themselves. But just as the KC needs registration fees income, breeders need puppy sales and stud-fee income. The owner of a Golden Retriever stud dog was once informed that his dog carried and transmitted an inherited disease affecting the brain; he refused to cooperate with his own veterinary surgeon, who, quite naturally, wished to contain the disease. The veterinary surgeon is under no legal obligation to report such an incident and all this stud dog's progeny can be registered with the KC. Who is going to stop such human folly?

Unwise Breeding

Once they reach sexual maturity, bitches can have two litters a year. If a bitch with a genetic defect has only four offspring a year, of which half are female, she could produce (and infect) well over 4,000 descendants in only seven years. Since show champions are not checked for behavioural defects and extensively bred from, we are creating wholly undesirable and quite needless problems for future dog owners. We *say* we love our dogs but surely we really *do* love our children; who is protecting them from dogs bred to a cosmetic design but not for mental stability? Unpredictable, unstable Rottweilers are produced by irresponsible breeders but so are unreliable golden Cockers and the general public don't know. *A dog's pedigree and its registration with the Kennel Club is simply meaningless in terms of quality.*

Battersea Dogs Home receives over 600 abandoned gundogs each year. We know that a quarter of all dogs taken to vets for destruction are taken there for behavioural reasons. How many of the abandoned gundogs had behavioural problems? Inherited behavioural problems can destroy the reputation of a breed faster and more lastingly than any inherited physical defect, as Rottweiler breeders have learned to their cost (10,000 registered in 1989, under half that number in 1998 and around 6,500 a year more recently). If we really care about dogs, the remedy is simple: all stud dogs with suspect temperament must be castrated, all breeding bitches with suspect temperament must be spayed. The Kennel Club must deregister any pedigree dog guilty of biting someone in unjustifiable circumstances *and* its past progeny, not just its future offspring. Sadly I cannot see that happening.

Popularity Penalty

It is a noticeable feature of statistics on breeds afflicted by hereditary defects that the most popular ones head the incident list proportionately and the less numerous breeds feature the least. In a wide-ranging Canadian study, Golden Retrievers were seventh in the list of most-afflicted breeds and sixth in the popularity stakes. Least-cited breeds were the German pointers, Welsh Springers, wire-haired Vizslas and Field Spaniels, none of which are over-bred. The same survey indicated that problems of temperament in Labrador and Golden Retrievers were far more prevalent than in the much less popular Curly-coated Retriever. Problems of temperament in English Springers, Irish and English Setters were far worse than in the less numerous Clumber Spaniel.

Dr Victoria Voith from the USA, who has studied mental illness in companion animals, has linked boredom and lack of employment with unacceptable aggression in dogs. Disturbed dogs that wreck the interiors of cars could be fighting boredom. A potential pack-leader lacking exercise may try to impose his will on members of his human family out of pent-up frustration. Both types need the working outlet to expend unused energy and undoubtedly have a spiritual need to carry out the function in the field they were purpose-bred to fulfil. Is it therefore fair to have as a companion breed a gundog that is

never ever required to work? Is it reasonable to buy a powerful, energetic, 'supercharged' Labrador with field trial champions behind it only for it to spend most of the day sitting on a doormat in the yard of a suburban house?

Danger of Complacency

Half a century ago, when I was working in Germany, the little German dog of one of my many German neighbours was savagely killed by the big English dog of one of my few English neighbours. The latter dog was a black Labrador – with hard, cruel eyes and the head of a Rottweiler. Relating this does not diminish my admiration for the *breed* of Labrador. Breeds don't misbehave; individual dogs do, partly through their breeding and partly through their upbringing and lifestyle. We can do something about all three if we address this problem. But, as usual with dogs, it will end up being someone else's problem. I am constantly amazed when highly intelligent parents go out and buy a puppy to live

ABOVE LEFT: Retriever looks for human direction.

LEFT: Brittany seeks human instruction.

with their family without one single check on its likely temperament. Such parents can spend hours verifying the safety features of the next car; both cars and dogs can harm children if safety checks are not made. We are all being far too complacent about the temperament of our gundog breeds; it is not in their nature to be sharp-tempered.

The explanation why the average collie is better trained than the average sporting dog is not far to seek. More work is put on him, but so gradually, that his brain can absorb and remember – he is kept up to the mark by having to do certain things daily, and not allowed to forget; he is not taken on a string half a dozen times a year and expected to do a dozen different things of which he never learned the rudiments.

The Keeper's Book by Sir Peter Jeffrey Mackie (1924)

There is so much that is paradoxical in the mentality of the modern-day shooting man that it is difficult to know what he expects of his dog. He will spend vast sums on a shoot and rearing a large head of game. He will give over £200 for a pair of guns, blaze away hundreds of cartridges at a shooting school to perfect his shooting, and give a long price for a dog only to ruin it in the first half-hour simply and solely because

in the art of understanding a dog's mind he is himself totally uneducated and probably worse.

The Early Life and Training of a Gundog by Lt Col. G.H. Badcock (1931)

A good shrill whistle, a good stout whip, a check cord and spiked collar for emergencies, and a plentiful command of language, and the thing is done. Is it? Follow this system and succeed in your object, and in nine cases out of ten you get a sulky slave, a senseless automaton, a mechanical apparatus. It may serve its turn, do its business as long as no complication occurs, but the moment you want something out of the common, presence of mind, thought, or great courage and perseverance, you are nowhere.

The Scientific Education of Dogs for the Gun by 'H.H.' (1920)

Valuing Our Shooting Dogs

Beauty and Utility

Dogs developed to support game shooting have long proved to be not only superb gundogs but admirable companion dogs and versatile service dogs too. Of all the groups of dog fashioned by man, the gundog group

Successful Labradors by Reuben Ward Binks, 1913.

LEFT: Shooting the Covers by Richard Ansdell 1885.

BELOW LEFT: Contented Golden Retriever.

can also make a claim to embrace the most handsome breeds available. Breeds like the Golden and Flat-coated Retrievers have glamour and charm, the Pointer has sheer style, the setters combine usefulness with handsomeness and the spaniels display energy and enthusiasm, as well as good looks. All these good-looking, valuable breeds developed in line with man's sporting preferences, with the retrievers coming later, as breeds, to meet a specific need. Gundog breeds introduced more recently, like the Weimaraner, the Vizsla, the Munsterlander, the GWHP and the Brittany, have perpetuated this combined appeal of utility and cosmetic distinction. Their performance deserves our valuing their contribution.

Changing Times

In modern marketing terms, a gundog breed is a gundog brand. Each has its own distinct identity and special features. The hugely popular breeds are under no pressure, beyond fashion, to protect their identity and so are often carelessly bred to satisfy demand, as some Labradors demonstrate. The unfashionable, overlooked breeds are often perpetuated by zealots and can become exaggerated as a result, as the bassetized Field Spaniels once showed. Of course, gundog breeds can be altered by changes in shooting styles, especially by subsequent demand from sportsmen. Harmful exaggeration has no place in the gundog breed lists; sportsmen gain no value, and perhaps high vets' bills, from Clumbers with loose eyelids and Field Spaniels with elongated spines. The changes we surely seek are sounder, healthier dogs than before, with the same field performance. The danger from over-popularity is from human behaviour, excessive breeding rates and ignorant breeding plans. If each gundog breed represents a distinct brand, then that brand needs to be valued, whether in type, in its health or in its ability to function *as a gundog*.

Changing Styles

A rough-shooter's dog needs wide-ranging skills, a wildfowler's dog needs the constitution and coat to ensure its mere survival. Battue shooting demands great marking talents and the softest of mouths, so that even the tiredest dog does not mark its game. Historically, game was shot by being walked up, the quarry being shot as it flew or ran away. But in the early to mid-1800s, sparked by the introduction of breech-loaders, a major change occurred. The guns remained stationary whilst the birds were driven over them by beaters. This style brought a great demand for retrievers and initiated the immense popularity of breeds like the Labrador and the Goldie. It also resulted in quite staggering numbers of game birds being shot – and retrieved!

Battue Shooting
Battue, or driven game, shooting seems to have been first introduced at Knowsley in the mid-1820s by the 12th Earl of Derby. One of his guests, the Viscountess Belgrave, related that the total bag for the 1825 season came to 27,000 head of game. In one shoot at Elveden in Suffolk on 5 November 1912, five guns brought down 2,507 pheasants and 806 partridges. At Hall Barn in Buckinghamshire on 18 December 1913, seven guns shot a bag of 3,937 pheasants. More recently, in one day's shooting at Broadlands in 1968, 2,139 pheasants were shot, Prince Charles alone accounting for 500 of them. If every bird on each of these days was retrieved by a dog, just imagine the stamina required, in such a short space of time. Were the dogs as valued as the bag? We write about gundogs needing sound anatomies, stressing the importance of shoulders, loins and limbs, but the sheer enthusiasm and utter determination required by the dogs during such intense activity, is awesome.

Physical Discipline
Sportsmen, too, were not always the best dog-owners. In his renowned sporting diaries, the strangely revered Colonel Hawker writes, on the 31 October 1814: 'The infamous behaviour of my water-dog spoiled all my amusement… I finished my day with shooting the dog, at the express wish of Mrs Hawker and to the general satisfaction of all who were with us.' This disgraceful, unforgivable act gives a whole new meaning to the descriptive expression 'dogs for shooting'! But truly can you expect more from a man who shot swans, wheatears, short-eared owls, fieldfares and woodpeckers, and found it amusing to call the gun he used to dispatch maimed birds, his

A 19th century training system.

'cripple-stopper'. He valued neither his gundogs nor his quarry; he was no sportsman.

Gundogs have always been at the mercy of single-minded so-called sportsmen. There was a shameful incident at a Pointer trial a decade or so ago, when one handler, disappointed by his dog's performance, suspended the animal on a choke chain and swung it through the air. 'Breaking' gundogs was for centuries the term used for their training. In his book *Dog Breaking*, of 1909, General W.N. Hutchinson writes: 'Consider coolly whether you are flagellating a thick-coated dog, or one with a skin not much coarser than your own. Pause between each cut; and that he may comprehend why he is punished…let your last strokes

Gamekeeper and gundogs, 1900 – shared contentment.

be milder and milder, until they fall in the gentlest manner...' It is never enough just to *use* gundogs. We simply have to attach importance to them. They need to be *valued*.

It is depressing to hear from someone who has sent his young gundog away to a professional trainer for 'special gundog training' that the dog has returned cowed, spiritless and fearful of even a slightly raised hand. Most dogs want to work; they need direction more than correction. In his perceptive *Gundog Sense and Sensibility* (1982) Wilson Stephens writes:

> For me, physical discipline is largely an uncharted area. Whenever possible, therefore, I seek to make my impression more directly on the mind. In this process the trainer has a valuable and negotiable asset in the confidence, even love, which the dog has come to place in him. I prefer to work on that...

I daresay that Colonel Hawker's water dog was wagging its tail with misplaced confidence when he shot it. He clearly placed no value on it.

Worrying Faults

It is depressing, too, to see essentially functional dogs, like gundogs, displaying so many faults in the show ring. Such basic faults as upright shoulders, weak loins, slab-sidedness and a lack of drive from the rear would seriously handicap a gundog in the shooting field, where function once decided form. Judges' critiques from recent shows illustrate the basic flaws in so many gundogs proudly exhibited by their owners. Irish Setters: 'Front movement crossed, plaited and hackneyed, this is due to badly constructed front assemblies, upright shoulders, narrow fronts and no depth of chest. Rear movement was appalling.' Gordon Setters: 'Movement in general was disappointing; close hind movement and lack of drive.' Another judge in this breed reported: 'I want to see some rib and substance, some forechest and heart room... I found more than a few bitches with lack of heart room and loose elbows...'. Are such dogs actually *valued*?

For any gundog breed to lack a working physique is disappointing to say the least; are we promoting glamour ahead of soundness? Dogs don't care what they look like, but they do suffer distress when we expect them to run and run with little lung room in their thoraxes, limited forward extension in front and a lack of power from the rear. A Pointer judge reported in a recent critique:

> The breed as a whole now seems to be suffering from poor hindquarters, ranging from straight stifles, no definition of hock joint, hocks set too high, poor width of thigh, steeply sloping croups...if we lose the

powerful back-ends our Pointers will no longer have the drive to propel them over the moors and stubble fields to enable them to do the job for which they were bred.

Should we not value the *working* anatomy? Are we not devaluing their sporting heritage?

Loss of Working Type

It is difficult to identify the logic in favouring a breed designed for a specific purpose, and therefore having the anatomy suitable for that, then breeding specimens to an alien design. Many Pointers that I see, even at Crufts, are quite unlike those depicted in past centuries. They lack substance; physically they are not sound gundogs, with narrow chests, straight shoulders and poor movement. This saddens me, for these were once superlative hunting dogs, famous in many countries for their prowess in the shooting field. I once watched a Pointer win at Crufts with a Hackney action, a feature forbidden in its breed standard. This is a standard that uses just three words on the stifles, stating that they must be 'well-turned'. Is such judging and such a word picture helping this distinguished breed? Are we devaluing their *function*?

The great Pointer expert William Arkwright, in his *The Pointer and his Predecessors*, of 1906, wrote: 'The Stifles, extending from the stifle-joint to the hock, must be well bent, since on the length of the outline of his hindquarters, between the hip-bones

and the hocks, will depend the endurance of the dog, as this formation, in conjunction with an arched loin, gives the maximum of speed with the minimum of labour...' I find those words valuable. Breed standards should be reasonably brief, but to devote just three words to the stifle does not give sufficient guidance to tyro breeders. This is a justly famous British gundog breed, deserving the very best custodianship, one to be valued.

In his informative *The Setter*, of 1872, the great setter pioneer breeder Edward Laverack gave his views on the 'formation of this breed', including these words: 'chest deep, *wide*, and ribs well sprung behind the shoulders... A setter should not rise or be too upright in the shoulder...' I don't see many wide-chested setters nowadays – most are noticeably slab-sided, which limits their lung room considerably. The Crufts judge of Irish Setters in 2001 wrote:

On the whole I was very disappointed with the quality of the dogs. Narrow fronts, lack of bone, upright shoulders, narrow chests with no heart or lung-room, weak back-ends, poor movement. I would be very surprised if many of these could work as a gundog, the job for which they are bred.

Their gundog heritage has manifestly been devalued.

BELOW LEFT: Handsome, stylish, but still sound Irish Setter.

BELOW: One of Derry Argue's excellent Llewellin Setters.

Lost Blood

The year before at Crufts, the English Setter judge recorded: 'Many of the dogs that were quite nice standing [but] fell apart on the move.' The movement of any setter should be a joy to behold: flowing, effortless, controlled power. It is more than disappointing for 'the best of the very best', as the Kennel Club describes the Crufts entry, to be so inadequate. Perhaps the stock of the gifted working setter breeder Derry Argue has a role in improving the breed. His Llewellin Setters are exported to knowledgeable overseas clients but are largely unknown to the show world. The Americans still keep the Llewellin blood separate and preserve it. We have lost the chalk-white Llanidloes Setter and never persevered with the Russian Setters once imported. They became devalued.

In his book, Laverack describes the Russian Setter as very high-couraged but obstinate, only kept in order and subjection by a large quantity of work and whip. He recounts how one owner was so disgusted with two of his dogs that he shot one and gave the other away. These dogs were credited with having 'an enormous quantity of long silky white hair' and you do see some over-coated, heavily furnished specimens in the show ring, but never in working stock. Setters are a most important element in our sporting dog heritage and it would be a disaster if they lost their functional anatomy in the pursuit of show-ring success. The functional anatomy is the soundest one, developed in a hard school; when devalued, it soon degrades a breed.

Favoured Breeds

Bird dogs' work may have been lessened by shifts in sporting preferences, but retriever work, especially with Labradors and Goldens, and spaniel work, particularly with English Springers, has actually expanded. The enormous success of these breeds may have led to some loss of true type but their success has been well justified. They are the favoured breeds of shooting men, despite the merits of the HPR breeds,

ABOVE LEFT: Clumber Spaniel gathering at the Ragley Game Fair 2010.

LEFT: Clive Rowlands with his Rhiwlas Field Spaniels.

now established here. Over-popularity has ruined many a breed and both the Lab and the Cocker community need to be vigilant. (One Labrador breeder regularly registers over fifty pups each year, clearly commercially.) We need also to support the minor spaniel breeds; I saw much to admire in the Field Spaniels of the late Clive and of Pam Rowlands, perpetuating the famous Rhiwlas line, and the working Clumbers of James Darley and the Zuricks.

Valued Companions

The shooting fields of Britain have bequeathed us some superlative sporting dogs and given to a wider world deservedly popular companion dogs. Before the invention of firearms, such dogs were retrieving duck and even spent bolts and arrows from water, enticing wildfowl into cages and 'freezing' game birds so that nets could be cast over them. They have indicated unseen quarry, put up game, flushed it, marked it, located it, retrieved it and delivered it to hand. In the past they have been whipped for getting it wrong, sometimes even shot. The modern use of electric collars has given them a new, and to me, unwanted experience. As always, a man's treatment of his dogs tells you a lot more of him than of his dogs.

Renewed Need for Empathy

I treasure my memories of a few brief hours on the Powys Estate with gamekeeper Peter Spilsby and his Field Spaniels and time spent with part-time gamekeeper the late Clive Rowlands on a nearby estate with his busy, energy-packed Field Spaniels.

ABOVE RIGHT: Peter Spilsby, gamekeeper on the Powys Estate, with his Field Spaniels.

RIGHT: Field Spaniels assemble for a scurry, organised by Clive Rowlands.

They were like little tanks in the way they penetrated the dense local cover. But even more noticeable was their rapport with their owner, whom they could not see; dog and man working in complete harmony.

I recall with pleasure, too, the first time I saw, in Germany, the all-rounders at work, the hunt-point-retrieve breeds in action. Wrongly described as utility gundogs, their skills are wide-ranging and demand much from a handler. Thankfully I know of no instance in which one has been shot by an intolerant owner but, if shooting becomes a new 'welfare' issue, some could well be. For over a thousand years these dogs have adapted to man's needs; I do hope we keep theirs in mind. Our training methods may now be more enlightened, I do hope our empathy is too. Our breeding methods need to be more enlightened too, benefiting from scientific advances.

Breeding Concerns

Inbreeding amongst purebred dogs is very much in the limelight in the early part of the twenty-first century and rightly so. Gundog breeds originating in a small genetic base need monitoring. The inbreeding coefficients (a low one is better – the higher the percentage, the closer the breeding) in gundog breeds have been identified and published. The KC's Mate Select system allows checks to be made on the genetic desirability of a proposed mating, merit apart. The coefficients of inbreeding (COIs) assessed for gundog breeds in 2010 gave some revealing (and some reassuring) figures, expressed as percentages:

Bracco Italiano 3.8 per cent, Brittany 3.6, Chesapeake Bay Retriever 4.8, Clumber Spaniel 17.7, Cocker Spaniel 9, Curly-coated Retriever 12.2, English Setter 10.6, English Springer Spaniel 8.7, Field Spaniel 15.4, Flat-coated Retriever 6.8, Langhaar 8.6, GSP 5.3, GWHP 4.3, Golden Retriever 9.5, Gordon Setter 10.7, Hungarian Vizsla 10 (with 5.2 for the wire-haired variety), Irish Setter 16.5 (with 6.8 for the Red and White), Irish Water Spaniel 13.4, Italian Spinone 6.7, Labrador Retriever 6.4, Large Munsterlander 6.6, Nova Scotia Duck Tolling Retriever 2.4, Pointer 9, Portuguese Water Dog 5.5, Slovakian Rough-haired Pointer 11.5, Sussex Spaniel 22.6, Weimaraner 8.7 and the Welsh Springer Spaniel 10.8.

These are *breed averages* and it would be wrong to apply these ratings to an individual in a breed; the KC website can make more precise measurements, based on pedigree names. In 2012, the new puppy contract launched by the British Veterinary Association's Animal Welfare Foundation, supported by the RSPCA and endorsed by the Advisory Council for the Welfare Issues of Dog Breeding, advised that puppies with an inbreeding coefficient of more than 12.5 per cent should be avoided.

Relative Values

To put these figures into context, all dogs in a breed are related. A mother-son mating would produce a 25 per cent COI, first cousins will have a 6.25 per cent COI, and within breeds variations can be found: Standard Poodles have varied from 6.25 to over 25

Maternal Affection by H.H. Couldery (1832–1893). We have a duty of care to the litters we breed.

per cent, with the former living four years longer than the latter. If you bred with two totally unrelated Labradors, then mated two of their offspring together, their pups' COI could theoretically be 25 per cent if they share the same grandparents. For many breeds, not just gundog ones, the average COI may be above 10 per cent, as common ancestors contribute. Of course a COI of 1 per cent doesn't *guarantee* better health than a measurement of 30 per cent. Some low-scoring breeds have serious genetic defects as bad genes manifest themselves.

The chances of inheriting a double dose of defective genes needs to be reduced. Without health checks the overuse of a defective sire can create long-term misery in any breed. Rushing to mate your bitch to the latest Crufts winner is not a rational act, nor always a compassionate one. It is important to note, moreover, that COIs are not all calculated from a common base; it would be more valuable, comparatively, if all were to be based on a five-generation survey. There would be greater clarity too if the advice to avoid breeding from stock with a COI of lower than 12.5 were altered to read *not more* than 12.5 per cent.

Health Concerns
As with all dogs, purebred, crossbred or mongrel, there are health issues to be faced. Some gundog breed clubs and breed councils have acted very responsibly on this and worked hard to trace carriers of inheritable defects or fund research into newly identified problems. It is not acceptable for

pedigree gundogs to win in the show ring and yet be carriers of inherited diseases. This situation has been tolerated for far too long and must now cease. A recent survey revealed that Labradors came second only to Bulldogs of the breeds most likely to need a caesarean section in order to give birth. Labradors can now inherit six different eye diseases, primary epilepsy, 'limber-tail' (coccygeal muscle damage), hip dysplasia, osteochondrosis and its very own degenerative disease: 'Labrador Retriever myopathy'. Of course there are plenty of perfectly healthy, well-bred dogs in this deservedly popular breed. But how do you know what you are buying? Far too many Labradors are carelessly bred, causing distress to both dog and owner. Demand has led to many more poor quality dogs being bred. Do we value our gundogs sufficiently?

That handsome breed, the Golden Retriever, also has inherited defects causing concern: multifocal retinal dysplasia and four other eye disorders, epilepsy and hip dysplasia. In America, the Golden Retriever and the Cocker Spaniel are the two breeds most commonly affected by juvenile cataracts. In one survey there, on unwanted aggression in breeds of dog, Golden and Labrador Retrievers and the golden Cocker Spaniel feature surprisingly high up in the listed breeds. Of course, the breeds that are far less popular display problems of temperament and carry harmful genes too. But they are not being over-bred; there are far fewer of them to live shortened lives and cause distress, and expense, to their owners.

A Sick Friend by Bernard de Gempt (Dutch, 1826–1879). We should NOT be breeding sickly gundogs.

Promoting Healthier Dogs

The fact that some gundog breeds have become too popular for their own good, whilst a compliment to their appeal, is a sad commentary on the lack of controls in the purebred dog industry. An enlightened kennel club in any country could improve canine health by simply declining to recognise breed clubs without a comprehensive health scheme and by insisting on mandatory health clearances for all breeding stock. The Swedish KC amongst others has successfully

introduced the latter step; the mother kennel club is being left behind. All that free-for-all in pedigree dog breeding has its appeal in a democratic society, but surely not if it allows flawed dogs to proliferate. The KC could lead the way by cancelling the registration of dogs carrying lethal genes; all that is achieved by perpetuating existing policies is an increased likelihood of purebred canine cripples, popular because of their breed rather than their virility. It's always reassuring to read the Drakeshead Labrador Stud advertisements and see that all of the five dogs available are not just field trial winners but elbow, hip and eye tested, as well as DNA tested for three of the inherited defects that can afflict the breed too. We should all learn to value the health of our gundogs.

Valuing a Gundog at Work

When I was a twenty-one-year-old platoon commander in the Malayan Emergency, over half a century ago, we used Labradors to track fleeing terrorists. Once, in a dried-out mangrove swamp, in exhausting circumstances, our tracker dog gave up, utterly spent, simply unable to go on. We understood its feelings well! We had choices: we could have shot it, abandoned it or just hit it over the head. We agreed to take it in turns to carry the exhausted dog, on an improvised Everest carrier – no mean feat

ABOVE LEFT: *No Walk Today (Continental School, 20th century) – the eyes alone make demands on us!*

LEFT: *Retrieving Gundog – do we truly value their service?*

anywhere, and doubly daunting there. But we silently acknowledged that the dog had, like us, endured the heat, the humidity, the flies, the thorns, lack of water and endlessly and exhaustingly climbing over dried, exposed mangrove roots. The dog was part of our team; as, in a very different shooting field, it could do things we could not, unquestioningly served us, and was therefore respected and valued. Carrying an exhausted Labrador in the jungle may not be a rational act but valuing your gundog, whatever the circumstances, always will be.

In sporting dogs the rage for narrow, long heads in pointer and setter has lessened the general intelligence of these breeds... Why is a broad head thus obnoxious? But perhaps the greatest difference between the old and the new is in spaniels. In the varieties of this beautiful breed we have seen dogs winning prizes repeatedly, which would not have hunted for ten minutes with straight shoulders, bowed legs, misshapen feet and weak loins; but their beautiful heads, shining smooth coats and great length! Well, look at the head of the spaniel, springer or Cocker, in one of Reinagle's or Cooper's pictures, full of life and expression!

Letter to *The Kennel Gazette*, September 1888

Of much greater importance is it to satisfy oneself that the particular animal springs from a *good kind,* and that from his structure he is fitted for the work required. There is no reason why a dog should not be both good-looking and a good worker. Many of our best dogs on the bench are capital workers, and only ignorance would hold the whole of our exhibition dogs are useless for sporting purposes.

The Keeper's Book by Sir Peter Jeffrey Mackie (1924)

Once an English Setter was sent to me to train. The dog appeared to be without ambition of any sort; and I was not surprised to discover that he had been a prize-winner at Crufts. Of all the dull-eyed, spineless, lethargic brutes I have ever handled that was the worst. I couldn't even make him chase a hare! I could just picture him being photographed with his owner holding out his tail with one hand and supporting him under his belly with the other, as most of these dogs are photographed (to stop them falling down?!).

Dogs and Guns, by R.V. Garton (1964)

I have been stirred to write of the strong relationship between man and dog by the elderly black Springer cross Labrador owned by a great friend, which is now in her 14th year. 'Giddy', as she is affectionately known, has been an outstanding deer dog over the years and matched in skill in this area with her game retrieving abilities. Where deer are concerned, I have seen her, over the years, sit stalwart and alert beneath a high seat, never moving a muscle even if a hare or pheasant strolled past... It is a sad fact that working gundogs have a relatively short spell of years in which they can serve our interests and it behoves us to return in full measure the affection in which they hold us, whether or not we are worthy of it.

'Nimrod', writing in *The Countryman's Weekly*, 4 July 2012

Gundogs On Parade – Showing Off Our Gundogs

Clever people soon fancied there was 'money in' the showing of so-called sporting dogs; and the show type strayed farther and farther from the lines of the old working pointer, until it touched the bottom about 1880, when the show-men, ignorant of the first principles of the pointer, could actually believe and applaud a writer who dared to sum him up thus:- 'How can I better describe him than by saying he should be formed to a great extent on the model of the foxhound.' (*The Dog,* 'Idstone', p.118). But by this time, Shows had multiplied like fever-rash – dog-showing had become a commercial profession – and doubtless the admixture of alien blood, alloying the gold, was found necessary to a dog that had to bear the constant strain of the show-bench. But what was the Kennel Club doing all that time, may be asked! Nothing, absolutely nothing.

The Pointer and his Predecessors by William Arkwright (1906)

Show-Ring Shortcomings

The annual Crufts Dog Show displays our gundogs – not the types that work best but each breed and its beau ideal. As I have previously stressed, it claims to exhibit 'the best of the very best', although the judges' critiques from recent shows hardly support that. More concerning, however, are the remarks made by the judges at Crufts 2011 on construction and therefore movement. Labrador Retrievers: 'Quite a few dogs that presented a glorious outline standing but reminded me more of a "Robin Reliant" on the move as they crossed their legs coming or were almost single-tracking going away. In front movement much of this can be put down to shortness and straightness of the upper arm'. Italian Spinoni: 'Movement overall was poor…'. Chesapeake Bay Retrievers: 'the same problem of close hind movement remains…'. Nova Scotia Duck Tolling Retrievers: 'I still found many with short upper arms which gave a short mincing action'. Bracchi Italiani: 'Heads were a cause for concern along with movement… Regretfully, I had to make the very difficult decision to withhold in both of the Puppy classes and from one exhibitor in a Junior class'. For a judge to withhold prizes at Crufts doesn't give you much confidence in the qualifying system set up by the Kennel Club.

This picture shows the arrival of 'Idstone' (the Victorian dog writer) with his Irish Setters.

English Setter at Crufts.

Large Munsterlander at Crufts.

Worrying comments from the 2010 show's judges include the following. Cocker Spaniel dogs: 'I can only conclude…some had achieved qualification merely by virtue of being present.' Flat-coated Retriever dogs: 'I was really worried about the front movement in the younger classes, they were all over the place with pinning front gait or else flicking out from the pasterns', and bitches: 'I am worried that some of the hind movement was not positive, with the hocks having no power, also some of the front

movement was not the best I have seen and this was not solely due to lack of exercise.' English Setters: 'a lot of exhibits were not as well-muscled as they should be, with flabby, soft rear ends and no second thigh muscle. An English Setter is a gundog and needs the exercise that will give them the required "well muscled" hindquarters required in the standard.' Golden Retrievers: 'we should watch for over angulation…the back legs should be under the body, not sweeping way behind…too much angulation is

RIGHT: Outstanding Pointer Sh Ch Five Bob Note, Best of Breed at Crufts, 2011.

BELOW LEFT: Pointer class at Ladies Kennel Association show, 1984.

BELOW RIGHT: Dutch Champion Pointer Majbritt vom Hammersheim.

no more or less a fault than too little.' Irish Red and White Setters: 'many Setters were completely splay-footed; at times I had to overlook this ugly fault in an otherwise sound specimen.' Not encouraging!

Here are some from the 2009 Crufts show on gundogs: GSPs: 'many of the exhibits had very short muzzles and broad skulls... I also noticed in many of the younger classes the appearance of long thin legs with no substance or width over the rump, very strange. If these faults are not corrected we are going to lose the appearance of the GSP and it will be unable to do the job it was bred to do.' Hungarian Vizslas: 'Heads of correct type and proportions were hard to find, short muzzles, snipy and lacking underjaw, round eyes and harsh expressions sadly becoming the norm.' Irish Setters: 'Movement continues to concern, mostly from behind and the lack of muscle-tone was staggering in this active breed.' Pointers: 'The movement on the majority of these dogs and bitches was quite unbelievable, from crossing in front, upright in pasterns, upright in shoulders and it became very soul-destroying watching so many bad unsound movers... How some of these bitches qualified for Crufts I will never know.' If the Crufts entry represents the *best* gundogs in the pedigree dog world, bring back the dropper!

Working Dog Presence

In the early days of Crufts, the Gamekeepers' Ring there was one of the busiest; the Gamekeepers' Association used to hold their Annual General Meeting at the show. But by the time gundogs as a Group had their own day at the show in 1987, the entries for the gamekeeper classes were low, with only seven for Labrador and Curly-coated Retrievers, none for Flat-coats and Goldies, six for Any Variety Sporting Spaniel and fourteen for Any Variety Gundog. In 1990, the BASC took over the running of the Gamekeepers' Ring and still do, introducing in time both new classes and trophies, including team events and young handler classes. They very commendably introduced classes for dogs that have worked regularly in the shooting field, with 140 entries in 2011 in working classes alone. The 'Northesk Memorial Trophy For Best Gundog' is held in the main arena and only winners from the gamekeeper classes can compete for it. Here the working anatomy is on parade.

Undesired Obesity

A regular comment from show ring judges in 2009 on the gundog entry concerned the exhibiting of overweight dogs, especially Labradors. Obesity in any working dog is a sin and any sensible judge should send such a dog to the back of the class, however shiny the coat. Labradors have long been known to be 'gross feeders', liable to put on flesh. Being overweight inhibits field performance and places needless extra demands on the heart of the dog. Extra demands are also made by the construction faults listed by the 2009 Crufts judges. Unsound movement, especially when rooted in incorrectly placed shoulders, limits endurance through the additional strain imposed on the forequarters. Setters can be racy but should never lack muscle tone. Strength in the back and limbs is fundamental for stamina on a long day in the shooting field. Such basic faults are of course present too in working dogs, but no sensible owner breeds from such stock. Winners at Crufts produce scores of offspring.

For the owner of even a show gundog not to keep his dog in good physical condition is a betrayal of the working origin of the breed. Crufts judges' reports in the recent past on Field and Clumber Spaniels respectively read: 'many were shown carrying too much weight', and 'I felt many were in soft condition...'. This source of criticism from show-ring judges on gundog breeds is not restricted to Crufts; at the North West Labrador Club's Championship show of 1996, the judge reported: 'There can't have been more than 20 bitches (in a high entry) who were a suitable weight for a working breed.' At the 2012 Manchester Championship Show, the Flat-coat judge reported, after lamenting the lack of hindquarter muscle: 'Several really nice dogs were shown overweight...' Obesity, however undesirable in a gundog breed, is easily rectified, while faulty movement indicates faulty construction, which is much more worrying.

Importance of Word Pictures

A Crufts-winning Pointer with a high-stepping, forward-reaching Hackney action, which I once witnessed, was in fact in breach of its own breed standard, as promulgated by the Kennel Club, which runs Crufts and appoints judges. This standard states very plainly, 'Definitely not a hackney action... Any departure from the foregoing points should be considered a fault...' So here was a specimen of one of our most famous gundog

Gordon Setter class.

South Eastern Welsh Springer Spaniel Club's Open Show 2012: Best in Show – Sh Ch Shandwick Premier Rose at Sarabande.

breeds winning at our most prestigious dog show of the year with an easily identified fault. What is the point of having a precisely worded standard if a dog can win in spite of it? What kind of gundog judge is it that cannot see such a basic fault in a working dog?

Other judges of show-ring gundogs are not slow to spot significant faults, as the following critiques from judges illustrate. North Riding Gundog Club's open show: 'I was appalled at the unsound action, especially in Golden Retrievers and Labradors, many of which looked so nice standing but fell to pieces on the move.' Other judges looking over Labradors at different shows wrote: 'The diversity of type and the prevalence of coarse heads and poor tails gives cause for concern for the future'; 'My main criticism is mouths. I found five from all the classes which were really bad'; 'I would like to mention incorrect mouths. I have never come across so many variations before and some were quite severely wrong.' A gundog's mouth is rather important! These remarks by judges were made about dogs bred to a carefully written standard and change hands for several hundreds of pounds.

Overlooked Flaws

A recent show critique on the Irish Setter used these words: 'Many had short necks or rather, the neck was the correct length, if only the shoulders and forequarters had been angulated correctly, … a *fault* that is being accepted as the correct standard…I hope the two entropians are not bred from.' Here are pedigree gundogs being bred with not only a fault in their basic

construction but with faulty genes too! In-growing eyelashes or entropion is a distressing eye condition in any breed; yet dogs suffering from this inherited defect can be shown under Kennel Club rules and win prizes. What a situation – gundog breeders knowingly perpetuating physically unsound dogs!

A well-known Labrador breeder, who prides herself on her dual-purpose dogs, once complained that the scheme to identify hip dysplasia in the breed was doing enormous damage to working Labradors. I would have thought that hip dysplasia was doing a certain amount of damage in the breed too! The desperately worrying situation over inherited diseases in dogs will only be changed through the fullest cooperation of all breeders. I would like to see the Kennel Club stipulate that all breeding stock *must* have their hips scored if their offspring are to be registered. What really is the point of spending two years training a dog to a good field standard only to find it disabled by an inherited defect?

It is surely not acceptable for pedigree gundogs to win in the show-ring and yet be carriers of inherited diseases. This situation has been tolerated for far too long and must now cease. It is also highly undesirable for dogs with glaring faults to be placed by judges lacking knowledge of functional animals. Gundogs in the conformation show-ring, where working qualities cannot be tested, really must move correctly and movement itself must be placed higher than any other judging point. Over the next few years, it will be illuminating to study the critiques of the gundog judges at Crufts and see what real progress is being achieved at the top of the pedigree dog world. I am more hopeful now than for several decades. Our gundog breeds deserve the very best custodianship.

Inspiration from Quality

When I was making a commercial video on the Labrador Retriever some years ago, I had the pleasure and privilege of seeing the dogs in the kennels of the late Gwen Broadley and, later, of Carole Coode. It was abundantly clear that both these breeders had a very clear idea of what an outstanding dog in their breed should look like. I think of them when I see overweight faulty Labs at shows and in the park. I am old enough too to recall the consistently high quality of the 'of Ware' Cockers and the Whitwell Pointers. Top-

quality dogs can be truly inspiring. But you shouldn't have to rely on your memory to be conscious of top-quality gundogs, they should be all around you – from inspired breeders, identified by competent judges and valued by experienced sportsmen.

In his valuable two-volume *The Dog Book* of 1906, the underrated Scottish writer, James Watson, describes quite scathingly those in the world of purebred dogs who fail to realize that a pedigree is only a piece of paper. He records a conversation with the great Irish Terrier breeder of one hundred years ago, William Graham, who cast his eye over a show entry of his time and declared: 'Some men show pedigrees; I show dogs and take the prizes.' Vero Shaw, the distinguished canine authority of that time, gave the view in a show report that, all too often, the

ABOVE: *Six 'of Ware' Cocker Spaniels.*

LEFT: *Ardaghin & Whitwell Pointers and Setters.*

pedigree was worth more than the dog. And to this day, you still hear an indifferent animal excused on the grounds that it 'has a good pedigree'. As James Watson observed: 'No one with any knowledge of the subject will breed to a dog merely on pedigree...a good dog makes a pedigree good, and not the other way.'

Flat-coated Retriever of the late 20th century. Photo: David Dalton.

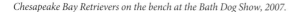

Chesapeake Bay Retrievers on the bench at the Bath Dog Show, 2007.

Curly-coated Retrievers benched at Bath Dog Show, 2007.

Reading Pedigree Forms

There used to be a saying in dog-breeding circles: no animal is well-bred unless it is good in itself. I haven't heard it spoken of as a received wisdom for some years. Much more important than the names on the written pedigree is the ability to 'read' it, that is translate the names into physical content. As the great Scottish Terrier breeder, W.L. McCandlish wrote in his book on the breed: 'The names in a pedigree form are merely cyphers, designating certain groupings of features and certain sources of blood, and pedigree is of no value unless the breeder can translate what these cyphers mean.' Yet even some quite experienced dog breeders get dazzled by names on forms, rather than by dogs, supported by blood from distinct ancestors. The eminent canine geneticist Malcolm Willis has written: '*Never* does pedigree information become more important than information on the dog itself.' We must always value dogs that are good in themselves.

Perhaps highly significant statements such as 'No animal is well-bred unless it is good in itself'; 'Never does pedigree information become more important than information on the dog itself'; 'Some men show pedigrees; I show dogs'; and 'a good dog makes the pedigree good, and not the other way' need to be given greater impact. The phrase 'become purely a fancier's dog' need not become immediately associated with deterioration, but be an acknowledgement that that breed is best-bred – and has wide-ranging, thoroughly comprehensive KC certification to indicate that. Quality assurance surely has to be the name of this purebred dog game. Show me the form – of the dog!

I believe that the award of champion status in gundogs has lost its value, in times when pedigree dogs often have to be protected from poor standards – of breeding, judging and amongst exhibitors. The title of champion should only be awarded *after* the dog has subsequently passed tests for temperament, carriage of inherited defects, inbreeding coefficients and morphology (that is harmful physical features, as at Crufts from 2012). The bestowing of champion status should only be awarded in a gundog breed after the dog has gained a working certificate at a working test in the field. The title of *Champion* really must mean something; cheap rosettes, and a superficial title such as Show Champion, lead to unworthy dogs

being bred from; a free-for-all in breeding doesn't benefit a breed; unreliable temperament presents an unwanted problem for the buying public – the pet market. Our dogs need protecting from bad breeders. Truly committed breed fanciers should welcome a title actually bringing all-round soundness with it, not just a name casually recorded in a stud book. If you are proud of your breed, why not strive for the very best stock?

The practical shooting man might well wonder what the pace of some of the fastest and most brilliant dogs would dwindle down to at the end of a long day on grouse. This staying power is the foundation of almost the most essential part of a pointer or setter, for a heavy-shouldered or slack-loined dog would be unable from his conformation to maintain pace and style in rough heather in Scotland, or over rough ground in the south; and yet on a brief trial such a dog might take a higher place than he would justify on a longer test. In America, the greatest attention and credit is paid to stamina and the consequent ability to maintain pace and style, and rightly so, as without this knowledge it is impossible to breed on correct lines.

Major Maurice Portal, writing in the Lonsdale Library's *Shooting by Moor, Field and Shore* (1929)

It is an undoubted fact that the major part of the sporting dogs exhibited have never been tested on game, but are merely specimens of external form… It is remarkable what numbers of miserable specimens often obtain prizes…you must bear in mind that the value of a dog does not consist in the number of prizes he may have taken at shows, but in the quality of his stock, and if he has improved the breed.

The Setter by Edward Laverack (1872)

I do not wish to suggest for a moment that as a dog-show club pure and simple the Kennel Club has done amiss, for (again like Gallio) it appears to police its kingdom effectually enough, and its registration of dogs' names and pedigrees is emphatically a benefit to all. It is as a guardian of the English working-dogs, and as a bulwark against the seething whirlpools of 'fancy', that it has proved such a failure.

The Pointer and his Predecessors by William Arkwright (1906)

Show Dogs

Field Dogs

ABOVE: *Field Irish Setter.*

LEFT: *Heavily furnished Irish Setter. Photo: Dogs in Canada magazine*

Heavily feathered Gordon Setter. Photo: Dogs in Canada magazine.

Field Gordon Setter.

Show Dogs

Show Springer.

Show Cocker.

Field Dogs

Field Springer. Photo: Kate Watson.

Working Cockers.

CONSERVING THE GUNDOG AS A SPORTING DOG

In the foregoing chapters, I set out firstly to show the immense value to the primitive hunter of the 'dogs of the net', the water dogs and the decoy dogs, and their subsequent adaptation to use with the gun. Then, I strove to establish how the gundog's role decided its design, as well as the vital importance of relating physique to function, not fashion. We boast of our gundogs' heritage; we must now honour it. Throughout the book, I have tried to make good use of the wisdom of past experts by quoting their exact words to make key points, points that stand the test of time. Sportsmen in past centuries were closer to their sport and their dogs than we are today. I have tried too to make full use of sporting art, which can be so revealing in illustrating breed type and breed change. The artist's eye picks up the key elements of the scene he witnesses, then immortalizes. In capturing the muscularity of the Pointer, the steadfastness of the setter, the vivacity of the spaniels and the controlled energy of the all-rounders, the sporting artist provides lasting testimony of the world of the sporting dog.

Important Inclusions

Often omitted in books on breeds, I have in this book made full use of the critiques of show-ring judges, most of them knowledgeable and experienced in their field, to highlight the worrying flaws they come across in the entry, even at Crufts. Some of these flaws appear to be historic, even endemic, in certain gundog breeds and this represents problems to be faced, not evaded. Guided by a respect for their function, we really must breed these quite admirable breeds to a

The Pointer 'Shot' by J.S. Cooper, 1831, depicting a far more muscular dog.

Two English Setters, attributed to Reuben Ward Binks, c.1905.

healthy phenotype and, with genetic advice, for the healthiest genotype we can achieve without losing breed type. But perhaps most importantly, we must shake off the shackles imposed largely by twentieth-century thinking on purebreeding. Breed type doesn't just exist in the genes of a breed but in the type those genes produce in combination. Our ancestors never hesitated to use the best dogs for breeding and not always *within a breed*. We have a moral duty to breed *sound* dogs ahead of pretty ones. I have made use of registration statistics to show how some gundog breeds have prospered down the years whilst some have not. If we prize our native gundog breeds we need to act soon to save some of them. We need a new man-dog covenant to safeguard our remarkably talented gundogs, as I outline below.

Reflecting Need

The division of most registered gundog breeds into a working type and a show variety is, however desirable to some and inevitable to others, to me regrettable. Some would claim that many working gundogs are just not handsome enough for the pet market, that the field trial dogs are too 'hot' even for rough-shooters and that working ability in a show dog is wasted anyway, so why get excited about it? It has been argued that there are in fact three varieties within some gundog breeds: field trial, working test and show bench types. This may well be true in some retriever breeds and, after all, every working and sporting breed evolved in the pursuit of function. Foxhound breeders adapt their pack to their hunting country, so why shouldn't our gundog breeds just reflect the sporting needs of their owners? Perhaps that is how four breeds of German pointer were created, three of the Weimaraner, at one time any number of setters, three of the Poodle and indeed two, by size, of the Munsterlander!

Sweeping generalizations are regularly made about the different varieties within a gundog breed, that on the one hand all show dogs have been ruined and, on the other, that all good working dogs are structurally sound. Yet we all know of some excellent dual-purpose gundogs and we all see dogs succeed in the field sometimes in spite of their anatomy. Strong working instincts are not automatically accompanied by a

German Long-haired Pointers.

The Large Munsterlander.

Working Cocker Spaniel – forever alert to activity.

Working Sussex Spaniel – always wanting to be busy.

strong sound physique. But surely it would be good to see *every* dog in each gundog breed not only possessing working skills but also conforming to the breed standard. Handsome is as handsome does is no recipe for breeding better dogs. Earlier, I have argued for the title of *Champion* to be reviewed, with harder and wider examinations to justify such a title. Appearance should *not* be the sole criterion. We should *all* be seeking sound, healthy, functionally capable, good-looking dogs. Of all dogs, gundogs *must* be functional.

Flawed Performance

This point is reinforced by my experience in past years when judging gundog working tests. Three come particularly to mind. The first concerned a test at the admirable Gamekeepers' Fair when held annually in April by the BASC at the Shugborough estate in Staffordshire that I then ran. This was a retriever test and involved some good working dogs, not all of which typified their breed. One yellow Labrador had a head that would not have disgraced a Foxhound. A whippety black Labrador really excelled whereas a handsome Golden Retriever just would not jump into the admittedly fast-flowing river. A hard-eyed Chesapeake leapt a good ten feet out into the river without hesitating; but I later noted that it had poor movement, perhaps from upright shoulders and short upper arms. In the end, even gifted working dogs have to be physically sound.

Handsome Limitations

The second involved a minor breeds spaniel working test – and there wasn't an ugly dog there. But apart from the late Clive Rowlands' Rhiwlas Field Spaniels, there was hardly a dog with nose and hunting enthusiasm. The third, for Curly-coated Retrievers, and also on this same country estate that I used to manage, tested some extremely sound dogs but proved too much of a test for the handlers, who didn't always know enough to keep ahead of or even control their dogs. In summary we had: handsome dogs which couldn't work; dogs that worked very competently but would never win a beauty contest; and owners/handlers who didn't know enough to coach whatever working instinct their dogs actually did have further forward. What can be done?

A Field Spaniel from the Rhiwlas line.

Parading Performance

Are field trials being conducted by the KC in a manner most likely to develop the most useful gundog? As long ago as December 1901, Leo Parsey was writing in *The Kennel Gazette*:

> At field trials the dogs engaged have no opportunity of giving proof of their steadiness under heavy fire, nor have they the chance of showing their perseverance and nose on winged birds where ground game is plentiful. Many of the dogs do not even see a bird fall to the shot, and only in exceptional cases have they the chance of testing their abilities in finding and retrieving a runner. Then, too, the excitement and jealousy of other dogs at a big shoot or heavy partridge or grouse drive is entirely absent, and the energy and stamina of the dog cannot be effectually tested… The only tests to which retrievers are subjected at field trials are of a simple and elementary nature…

Do his words have application today? Are we testing our gundogs in the most appropriate way? Why don't real gundog men take over? Not just the conducting, but designing the whole system of gundog field trials?

Most sensible gundog men are full of admiration for show people who try to work their dogs. We all love a handsome dog; but a handsome useless dog has little value for me. As Wilson Stephens once memorably remarked on this subject: 'They didn't send male models to recapture the Falklands.' (As a one-time member of 3 PARA, I know only too well that none of us were ever chosen for our looks!) Perhaps the ability of a gundog to carry the title of show champion without a working certificate, a health check, a temperament test and a morphological examination is itself creating not just a wider gap between show and working dogs, but between sound dogs and rosette winners that may not be sound.

Winners Bred From

It is both worrying and potentially damaging to a breed when a gundog wins in the show ring with serious anatomical faults for a functional animal. When conformation to a wholly physical blueprint, the breed standard, is the only criterion, it is vital for sound dogs to win. They get bred from the most. I have benefited from the immense number of books on gundogs, listed in the Bibliography, written across several centuries, by real experts. Are today's gundog breeders benefiting too? Mary Roslin Williams, for example, in her book *Advanced Labrador Breeding* of 1988, provides clear, convincing guidance on the working anatomy desirable in a functional gundog.

Langhaars at a Dutch show.

English Springers – ready to demonstrate their working skills.

A brace of Hertha Pointers in Denmark.

RIGHT: *Scrambling For Dinner by W.H.H. Trood, 1893 – we owe such pups a healthy future.*

BELOW RIGHT: *These appealing Cocker Spaniel pups will depend on us for their quality of life.*

She points out the dangers of 'flashy' dogs, with upright shoulders, straight elbows, a high-stepping Hackney action, too short a body, lacking a waterproof coat and exhibiting too much hock action in the trot, and then explains the disadvantages of these features in a working gundog. Yet a few years ago at Crufts, a Pointer won not only its breed class but the whole Gundog Group with a pronounced Hackney action, a feature condemned in its own breed standard. This occurred under a famous judge who breeds well-known retrievers. How long would such a Pointer last on a grouse moor with such a defect? Surely the whole point when judging a gundog in the show ring is to consider whether its anatomy allows it to carry out its traditional field function. Otherwise it doesn't belong to that breed of gundog. And Crufts winners are extensively bred from, winning sires especially.

Critical Comments

If this were an isolated case, it could be overlooked, but it is not. Here are some critiques from the judges themselves at shows in recent years. German Wire-haired Pointers at the 1996 Gundog Breeds Association of Scotland show: 'In the last five years the breed has altered dramatically and not for the better I hasten to add. At least 50 per cent of the breed is incorrect to the standard and this has resulted in some poor quality dogs winning championship certificates.' Labrador Retrievers at the 1996 North West Labrador Club Championship Show: 'The true Lab head and expression seems to have gone… Feet are distinctly odd at the moment throughout the breed… There can't have been more than about 20 bitches who were a suitable weight for a working breed… Coats surprised me no end… They gave an impression of density until you put your hand on them.' German Short-haired Pointers at a 1996 show: 'I was pleased to have 122 exhibits making 129 entries. The disappointment was the poor standard overall… They cannot perform the intended function in the field unless their construction is correct. They were after all bred for working.' Do the exhibitors of these dogs actually know a bad dog from a good one?

Critical comments on the last-named breed continued at the 1997 Manchester Championship show: 'very few of the exhibits before me at this event actually displayed any drive or satisfactory rear end movement'. Other comments at 1996 shows included these words, on Pointers: 'Movement left a lot to be desired' and at a different show, with a record entry: 'Are we becoming a breed of cardboard cut outs?… it must look and act like a pointer, or we will lose the characteristics of the breed we love'; on Labradors: 'What worried me…was the continued deterioration in head quality… Movement was, as I expected variable;' and at another show: 'Front movement still needs our attention, this stems mainly from a short straight upper arm or upright shoulders.' (How many pups have been bred from these flawed exhibits since then?)

Such worrying comments come from dog show judges who are so often accused of being too tolerant rather than hyper-critical. If the dogs drawing these comments are 'show quality', what is the quality like in those dogs sold by breeders to the pet market because they lack quality? If these dogs in the show critiques are representative of their particular breeds, what a commentary on pedigree dog breeders. There are clearly far too many people producing puppies for sale nowadays rather than breeding dogs. One hundred years ago, if a gundog was unable to perform in the field for any reason then it was culled. Today it would be bred from. This stems from a dog now being valued for what it looks like rather than for what it can do.

Where to Buy?

Where do you advise the pet-owner seeking a companion gundog to go for one? The Kennel Club advises us to go to an *assured* breeder. But regularly in *The Kennel Gazette*, the KC's own monthly publication, there are cases of breeders being banned for cruelty to their own dogs, cheating purchasers of puppies, falsifying hip scores, reneging on sale terms and otherwise acting discreditably. Unlike our ancestors, who developed our splendid gundog breeds, we talk more proudly of a dog's pedigree, a piece of paper, than the dog.

A Danish geneticist once went through his own country's dog-breeding records and found that, on genetic grounds alone, one in ten of the breeding records could not be correct. A recent test on registrations in the United States found that 13 per cent were false. Our Kennel Club carries out no rigorous formal routine checks on the validity of its pedigrees – just takes the registration fee! In the United States, a number of scientific institutions are working hard to improve the genetic health of breeds of purebred dogs. The Institute of Genetic Disease Control in Animals at the School of Veterinary Medicine at the University of California and the School of Veterinary Medicine at Purdue University both find, however, that their biggest obstacle in research lies with breed clubs. Breed

This charming pup will benefit from the work of an effective breed club.

A healthy pup, but will it have a healthy future?

clubs there simply will not provide honest, reliable information to assist research, perhaps guarding their wallets more than their breed – a breed under their stewardship.

Breeding for Virility

A study a few years ago by a group of distinguished Canadian veterinary surgeons concluded with these words: 'The next hundred years look rather bleak for the pure-bred dog industry unless dramatic changes are introduced. We have a problem which if not addressed and speedily rectified, may destroy for all time many beautiful breeds of dog. All dog lovers share the blame for not acting...' They were referring to the practice of breeding dogs to a harmful design and to the failure to face the challenge posed by inheritable diseases. Breeding for virility should be our watchword.

Perpetuating Soundness
If we do not breed for soundness, then we are betraying an inherited trust, the belief that we too would care for our gundogs and perpetuate them in their ancestral mould. But we have been reckless with the genotype as well as their phenotype. Cocker Spaniels can now inherit ectropion, entropion, a bleeding disorder known as factor X deficiency, progressive retinal atrophy, distichiasis and three different skeletal anomalies. How many *mandatory* control schemes have been set up to reduce their incidence? Not one. Commendably, the KC now has a Dog Health Group looking at the number of litters registered to one bitch, veterinary inspections of Best of Breed winners in certain breeds – one of them, the Clumber Spaniel, being a gundog breed – and has introduced the Mate-Select system to guard against unknowing inbreeding.

Hip dysplasia is a crippling disease affecting a number of gundog breeds, especially Labradors and Golden Retrievers. Every year another 50,000 retrievers are registered with the Kennel Club. They come from breeding stock only a tiny number of which has been hip scored. Who knows what their hips will be like? Why shouldn't their purchasers get their money back if these pups develop hip dysplasia in due course? Most of them will be too distressed by their dog's suffering even to try.

The literally cruel fact is that nobody cares enough to lobby for *mandatory* clearances for all pedigree dog breeding stock. This does nothing for subject creatures in our care. It does nothing to perpetuate pedigree dogs as sound healthy animals for working use or as companion dogs. We should be thoroughly ashamed of the way we breed our gundogs and even more ashamed by our total failure to safeguard their health and well-being. We are a nation of dog-owners, not dog-lovers. We have lost our way.

ABOVE: *This Curly pup was very well bred – but how many are?*

LEFT: *An endearing pup deserving a disease-free future.*

The Way Forward

There is a way back; but it is conscience-led not wallet-led. Kennel Club registrations are not being sustained; since 1996, when over 270,000 registrations were processed, the KC has regularly lost thousands in annual registrations. The gundog group accounts for around 100,000 of these registrations, easily the largest group. If the Countryside Alliance or BASC made themselves responsible for such registrations and maintained the same scale of costs, they would receive the best part of a million pounds. Quite a thought! Think of the health schemes and sporting competitions that could be financed by such income.

Of course, owners of gundogs who are solely interested in showing their dogs at KC-licensed shows will still want to register their dogs with them. But most dogs registered are just pets. These, together with gundogs intended for work, would probably make up around 55 per cent of gundogs registered. If these alone came over to a new scheme, they would still bring with them well over £500,000 in revenue, a sum worth more than a passing thought.

Sponsoring Sporting Dogs

The fashion of registering sporting dogs with the KC should have gone 'out of fashion' a long time ago. Owners of sporting dogs have been slow to realize that the Kennel Club itself is slowly but surely going out of fashion. Gundog fanciers need to ensure that our native breeds don't go out of fashion too. Thirty years ago I tried hard to stir the consciences of the gundog fraternity in an article in *Shooting Times* entitled 'Do we need the Kennel Club?' pointing out the value of the International Sheepdog Society to the working sheepdog, the National Greyhound Racing Club to the racing greyhound and the Associations of Masters to packhounds, despite their disassociation from the KC. I was inundated with letters of support and the editor's *Letters* page vastly oversubscribed. But the support of such notables as Peter Moxon, Derry Argue and Diana Bovill was not reinforced by the field sports organizations, to my deep regret.

Commenting on my article, the editor of *Our Dogs* wrote that, 'The gundog section of dogdom, particularly that part of it concerned with field trials rather than show competition, has always shown great independence of spirit.' I wish that 'great independence

of spirit' in the field trials world had only matched that of their counterparts in the sheepdog, greyhound and packhound world down the years. Diana Bovill, in her letter to the editor, wrote: 'Having for about twenty years watched and studied the Kennel Club in relation to field trials, I do not think one can easily overestimate the evils which spring from autocracy and privilege.' In the late 1920s, a gundog breakaway was planned and only averted at the last moment by the clever intervention of the Earl of Chesterfield and by taking the rebels' general, the redoubtable Lady Howe, on to the field trial committee, the first and only woman to serve on any KC committee for more than forty years. Are Diana Bovill's words that wrong?

Ministerial Confusion

Subsequently I wrote another piece for the same sporting magazine, pointing out that in Canada, the monopoly of their Kennel Club has now been broken – by law. Sadly, in this country two quite separate ministries, the Home Office and the Department of the Environment, Food and Rural Affairs, neither of them noted for their vision or surefootedness, seem to dabble in the welfare of the domestic dog, unlike the Canadian situation. But the welfare of our gundogs – the control of psychopathic dogs, the eradication of inheritable diseases, the restriction of back-street breeders and the promotion of well-bred, physically sound, functional, working dogs to support us in the field *is* the business of *all* of us who have had the privilege of working such dogs. Master breeders of the last century passed these revered sporting breeds into our hands during our lifetime, in the belief that we too would carry their torch and then perpetuate these splendid animals for the benefit of those who come after us. We are betraying that trust.

After the publication of that second article, several gundog society secretaries wrote to me expressing support for a gundog breakaway from the KC. I asked them to write to the BASC; perhaps I was wrong. But all of us who admire field prowess in gundogs have to accept the need for change. The destiny of our gundog breeds, as breeds, must be recaptured by those who use them as functional animals. Perhaps the new thinking at the KC, in the light of the immensely influential TV programme *Pedigree Dogs Exposed* of 2008, will restore our faith, but valuable time has been lost over safeguarding the future of our precious gundog breeds.

RIGHT: *Bracchi Italiani – a welcome foreign breed, but not at the expense of native ones.*

BELOW RIGHT: *Italian Spinone and a Hungarian Vizsla, notable additions to our gundog list.*

If we did have a separate working gundog studbook, perhaps then we could work to eliminate entropion in Clumbers, inherited canine cataracts in Labradors, hip dysplasia in Golden Retrievers, central progressive atrophy in Chesapeakes and PRA in all too many gundog breeds. The studbook can play a leading role in such work – if we are determined, that is, to work towards the reduction rather the limp acceptance of such flawed stock. We would no longer need forty-four words to describe the tail of the Labrador and could work to restore true type and the correct temperament in our gundog breeds. We might even find genuinely *yellow* Labradors and *truly Golden* Retrievers being bred again! And, after all, do the American shooting men allow the show dog people over there to run their sport? No, they do not and that alone is a lesson for us.

Debrett Analogy

One secretary of the KC, with regrettable complacency, likened his registration department's role with that of Debretts; in other words, to record statements of fact not evidence of quality. All of us with responsibilities towards captive animals need to act more honourably than that; those that feature in Debretts are free not to choose diseased partners. A machine can record facts; humans have a higher duty towards dumb animals bred for their use. We now have to raise our level of thinking, act responsibly towards dependent creatures which exist to serve us, keep faith with breed creators like Llewellin, Laverack, Boughey, Phillips, Tweedmouth, Lloyd and McCarthy and obey our consciences. Can any caring person sleep well when 600 unwanted pedigree gundogs end up in Battersea Dogs Home alone each year? More and more dogs means more and more money coming into the registration department of the KC to be passed on to support its social activities – and working gundog men actually go on paying up!

Look at the early photographs of our gundog breeds and then ask yourself: 'Have our gundog breeds gained anything at all from past KC patronage?' Then think of the capability that the desktop computer has given us to record, register and correlate the statistics we feed into it. A working gundog register/studbook could be established by any enterprising gundog society secretary, but how much better it would be if the BASC took on the task – with the fees being used for the benefit of our country sports as a whole. We have experienced some 150 years of KC rule and seen nothing so far but ever-increasing costs, deteriorating breeds and show-ring bias.

Only a combination of apathy and a clinging to the status quo is preventing working gundog men from running their own ship. There is no practical reason why they should not do so without further delay. There is every moral reason for them to do so as soon as possible. Failing to take such an initiative might give the less ethical and the apathetic few sleepless nights, but who *is* going to safeguard the future of our precious gundogs? My recurring nightmare is waking to find myself in the year 2020 to witness a Rottweiler-headed, white-coated, hard-eyed, hound-like Labrador Retriever, with clicking hips and poor eyesight, (but KC-registered and with 'an excellent pedigree') winning a field trial, not on merit, but because the other entrants were even worse! Come on, you allegedly hard-headed gundog men, wake up and do your duty!

Road to Ruin

Sadly gundog breeds that become highly popular are more likely to be carelessly bred and thoughtlessly owned. For every comment on Labradors at field trials resembling 'black Whippets' twenty could be made on fat Labradors in suburban gardens. It is sadder still to see both the Labrador and the Golden Retriever featuring high in breed listings for dogs with unacceptable temperaments. In some places in North America both breeds are banned under local so-called dangerous dog legislation. Popularity has its perils; when demand is high, standards can be lowered. The over-use of successful sires, which have not been screened for inheritable defects, is surely the road to ruin.

Ambition Needed

Whilst unpopularity need not lead to lower standards, a reduced gene pool, the lack of a major leading kennel and declining field employment can all add up to diminished quality. Just as the HPR breeds have been favoured by individuals ambitious for their dogs, so surely could the minor native gundog breeds. If the German Wire-haired Pointer Braithewaite Hanky Panky, owned by Anne Collen and bred by David Brigden, can beat fifty-five other dogs to become an International Working Trials Champion, can this not encourage other breeds to follow suit? Natural working ability has to be matched by expert handling of course, but how ambitious are the other breed

Retriever Trial – a vital activity for willing dogs.

enthusiasts? We need more enthusiasts like Peter O'Driscoll, who runs training courses for Pointer and setter owners at Edenmouth in the Scottish borders, both to offer a chance to learn about the working side and for owners, especially newcomers, to gain experience with their *own gun*dogs.

New Tests Abroad

It may not be 'fashionable' to enter gundogs in such working trials but new competitions attract talent from unfamiliar sources. In America, the United Kennel Club has announced the expansion of its extremely successful Hunting Retriever Program with a new Started Hunting Retriever title in 2012. Its object is to attract those who support hunting and promote the use of hunting dogs, the fourth title available for hunting retrievers from the UKC. This shows the advantage of having more than one kennel club and of having one more interested in working dogs. This is a fashion we could benefit from.

With their earth dog, Airedale and Beagle trials, for example, the Americans are ahead of us in promoting the use of working dogs across a wider spectrum. The HPR breeds could by their nature be entered for a range of working trials, not just those for gundogs. Here is a group of dogs that can follow

wounded game or track deer and boar, work with the falcon, quarter ground close or wide, hold game on point, flush on command, mark and retrieve shot game, work in water and dense cover, withstand the cold and wet, and yet provide companionable loyalty and affection for their owners. Versatile breeds need a whole range of tests if they are to show their mettle and be fully exercised. And when a gundog breed

ABOVE RIGHT: Gundog demonstration – important event for tyro gundog owners.

RIGHT: Working Tests ensure working instincts are aroused.

becomes a much-desired brand of dog, it's time for better dogs not lesser ones.

New Field Tests Required at Home

Is it enough for us merely to follow fashion in gundogs in Britain and restrict our gundogs to the same old annual trials and working tests? The current campaign against any kind of sporting activity that involves hunting with dogs may in time force us towards different forms of trials and tests. Falconry, hound trailing, lure chasing, tracking and water rescue all offer challenges to sporting dogs. We should never be content just to perpetuate last year's or the last century's competitions. Our dogs would surely benefit from more pioneering initiatives over field tests and less of the stultifying status quo! The use of specialist breeds that excel should not exclude the use of gifted dogs with talent wastefully buried. This might even give new life to our struggling native minor gundog breeds, our lost brands. I look forward to annual tests for decoy dogs, water dogs and hawking dogs!

The Future

To be fair to the KC, however, it is only right to commend them for recently increasing their efforts in the working gundog field: in 2011 the KC licensed some 700 field trials, a number exceeded by unlicensed working tests; in 2012, they announced four special gundog training days for novice handlers – right across the UK, as well as their annual working tests for retrievers, HPRs and spaniels, combined with an international team event. The KC now encourages show-ring judges to attend field events to see how gundogs function, but it's vital that they attend the trial *for their breed*, not one for another gundog type with a different function. It's vitally important for our gundogs that the KC continues to bring some vision and compassion, as well as scientific realism, into their custodianship of pedigree gundog breeds. It must move on in this sphere of its activities from *ancien regime* to proactive progression.

The BASC needs to become much more involved in the breeding, trialling, testing (both for heath and field competence reasons) and the wider working gundog scene. The old expression an 'eye for a dog', or a talent for identifying outstanding dogs, has never been 'bred in the bone' in certain gifted individuals but shaped by the intellect, however instinctive this has appeared to be. Show-ring judges and working dog breeders need to have the *knowledge* to make decisions, not just the authority to make them. It was enlightening to read recently of distinguished Labrador breeder and judge Carole Coode that even after forty-five years of owning the breed, she still studies the breed standard before each judging appointment. We need better informed training

Working Tests need to be wider in scope.

Labrador Retriever At Work coloured etching by C. Vernon Stokes – the service to man of our gundogs make shooting the sport it is.

techniques – no more 'dog-*breaking*' – and only *truly* informed breeding schemes, related to health tests, coefficients of inbreeding and sound morphology, regarding the dog's genotype as important as its phenotype. We need a gundog covenant.

Gundog Covenant

In the preceding chapters, I have striven to highlight the immense value of the gundog to man, both as a working animal in the sporting field, as a highly effective service dog, and, not least, as a much appreciated companion dog. Now is the time, in the best interests of the admirable man-gundog relationship, to establish a newly framed partnership, what I have dubbed the Gundog Covenant. This I list as a three-fold commitment:

1. To conduct better-informed breeding systems, with reliance on health testing, veterinary advice on anatomical soundness and genetic advice on inbreeding ratios. It's the breeders who make or break the gundog breeds.

2. To observe the requirement for:

   a. A healthy genotype, so that short-lived sickly dogs are less likely;
   b. A truly functional phenotype, placing field usefulness ahead of show-ring fashion;
   c. A rational approach to so-called 'breed points', in which minor physical features can dominate the overall need for basic soundness in construction and movement. Gundogs can do without the handicap of over-long ears, excessive coats, heavy bone and loose eyelids.

3. To acknowledge the spiritual needs of gundogs, their fundamental requirement for exercise, their innate desire to seek scent from external stimuli and the exhilaration they experience in working with their owner, even in small, quite humble ways.

In this book I celebrate the gundogs of the world, giving praise where it is due to breeds from overseas. I welcome them here and admire their capabilities. But I worry much more about the future for some of our native gundog breeds, part of our sporting heritage and so worthy of our patronage.

If charity starts at home, let's promote our gundogs, respected the world over not just in the field but as companions too. All our distinguished gundog breeds thoroughly deserve our total commitment to their best interests.

Our gundogs look to us for enlightened, informed and dedicated custodianship.

POINTS OF THE DOG

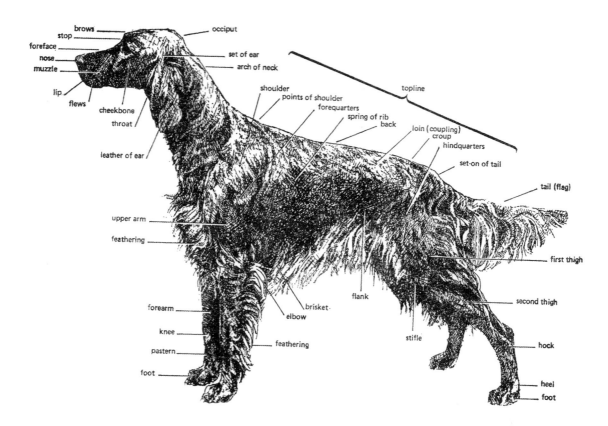

Points of the Dog (courtesy of Susan Oakley & Hutchinson Publishing Group).

GLOSSARY OF TERMS

Action Movement; the way a dog moves

Angulation The degree of slope or angle of the shoulder blade in the forequarters and in the sharp angles of the inter-related bones in the hindquarters – thigh, hock and metatarsus

Back Area of the dog between the withers and the root of tail

Balanced Symmetrically proportioned

Barrel-hocks Hocks turned outwards resulting in feet with inward-pointing toes (similar to bandy legs)

Barrel-ribbed Well-rounded rib cage

Blanket The coat colour on the back from the withers to the rump

Blaze A white patch of hair in the centre of the face, usually between the eyes

Bloom The sheen of a coat in prime condition

Bodied-up Well developed in maturity

Brace A pair, a couple

Breed points Characteristic physical features of a breed, often exaggerated by breed fanciers

Brisket The part of the body in front of the chest

Button ear The ear flap folding forward, usually towards the eye

Cat-foot The rounded, shorter-toed, compact type of foot

Champion A dog achieving this level of merit under KC-approved judges

Chest The area from the brisket up to the belly, underneath the dog

Chiselled Clean cut, especially in the head

Chopping Exaggerated forward movement through abbreviated reach

Close-coupled Comparatively short from the last rib to the leading edge of the thigh

Coarse Lacking refinement

Cobby Short-bodied, compact in torso

Conformation The relationship between the physical appearance of a dog and the imagined perfect mould for that breed or type

Couples Connection of hindquarters to torso

Cow-hocks Hocks turned towards each other (similar to knock-knees)

Crossbred Having parents from two different breeds

Croup (rump) Region of the pelvic girdle formed by the sacrum and the surrounding tissue

Dewlaps Loose, pendulous skin under the throat

Down at pastern Weak or faulty metacarpus set at an angle to the vertical

Drive A solid thrust from the hindquarters, denoting strength of locomotion

Drop ear The ends of the ear folded or falling forward

Dropper Cross between a Pointer and a retriever

Elbows out Elbows positioned away from the body

Even bite Meeting of both sets of front teeth at edges with no overlap

Feathering Distinctly longer hair on rear line of legs, back of ears and along underside of tail

Flank The side of the body between the last rib and the hip

Flat-sided A noticeable lack of roundness in the rib cage

Forearm Part of foreleg extending from elbow to pastern

Forequarters Front part of dog excluding head and neck

Front Forepart of body viewed from the head-on position

Furnishings Long hair on ears, trailing edge of legs and under part of tail

Gait Pattern or rhythm of footsteps

Gallop The fastest gait; a four-beat rhythm, propelling the dog at great speed, with all four feet off the ground during the seeking of sheer pace

Grizzle Bluish-grey or steel-grey in coat colour

Hackney action High-stepping action in the front legs (named after the carriage horse)

Hard-mouthed Too much pressure of grip in the dog's muzzle when carrying game, sometimes leading to damage to it

Hare-foot A longer, narrower foot, usually with an elongated third digit

Haunch Rump or buttock; bones of that area

Height Distance or measurement from the withers to ground contact in the standing dog

Hock Joint on the hind leg between the knee and the fetlock; the heel in humans.

Hound-marked Coat colouring involving a mixture of classic Foxhound coat colours – white, black and tan – in varying proportions, usually mainly white, especially underneath

Hound tail Tail carried on high, up above the rump

Irish spotting White markings on solid coat, usually on the blaze, throat and toes

Knee The joint attaching fore-pastern and forearm

Layback The angle of the shoulder compared to the vertical

Lay of shoulder Angled position of the shoulder

Leather The flap of the ear

Level back The line of the back is horizontal, parallel to the ground

Level bite (pincer-bite) The front teeth of both jaws meeting exactly

Loaded shoulders When the shoulder blades are pushed outwards by over-muscled development (often confused in the show ring with well-muscled shoulders on a supremely fit dog)

Lumber Superfluous flesh and/or cumbersome movement arising from lack of condition or faulty construction

Mask Dark shading on the foreface, most usually on a tan or red-tan dog

Moving close When the hind limbs move too near each other

Occiput The peak of the skull.

Out at elbow *See* elbows out

Over-reaching Faulty gait in which the hind feet pass the fore feet on the outside due to hyper-angulation in the hindquarters

Overshot jaw The front upper set of teeth overlapping the lower set

Oversprung ribs Exaggerated curvature of rib cage

Pace Rate of movement, usually speed

Padding A Hackney action due to lack of angulation in forequarters

Paddling A heavy, clumsy, threshing action in the forelegs with the feet too wide of the body on the move

Pastern Lowest section of the leg, below the knee or hock

Pedigree The dog's record of past breeding; sometimes used as shorthand for purebreeding

Pile Dense undercoat of softer hair

Pincer bite *See* level bite

Plaiting (or weaving or crossing) The movement of one front leg across the path of the other front leg on the move

Prick ear Ear carriage in which the ear is erect and usually pointed at tip

Racy Lightly built and leggier than normal in the breed

Ribbed-up Long last rib

Roach- or carp-backed A back arched convexly along the spine, especially in the hindmost section

Root of the tail Where the tail joins the dog's back

Rose ear A small drop ear with the leather folding over and back, often showing the inner ear.

Saddle A solid area of colour extending over the shoulders and back

Saddle-backed A sagging back from extreme length or weak musculature

Scissor bite The outer side of the lower incisors touches the inner side of the upper incisors

Second thigh The (calf) muscle between the stifle and the hock in the hindquarters

Self-coloured A solid or single-coloured coat

Set on Where the root of the tail is positioned in the hindquarters

Shelly Weedy and narrow-boned, lacking substance

Short-coupled *See* close-coupled

Shoulder layback *See* layback

Sickle-hocked Lack of extension in the hock on the rear drive

Slab-sided Flat ribs, with too little spring from the spinal column

Snipiness Condition in which the muzzle is too pointed, weak and lacking strength right to the nose end

Soft-mouthed The degree of muzzle tension that ensures the carried game is unmarked

Soundness Correct physical conformation and movement

Splay feet Flat, open-toed, widely spread feet

Spring of rib The extent to which the ribs are well-rounded

Stance Standing position, usually when formally presented

Standard The written word picture of a breed

Stifle The joint in the hind leg between the upper and lower thigh, equating to the knee in man, sadly weak in some breeds

Stop The depression at the junction of the nasal bone and the skull between the eyes

Straight-hocked Lacking in angulation of the hock joint

Straight-shouldered Straight up and down shoulder blades, lacking angulation or layback

Strain A family line throwing offspring of a set type

Symmetry Balance and correct proportions of anatomy

Throatiness An excess of loose skin at the front of the neck

Tied at the elbows When the elbows are set too close under the body, thereby restricting freedom of movement

Topline The dog's outline from just behind the withers to the rump

Trot A rhythmical two-beat gait, with hind- and forequarters working in unison

Tuck-up Concave underline of torso, between last rib and hindquarters, lack of discernible belly

Type Characteristic attributes distinguishing a breed or strain of a breed

Undershot Malformation of the jaw, projecting the lower jaw and incisors beyond the upper (puppies with this condition, they appear to be grinning)

Upper arm The foreleg bone between the shoulder blade and the elbow

Upright shoulders Too straight an angle in the shoulder joint, also called steep in shoulders, usually giving a shortened front stride and a short-necked appearance.

Variety A subdivision of a breed

Well-angulated Well-defined angle in the thigh-hock-metatarsus area

Well-coupled Well made in the area from the withers to the hip bones

Well-knit Neat and compactly constructed and connected

Well-laid Soundly placed and correctly angled

Well-laid back shoulders Oblique shoulders ideally slanting at 45 degrees to the ground

Well let-down Hocks close to the ground; having low hocks as a result of long muscles in what in humans is the calf. (This is an often misunderstood term; in both racehorses and sporting dogs, the seeking of long cannon bones led to the use of this expression. It was never intended to promote short rear pasterns)

Well ribbed-up Ribs neither too long nor too wide apart; compact

Well-sprung With noticeably rounded ribs

Well tucked-up Absence of visible abdomen

Wheel back Excessive roaching, marked arching over the loins

Wire-haired A coat of bristly crispness to the touch, hard in texture

Withers The highest point on the body of a standing dog, immediately behind the neck, above the shoulders

Yawing (crabbing) Body moving at an angle to the legs' line of movement

BIBLIOGRAPHY

Arkwright, William, *The Pointer and his Predecessors* (Arthur L. Humphreys, 1906)

'Bach', *Training Dogs* (The Stock-Keeper, 1896)

Badcock, Lt Col G.H. *The Early Life and Training of a Gundog* (Watmoughs Ltd, 1931)

Barton, Frank Townend, *Our Dogs and All About Them* (Jarrolds, 1938)

Blaine, Delabere, *An Encyclopaedia of Rural Sports* (Longman, 1870)

Brander, Michael, *Hunting and Shooting from earliest times to the present day* (Weidenfeld & Nicolson, 1971)

Burgoin, Gillian, *Guide to the Weimaraner* (Boydell, 1985)

Caius, Doctor, *Of English Dogs* (1576)

Cassell's Popular Natural History (Cassell, Petter & Galpin, 1890)

Castaing, Jean, *Les Chiens d'Arret* (Edition du Message, 1960)

Charlesworth, W.M., *Golden Retrievers* (Williams & Norgate, 1952)

de Chimay, Jacqueline, *Plaisirs de la Chasse* (Librairie Hachette, 1960)

Clark, Ross and Stainer, John (eds), *Medical and Genetic Aspects of Purebred Dogs* (Forum, 1994)

Compton, Herbert, *The Twentieth Century Dog* (Grant Richards, 1904)

The Countryman's Weekly, 2012

Croxton Smith, Arthur, *Sporting Dogs* (Country Life Ltd, 1938)

Croxton Smith, Arthur, *British Dogs,* (Collins, 1945)

Croxton Smith, Arthur, *Dogs since 1900,* (Dakers, 1950)

Dalziel, Hugh, *British Dogs* (1888)

Daniel, Rev. W.B., *Rural Sports* (1801)

Davies, C.J., *The Theory and Practice of Breeding to Type* 1928; new edition Day, James Wentworth, *The Dog in Sport* (Harrap, 1938)

Drury, William, *British Dogs* (Upcott Gill, 1903)

Edward, Duke of York, *The Master of Game* (1410)

Edwards, Sydenham, *Cynographica Britannica* (1800)

Fairfax, Thomas, *The Complete Sportsman* (1689)

The Field, 1902, 1909, 1941

de Foix, Gaston, *Livre de Chasse* (1387)

Garton R.V., *Dogs and Guns,* (Geoffrey Bles, 1964)

Gay, John, *Rural Sports* (1711)

Glyn, Sir Richard, *Champion Dogs of the World* (Harrap, 1967)

Gottlieb, Gay, *The Hungarian Vizsla* (Nimrod, 1985)

Graham, Joseph, *The Sporting Dog* (1904)

'H.H', *The Scientific Education of Dogs for the Gun* (Sampson Low, 1920)

Hall Jones, Roger, *The Complete Book of Gundogs in Britain* (Barrie & Jenkins, 1974)

Heaton, Andrew, *Duck Decoys* (Shire Publications, 2001)

Hubbard, Clifford, *Working Dogs of the World* (1947)

Hubbard, Clifford L.B., *Dogs in Britain* (Macmillan, 1948)

Hutchinson, General WN, *Dog Breaking* (John Murray, 1909)

Hudson, David, *Working Pointers and Setters* (Swan Hill Press, 2004)

'Idstone', *The Dog* (1872)

Jackson, Tony, *Hunter-Pointer-Retriever, The Continental Gundog* (Ashford, 1989)

Jesse, George R., *Researches into the History of the British Dog* (Hardwicke, 1866)

The Kennel Gazette, 1884, 1888, 1889, 1890

Laughton, Nancy, *A Review of the Flat-coated Retriever* (Pelham, 1968)

Laverack, Edward, *The Setter* (Longmans Green and Co., 1872)

Lawrence, Richard, *The Complete Farrier* (1815)

Layton, David, *All Purpose Gundog* (The Standfast Press, 1977)

Lee, Rawdon, *Modern Dogs – Sporting Division* (1906)

Leighton, Robert, *The New Book of the Dog,* (Cassell & Co., 1912)

Leighton-Boyce, Gilbert, *A Survey of Early Setters* (1985)

Lepeudry, Jean-Michel, *Hunting Dogs from around the World* (Barron's Educational Series, 1997)

Lloyd, H.S., *The Cocker Spaniel* (Our Dogs, 1924).

Lloyd, Freeman, *All Spaniels, their breeding, rearing, training, bench show points and characteristics* (Freeman Lloyd, New York, 1930)

McCandlish, W.L., *The Scottish Terrier* (Our Dogs, 1926)

Mackie, Sir Peter Jeffrey, *The Keeper's Book* (Foulis & Co., 1924)

Martinez de Espinar, Alonzo, *Arte de Ballesteria y Monteria* (1644)

Mason, Joan, *Flat-coated Retrievers Today* (Ringpress, 1996)

Maxwell, C. Bede, *The Truth about Sporting Dogs* (Pelham, 1972)

Miller, Warren Hastings, *The American Hunting Dog, modern strains of bird dogs and hounds, and their field training* (George H. Doran, New York, 1919)

Morris, Desmond, *Dogs – The Ultimate Dictionary of over 1,000 Dog Breeds* (Ebury Press, 2001)

Moxon P.R.A., *Gundogs – Training and Field Trials,* (Swan Hill, 1998 reprint)

Page, Thomas, *The Art of Shooting Flying* (1767)

Parker, Eric (ed.), *Shooting by Moor, Field and Shore,* Lonsdale Library Vol. III (Seeley, Service & Co., 1929)

Parker, Eric, *Shooting Days,* (Philip Allan, 1932)

'Pathfinder' and Hugh Dalziel, *Breaking and Training Dogs* (The Bazaar, 1906)

Payne-Gallwey, Ralph, *The Book of Duck Decoys* (1886)

Petch, Paddy, *The Complete Flat Coated Retriever* (Boydell, 1988)

Pferd III, William, *The Welsh Springer Spaniel: History, Selection, Training and Care* (A.S. Barnes, 1975)

Pollard, H.B., *The Mystery of Scent* (1929)

Phillips C.A. & Cane, R. Claude, *The Sporting Spaniel* (Our Dogs, 1924)

de Raad, A.H., *Jachthonden rassen-africhting* (Uitgeversmaatschappij, 1990)

Rawlings, Leslie, *Gamekeeper – Memories of a Country Childhood* (Boydell, 1977)

Ribblesdale, Lord, *The Queen's Hounds and Stag-Hunting Recollections* (1897)

Ritchie, Carson I.A., *The British Dog* (Robert Hale, 1981)

Ruffer, Jonathan Garnier, *The Big Shots, Edwardian Shooting Parties* (Viking, 1978)

Scott, Lt-Col Lord George and Middleton, Sir John, *The Labrador Dog – its Home and History* (1936)

Seall, Judi, *The History of Retrievers, compiled from the scrapbooks of H Reginald Cooke,* (Judi Seall, 2001)

Shaw, Vero *The Illustrated Book of the Dog* (1880)

Smyth, R.H., *The Mind of the Dog* (1958)

Smythe, R.H., *The Dog: Structure and Movement* (Foulsham, 1970)

Sporting Review, 1839

Stephens, Wilson, *Gundog Sense and Sensibility* (Pelham, 1982)

'Stonehenge', *Manual of British Rural Sports* (1856)

'Stonehenge', *Dogs of the British Islands,* (Horace Cox, 1878)

Stonex, Elma, *The Golden Retriever Handbook* (Nicholson & Watson, 1953)

Strebel, Richard, *Die Deutschen Hunde* (Munich, 1904)

Taplin, William, *The Sportsman's Cabinet* (J. Cundee, 1803)

Teasdale-Buckell, G.T., *The Complete Shot* (Methuen, 1907)

Watson, James, *The Dog Book* (1906)

Webb, H., *Dogs: their points, whims, instincts and peculiarities* (Dean & Son, 1883)

'Wildfowler', *Dog Breaking* (Burlington, 1915)

Williams, Mary Roslin, *Advanced Labrador Breeding* (Witherby, 1988)

Willock, Colin D., *The Farmer's Book of Field Sports* (Vista Books, 1961)

Wolters, Richard, *The Labrador Retriever – The History…The People* (Petersen Prints, LA, 1981)

Wood, Carl P., *The Gun Digest Book of Sporting Dogs* (Dbi Books, 1985)

Youatt, William, *The Dog* (1845)

INDEX